'These collected memories of an extraordinary educator form a deep critique of the marketization of education. For this wartime resistance fighter, despair was not an option. Harry Rée's ideas of public service and lifelong learning remain a beacon.

Beverley Naidoo, Writer

'Jonathan Daube has woven a multitude of personal memories into a coherent picture of this Educator Most Extraordinary. This is the Harry Rée whom I remember with such affection and gratitude.'

George Walker, former Director General, International Baccalaureate

'Harry Rée was a humane, open-minded, generous-spirited and engaging educationalist. He thoroughly merits Jonathan Daube's humane, open-minded, generous-spirited and engaging account of his influential life.'

Professor Eric Midwinter, Social Historian and Educationalist

Educator Most Extraordinary

IOE Press

Be ashamed to die until you have won some victory for humanity.
Horace Mann, 1859

Be truthful, gentle and fearless.
Mohandas Gandhi

*I think Harry mattered to so many of us because each of us separately
seemed to matter to him. I have no idea how he managed it.*
Ben Foley

The pre-eminent educationalist of the post-war years.
Education, May 1992

Educator Most Extraordinary

The life and achievements of
Harry Rée, 1914–1991

Jonathan M. Daube

UCL Institute of Education Press

First published in 2017 by the UCL Institute of Education Press, 20 Bedford Way, London WC1H 0AL

www.ucl-ioe-press.com

British Library Cataloguing in Publication Data:
A catalogue record for this publication is available from the British Library

ISBN
978-1-78277-212-5 (paperback)
978-1-78277-187-6 (PDF eBook)

Typeset by Quadrant Infotech (India) Pvt Ltd
Printed by CPI Group (UK) Ltd, Croydon, CR0 4YY
Cover image reproduced by kind permission of Caroline Forbes

Contents

Acknowledgements

I am grateful to so many people ... family and friends ... for both encouragement and help. Above all, my wife Linda indulged me as I spent many, many hours with Harry and his world. And Harry's children never ever made editorial suggestions.

I am both amazed and moved – 'gobsmacked' may be the right word – by the sheer number of people who have responded to pleading emails. Many have sent encouraging messages or suggested whom else I might approach; most have written substantively. Some have decided, generously, to go through letters they received from Harry over the years. Some have preferred face-to-face or telephone conversation to emailing. I have been in touch with about 300 individuals.

Clearly, the reminder of Harry Rée brought joy to many hearts as people recalled his *joie de vivre*, his capacity for friendship and his total commitment to others. I was especially moved by the 20-plus Bradford Grammar School Old Boys who wrote about events between 1946 and 1951. I was constantly reminded why I was bowled over by Harry as a starry-eyed 20-year-old: I wasn't wrong!

There is no way I can, in the listing that follows, discriminate between those who took the time to write mini-articles, those in the cheering section and those in-between. I owe them all.

Harry would look at you quizzically; possibly a bit taken aback – not that Harry was ever taken aback – by the sheer number, the love, the affection and the details of the memories. For sure, he had an impact: he made a difference.

And I need to say something about the historians, archivists and librarians, few of whom I know personally. What a wonderful group.

In what follows, I have tried to list people in a sensible way. I apologize where it doesn't seem to make sense.

Historians, archivists and librarians

Paul Addison; Sarah Aitchison, Archivist, Institute of Education, University of London; Alexandra Aslett, Librarian and Archivist, St Paul's School, London; Stephen J. Ball, Institute of Education; Jonathan Bell, Advice and Information Officer, Liberty; Maike Bruhns, Hamburg art historian; Niklaus Bütikofer, Archivist, University of Bern; Helen Chapman; Peter Charlton, Editor, *Yorkshire Post*; James P. Coatman, Manchester Literary and Philosophical Society; Fiona Colbert, Biographical Librarian, St John's College, Cambridge; Kate Dodd, Academic Registrar, University of York; Sarah Dodsworth, Master's Assistant, St John's College, Cambridge; Chris Fletcher, Greater Manchester Chamber of Commerce; Charles Fonge, University Archivist and Records Manager, Borthwick Institute, University of York; M.R.D. Foot CBE, Official SOE historian; Janet Friedlander, Information Officer, National Union of Teachers; Christi Geisinger, Library Associate, Manchester Community College; Margaret Grace, Archivist, Beaconsfield and District Historical Society; Rosemary Hanes, Reference Librarian, Library of Congress; Simone Harris, Customer Service Assistant, Bromley Local Studies Library; Katie Harrison, Librarian, Bradford Grammar School; Sir Max Hastings; Peter, Lord Hennessy; John Horsfield, Retired History Master, Manchester Grammar School; Claire Jackson, Archive Volunteer, Barnet Local Studies and Archives; Tony Jenkins, author of *A Pacifist at War, The Silence of Francis Cammaerts;* James King, Senior Archivist, University of Warwick; Diane Livesey, Correspondence Clerk, Watford Quakers; Jayne Marsden, *Yorkshire Post;* Amanda Mason, Historian, Department of Research and Information, Imperial War Museum; Callum McKean, news reference team, British Library; Elspeth Millar, Archive Assistant, Oral History and National Life Stories, British Library; David Moore, author, *Haec Egimus*, 2011 (Bradford Grammar School); Michael Morrogh, Head of History and School Archivist, Shrewsbury School; Jackie Parcell, Watford Grammar School; Julian Perfect, Honorary Librarian, Society of Chemical Industry, London; Sue Plant, P.A. to the headmistress, Bedford High School for Girls; Kay Rees; Julian Reid, archivist, Merton College, Oxford; Sheldon Rothblatt, Professor Emeritus of History, University of California, Berkeley; Sue Sampson, Senior Archivist, Cambridgeshire Archives; Sue South, Librarian, Bradford Grammar School; Katy Stoddard, *The Guardian*; Wallace Vincent, Secretary, Special Forces Club; June Wailling, Archivist, Centre for Buckinghamshire Studies; Jeff Walden, Archives Researcher, BBC; Julia Walworth, Fellow librarian, Merton College, Oxford; Koleen Wright, Bradford Grammar School.

Family
Douglas Gill; Harriet Gill, first grandchild; Rebecca Gill, grand-daughter and mother of first great-grandchild; Pamela Lowe, niece; Philip Rée Mallinson, (American) nephew; Brian Rée, son; David Rée; Hugo Rée, (Australian) nephew; Janet Rée, daughter; Jonathan Rée, son; Peta (Garrett) Rée, wife; Charles Swallow, nephew; Lisa Vine, niece.

Turkish experts
Matthew Daube; Erika Gilson, Professor, Princeton University; Gottfried Hagen, Associate Professor of Turkish Studies, University of Michigan; M. Şükrü Hanioğlu, Garrett Professor and Chair, Department of Near Eastern Studies, Princeton University; Sylvia Önder, Assistant Professor, Georgetown University; Alice Savage, Dean Emeritus of Academic Affairs, Manchester Community College; Uli Şamiloğlu, Professor and Director of Middle Eastern Studies, University of Wisconsin-Madison.

Bradford Grammar School Old Boys (and before)
Bernard Barker; Peter J.M. Bell; Roger P. Bland; Roger M. Charnley; John Cureton; Peter Drumm; George Feather; John Field; David Finney; Denis M. Foster; John Grange; Hilary Green; John Hicks; John Hill; Paul Hockney; Barry Hoffbrand; Victor Hoffbrand; Michael Ludgate; Steve Parsons; Norman Pedgrift; David Rands; Pierre A. Richterich; Tom Seekings; Philip Selby; George E. Smart; David Swallow; David R. Watson; Peter White; Ian Wilson.

From Watford days
Eric Albone; Jack Altman; Chris Anthony; Ron Armstrong; Ian Ashcroft; Robin Attfield; Adrian C. Bailey; Bill Bailey; Chris Bailey; David Bentley; Mike Benton; Alfred Bradley; Fred Bridgland; Ian Brown; Martin C. Cartwright; John Collins; Peter Dilloway; Tim Edwards; Keith Emmans; Thelma Emmans; Jim Feeney; Stuart Field; Michael Fitzpatrick; Ben Foley; Margaret Foreman; Michael Gray; Shirley Greenman; Barrie Hall; A.H. (Chelly) Halsey; Michael Harloe; David Harman; Rt. Rev. John Hind; Sir John Holman; Graham Huggins; Ralph Ibbott; Ian Jarritt; Norman Jarritt; Jonathan Kiek; John Law; David Lim; John Mann; Chris Manning; Takako Mendl; Jack Page; David Pinchin; Stephen Plaice; Roger Pooley; Martin Post; Christopher Price; Bishop Anthony Priddis; Sir Ian Prosser; Michael Rosen; Chris Smith; Jane Steedman; Mark Steedman; Peter Swan; Peter Taylor-Goolby; Stephen Thake; Jill Thistlethwaite; Maureen Thomas; Mary Turner; George Walker; Lisa Wells; Michael T. Wilson.

From York days
Alasdair Brown; Harry Creaser; Jeremy Cunningham; John Currey; Bob Finch; David Foster; Tony Gelsthorpe; Sir Peter Hall; David Hargreaves; Peter Hollindale; Fred Inglis; Oliver James; Chris Kyriacou; Ian Lister; Bob Moon; Caroline Moseley; Beverley Naidoo; John Pratt; Anne Riddell;

Carolyn Royds; David Smith; Laurie Taylor; Sir William Taylor; David Waddington; Nicole Ward; Judy Weyman.

From Woodberry Down days

Sir Tim Brighouse; Simon Clements; Judith Hemming; Ingrid Lunt; Linda Marland; Jon Nixon; Andrew Puddephatt; Joan Shapiro; Michael Simons; Nigel Wright.

Mostly Post-York: from Colt Park days; and before

Susan Addinell; Richard Aldrich; Baroness Blackstone; Leslie Baruch Brent; Gabriel Chanan; Anna Coote; Anne Corbett; Anne Davies; Madeleine de Little; Mary Evans; Geoffrey Fallows; Colin Farrell; John Farrer; Colin Fletcher; Jim Foley; Caroline Forbes; Tyler Forbes; Nigel Gann; Vivian Griffiths; Stephen P. Hersh; Lucy Hodges; Janni Howker; Chris Husbands; Tony Jeffs; Harry Judge; Michel Lemosse; Tony Little; Margaret Maden; Ian Martin; Gary McCullogh; Eric Midwinter; Peter Mitchell; Graham Mort; Peter Mortimore; Sam Murray; Sir Peter Newsam; Ailsa O'Brien; Ursula Owen; Ann Page; Bruce Page; Jonathan Palmer; Liz Peretz; Deborah Ravetz; John Rennie; Peter Renshaw; Patricia Rowan; Tom Schuller; Tom Thompson; Gillian Tindall; Nick Tucker; George Varnava; Pippa Warin; Baroness Warnock; Peter Wilby; Cathy Wood; Terry Wrigley.

Introduction

What was so extraordinary about Harry?

I first met Harry Rée at the impressionable age of 19, and I am still impressed. The notion of writing about him first came to me shortly after his death in 1991. I had hoped that his close and dear friend Edward Blishen would do the heavy lifting and I would be his little helper, but Edward's health began to deteriorate shortly after we began exchanging letters and thoughts, and he died in 1996.

As long ago as July 1992, Edward was writing to me about 'celebrating Harry's multiple Harryishness'. The next year, it was, 'I think it is over to you.' And in October 1994, he wrote, 'He will have his hour. I doubt if I'll be around then … but you will be.'

So what was it in Harry Rée that has kept me admiringly curious for almost 60 years, most of them spent over 3,000 miles away?

From my first day as a student teacher at Watford Grammar School, Harry trusted me totally. Maybe he had too much faith in people. But what a motivator!

He practised what he preached. Actually, he didn't preach much. But he was a great persuader. Eric Midwinter, basically agreeing, writes: 'he never "preached", whereas we certainly did beat the drum and bang the tambourine'. Nicole Ward Jouve put it this way: 'Albert Schweitzer said that preaching by example is not only the best way; it is the only way.' As I observed on my first day, he taught half a timetable, which was extraordinary for the headmaster of a largish and well-known school.

He had enormous faith in the power of education for good and the ability of all kinds of people to find meaning in their lives through education. From that first day, I felt I was part of a crusade, though I would not have put it in those terms.

Harry took intelligent risks. When, 30 years after we first met, I resigned from a position before I had secured another job, I thought of him: what might he have done had he been in my shoes?

He had a broader view of the world than anyone I had yet encountered. I can still recall my amazement on 11 November 1957, when the headmaster prayed for Germans and Italians as well as Britons and French, which was dramatically noteworthy in the UK at that time.

All this, and more, added up to someone who had an enormous influence on my life and, as I was to re-discover as I worked on this book, many, many other lives. In no way has he become irrelevant with time. What follows, then, is an attempt to share the life and thought of an unusual, charismatic man. What is it about Harry, I ask myself, that I want people to know, especially young people who might become teachers if inspired? (Alasdair Brown describes Harry as 'an iconic inspirer'.) Of course, this ageing author is not only much older than the impressionable youth of September 1957; he is also very different and living in a different world. Whether he is wiser or not is for others to judge; for sure, he will do his utmost to be fair to someone who can no longer speak for himself.

About the author

Jonathan M. Daube was born and educated in the UK, taking his first degree at the University of Aberdeen and his teacher training at the Institute of Education, London. He emigrated to the United States in 1963, receiving his doctorate at Harvard University. He has been an English teacher in both countries, and spent 1968–70 at the University of Malawi. Later he served as a school superintendent in Massachusetts; a graduate school director in Ohio; and a community college president at Berkshire Community College, Massachusetts, and at Manchester Community College, Connecticut, from 1987 to 2008. He has been a member of the board of directors of the Association of American Colleges and Universities, and in 2007 was elected President of the University of Aberdeen Foundation, a position he held for five years. He has taught part-time at the schools of education of the universities of Connecticut and Massachusetts, and currently serves on the regional advisory councils of Middlesex and Naugatuck Valley Community Colleges, Connecticut.

Chapter 1

Antecedents

Harry Alfred Rée was born on Thursday 15 October 1914, two months after the beginning of what his family would later know as the Great War. I don't think his first name meant much to him, but he must have been chuffed when his first grandchild, born in 1970, was named Harriet. For sure, he did not turn out to be any Tom, Dick or Harry.

George V was on the British throne and Herbert Henry Asquith was the (Liberal) prime minister. Woodrow Wilson was the (Democratic) president of the United States. The name 'Harry' was in the family: his great-grandfather had been named Harry, and 'Alfred' was, of course, his father's name.

He was the eighth of eight. There were five sisters and three brothers, born between 1901 and 1914. Two of his sisters outlived him. All of the eight married: Eric, who died in Algeria in 1943, and Harry, both married twice following the deaths of their first wives, and every one of them had children. Their parents, with 24 grandchildren, 40 great-grandchildren and numerous great-greats, might be amazed at the sheer number of living descendants. A century after he was born, Harry himself would have three children, five grandchildren and four great-grandchildren.

And it should be noted that Harry was not the only Rée headmaster. His oldest brother, Edward Anton Rée, ran the Chesterton Boys' Preparatory School in Seaford, Sussex, a town full of preparatory schools. He died in 1949, a very short time before Harry went for the headship of Watford Grammar School. Edward had been taken prisoner at Dunkirk and spent much of the War in PoW camps, where he took an active role in entertainments. He contracted tuberculosis and, despite early repatriation via the Red Cross, died at the age of 47. Harry's nephew Charles John Swallow, son of Irene Dupont Rée Swallow, went to the Chesterton Prep. School. Swallow tells us that while at Oxford, Edward had 'spent more time carousing in Vincent's than attending to his studies'.[1]

Harry's origins were possibly Alsatian (whether French or German is uncertain), American, Danish and North German; Christian and Jewish.

---

1   Vincent's is a club that still exists at 1A King Edward Street, Oxford. Its members unapologetically describe it as elitist and selective. The website declares, 'Collar and tie are to be worn in the evening. No mobile telephones are to be used at any time.'

According to Marcus Binney, 'he joked that he was not English at all'. And in an interview in 1985, he was to describe himself as a mongrel. His mother Lavinia Elizabeth Dimmick was 40 when he was born. She died in 1946, so saw him as husband, parent, war hero and teacher, but not as headmaster or professor. Francis Cammaerts described her, after Harry's death, as 'a most attractive woman'.

In 1988, Dr Liz Peretz interviewed Harry at his home in Colt Park, near Ingleton, North Yorkshire, for the British Library Sound Archives National Life Stories Project. The transcript contains an appalling number of errors, lapses and 'inaudibles', but Harry does tell his mother's story, and with considerable affection.[2]

His mother was American, so he could have claimed United States citizenship at any time in his life.[3] Her father, Edward Dimmick, was a native of Wayne County, Pennsylvania: a lawyer who was admitted to the bar in 1865, he became City Controller of Scranton, Pennsylvania, around 1886. Harry's maternal grandmother died when she was very young, so Dimmick married his deceased wife's younger sister, who helped bring up his daughter Lavinia.

Harry's mother was not only American, she was also a Dupont, with a fair amount of contact with the main family in Wilmington, Delaware. Even today, a foundation in Delaware updates the Dupont family tree, which includes Harry and all his descendants. Lavinia Dimmick was also a traditional Anglican, but later in his life, Harry was to confirm in writing, 'I am not a Christian.'

According to her obituary in the *Manchester Guardian*:[4]

> Mrs Lavinia Rée ... a keen worker for several educational and cultural causes in Manchester, was killed in a bus accident at the junction of Mauldeth Road, Withington, where she lived, and Wilmslow Road. ... an American citizen ... For 20 years she was the chairman of the Princess Christian College in Fallowfield,[5] a member of the council of Langdale Hall, a university residence for women students. She also served on the committee of the Manchester branch of the NSPCC,[6] and on the committee of the

---

2 Both the audio tapes and the transcript are available at the British Library and can be purchased.
3 In 1983, he was to acquire an American daughter-in-law.
4 23 September 1946.
5 The college was for the training of nannies at 26 Wilbraham Road; less than a mile from her home.
6 National Society for the Prevention of Cruelty to Children, founded 1884.

Manchester branch of the English-Speaking Union,[7] and was chairman of its hospitality committee.

Two days later, 'F.E.C.' wrote:

> It would be a pity if a catalogue of good causes ... should obscure the rich and warm humanity which characterized Lavinia Rée. As a devout churchwoman, her concern was not solely for humanity at large ... but it was individual men and women, boys and girls for whom she cared. Tall and with a youthful walk which belied her years, she also had a sense of fun which endeared her to the young: seeing her with her grandchildren it was obvious that she was the most delightful of grandmothers, and an old student of Langdale Hall has recalled that the parties Mrs Rée gave to the students there were the best she ever attended.

Harry's nephew Hugo Rée, son of Eric (who died in 1943), confirms the role of religion in her life, describing her as a 'very religious woman who disapproved of overt shows of emotion'.

Jonathan Rée has put together a list of ancestors that goes back to 1728: Harry's paternal grandfather Isidor was from Germany, a wool merchant from Hamburg who set up a business in Bradford, where Harry was to live from 1946 to 1951. So Harry's father, Alfred Rée, was a Yorkshireman born in Leeds.

Alfred went to Bradford Grammar School, where Harry was to teach after the War, long after his father's death. From an early age, Alfred was interested in chemistry. He could not find the courses he wanted in the UK, so, according to Harry, he went to study in Germany and in Leiden, Netherlands. His obituary in the *Manchester Guardian* mentions the Universities of Geneva and Munich. Interestingly, the record shows that Alfred Rée received his doctorate from the University of Berne, Switzerland, in 1886, when he was 22 years old. He did not spend much time studying there, but took his doctoral examination on 6 March of that year. The title of his thesis (Did Harry know this? Could he have pronounced it?) was *Ueber β-Sulfophtalsäure*, published by Stämpfli in Berne in 1886.

Alfred returned to England in his early twenties to set up a dye works in Manchester, living in a sort of club in the centre of the city that had rooms and dining facilities. At the turn of the century, W.H. Claus and Rée of Clayton, three miles east of the centre of Manchester, were co-owners of a

---

7   Founded 1918.

plant that manufactured aniline dyes, and in 1904, Dr Rée testified at length before the parliamentary Industrial Alcohol Committee.

When he was in his mid-thirties and still a bachelor, Harry recalled in 1988, he met a young American woman who was visiting, and was smitten. He saw her a couple of times in Manchester, then visited her in London before she returned to the United States from Tilbury, Essex. He arranged for a letter to be left for her on the boat in which he proposed marriage.

When his intended got back to America, she wrote, 'I'm terribly sorry, there must be some mistake, perhaps American girls are more forward than English ones.' The answer was no! Alfred wrote back, 'I'm so sorry, may I go on writing to you?' The family still has those letters. 'Dear Doctor Rée, yes of course we can go on corresponding.' And letters went back and forth for two or three years. Finally, 'Dear Doctor Rée' became 'To my darling Alfred,' and they got married (Harry says in 1898, the Dupont records and Mrs Rée's obituary both say 1900) in Pennsylvania. Her *Manchester Guardian* obituary describes her as an American citizen.

Dr Rée's obituary tells a slightly different story:

> He travelled in the United States. It was on one of his early visits there that he met his wife. His interest in international affairs was already large, and his marriage perhaps strengthened its American side. … His home was one in which many Americans found a cordial welcome.

They returned pronto to Manchester, since he was a conscientious businessman, and settled at 15 Mauldeth Road. Alfred soon retired.

The letters that Alfred Rée and his bride exchanged were transcribed in 1976, at the behest of Pamela Lowe. Both of them were very much of their time. For example, as they write back and forth for two years or more, there is no mention of the goings-on in England or the United States or internationally, apart from these exceptions: on 18 November 1899, Lavinia writes, 'I was so disgusted with the French through the Dreyfus affair,' and on 9 November of the same year:

> I am *so* interested in the outcome of the South African struggle, and *so* disappointed that England did not sweep everything before her at the first blow. What with our troubles in the Philippines and yours in the Transvaal the Anglo Saxons seem to have their hands pretty full.

And on 12 April 1900, Alfred refers to the *Manchester Guardian* as 'the only pro-Boer paper in the Kingdom'. There is no mention of citizenship.

Presumably Lavinia became a British subject upon her marriage; and passports may not have been required in those days.

Alfred agitates mightily for Lavinia to send a photograph, and he has almost an obsession with dates, pushing hard for the wedding date to be as soon as possible. Nearer the agreed-upon date, Lavinia offers to find Alfred a best man, and he accepts.

On 9 December 1899, Alfred writes, 'We are certainly of Jewish origin', eliciting no response, but on 2 April 1900, Lavinia writes, 'My father's family have been American since 1835. ... The du Ponts ... came to this country in 1800. ... Nor am I a Yankee.'

They discuss religion. Alfred comes across as a respectful agnostic, Lavinia as a believer, but neither is a preacher. Alfred does opine, 'People with nothing to do, have never any time for anything.' On 7 March 1900, Alfred refers to 'those darkie songs you sang'. Alfred read *Dombey and Son* and *Anna Karenina*; Lavinia the Browning letters and John Ruskin. There is no mention of sex.

He must have sold his business for quite a sum, since he did not do any more paid work for the rest of his days. Instead, he went into what he would have called 'public work'. He served on a committee for the Manchester College of Technology,[8] and was on the board of Imperial Chemical Industries[9].

Alfred Rée was president of the Manchester Chamber of Commerce in 1924–5, and a director for many years. A press clipping from those days describes the Manchester Chamber as among the first half-dozen of the world's greatest chambers and goes on: 'At its head today is a doctor of philosophy and scientific chemist. ... The Chamber embodies in its President the business interests and the civic interests of a great community.' Dr Rée's ideas, quoth the author, coincided exactly with those of President Coolidge:

> His office was in the noisiest spot in the noisiest city in the kingdom[10] ... the worst room in the country in which to talk, listen or think. ... There is nothing fussy or ostentatious about Dr Rée ... He is himself the essence of modesty. ... Dr Rée never smokes while at work ... The nearest approach to a hobby he could boast of was a daily walk of about ten miles, and a week-end in the country on his bicycle. He and his family – 'about eight

---

8   Part of the University of Manchester since 2004, having been UMIST (University of Manchester Institute of Science and Technology) for many years.
9   Which was soon to become the largest manufacturing company in the British Empire.
10 The office was in the Guildhall Chambers, Lloyd Street, between Deansgate and Princess Street.

or ten of us' – he laughed, 'cycle into the country every week-end the weather permits. I have no ambition to possess a motor car.'[11]

The author of his *Manchester Guardian* obituary wrote:

His modesty prevented him from being well known to the public. A friend describes him as 'entirely impersonal and unambitious' in all his work. This quality made him one of the most popular members of the chamber …[12]

There is a report of a presidential address that was devoted to the subject of patent law reform. Dr Rée said that the number of well-trained chemists 'in this country' was only one-fortieth of the number in Germany and one-fiftieth of the number in Switzerland. It was high time, he said, that the old prejudice against the study of chemistry should be overcome. It is intriguing that this address was delivered in May 1917, at the height of the First World War, and by the descendant of a German immigrant.[13] Dr Rée, with his foreign-sounding name and his doctorate from Switzerland, must have been very well accepted: *Nature* (1917) reports a meeting of 500 persons at the Manchester School of Technology, which he chaired, where a British Association of Chemists was inaugurated.

The sheer number of organizations to which Dr Rée belonged, usually in some leadership capacity, is impressive, and one thinks of the number of causes his son Harry was to embrace decades later.

Herewith a partial listing:

• English-Speaking Union: supporter of Lord Derby when it was being formed
• University of Manchester: treasurer
• Manchester (Municipal) College of Technology: chairman, chemical section
• Manchester Education Committee: co-opted member from 1920 until his death
• Manchester Literary and Philosophical Society: elected an 'ordinary' member in 1888 and remaining a member until at least 1916
• Board of Trade[14]: inspector of research for three years

---

11 All efforts to identify the provenance of this newspaper cutting have so far been unsuccessful.
12 24 February 1933.
13 It was a couple of months later that the Royal Family switched from Saxe-Coburg-Gotha to the 'House of Windsor' and the Battenbergs changed their names to Mountbatten.
14 Now the Department of Business, Innovation and Skills.

- Imperial Chemical Industries (ICI)
- Federation of British Industries: represented the chemical section in a deputation to the French Government, 1919
- Manchester Chamber of Commerce
- International Chamber of Commerce: representing the Manchester Chamber at its first meeting in Paris in 1920
- Association of British Chemical Manufacturers: active in its formation, becoming a member of its council in 1916
- British Association of Chemists: first chairman
- British Dyestuffs Corporation: member
- Joint Committee of the Cotton Trade Organisations: first chairman, 1924
- Society of Chemical Industry: vice president
- Society of Dyers and Colourists: president, 1916–18

In 1984, Maurice Tordoff put together a sturdy volume entitled *The Servant of Colour, A history of the Society of Dyers and Colourists 1884–1984*, in which Alfred Rée is mentioned at least seven times. In 1898 he was paid two guineas[15] for an article on the Patent Act, and in 1917 he delivered his second presidential address, in which he offered 'a few reflections on matters connected with the British coal tar colour industry'.

He died at home, probably of cancer, at the age of 68, and Harry remembered him being cremated. His wife died 13 years later.

Dr Rée left a document with his daughter Helen Rée Fairclough, Harry's youngest sister, in which he wrote that 'some people of the name of Rée migrated from Alsace to the northern parts of Europe' in the seventeenth century. Ruben Rée died in 1659, and his grave is in an old disused cemetery in Altona. Altona is now the westernmost urban borough of Hamburg, Germany. From 1640 until 1864, it was under the administration of the Danish monarchy; and because of the severe restrictions on the number of Jews allowed to live in Hamburg, a major Jewish community developed there.

If there is an Alsatian connection, it dates back almost 400 years. Harry's son Jonathan writes:

> The confusion arises from the vaguely French appearance of the name Rée. But there are no French people of that name, though several in Denmark and (before Hitler) in Germany. Several early Rées were also called Herschel or Hirsch, and a friend of mine, who specializes in the history of Jews, came up with the best

---

15   Equivalent to about £230 in 2016.

explanation I have heard. Hirsch means a deer, or a kind of deer
in German, and Ré means a kind of deer in French, so when
Jews were required to adopt family names in Europe, around the
beginning of the eighteenth century, they seem to have opted for
Rée, perhaps to cover their tracks and make themselves sound as
if they were French. Cunning or what?

Jonathan Rée's document continues: 'Harry [our Harry's great-grandfather]
was born in Altona in 1805. He was a paper manufacturer and later an
agent for Reuters', which began in the middle of the nineteenth century:

> His eldest son Isidor Rée [Harry's grandfather] was born in
> Hamburg in 1830, and migrated to Leeds about 1855. ... He
> was in business as a wool stapler, first in Leeds and later on in
> the early 70s he moved his business to Bradford, but lived in
> Apperley Bridge until his death in 1905. ... When he [Isidor]
> retired from active business life at the end of the 80s, he devoted
> himself almost exclusively to ... charitable affairs ... in and
> near Bradford. ... His numerous kind deeds were of an entirely
> unostentatious character. My own mother, Meta Rée, died very
> early at the age of 27.

Isidor died in 1905 and was buried in the cemetery of St Peter's Church,
Rawdon, Leeds, Yorkshire.

To this day, there is a Rée Park in Aarhus, the second-largest city
in Denmark, and about 350 kilometres from Hamburg. There is an 11-
page document entitled *Hartvig Philip Ree and his Family*, 'published at
the instigation of Edward Ree, stock-broker, director of the land bank of
the Danish Isles.' I do not know when this paper was printed. It describes
Hartvig Philip Ree as 'a merchant with liberal ideas and a very cultured
mind, gifted with thorough knowledge'. He was born in 1778 and died in
1859. He studied Hebrew, and 'at one of the king's visits he had the honour
of being named the Jewish community's spokesperson and in the name of
this community he gave speech to the king[16] in French'.

Back to Alfred Rée:

> My mother's father [Harry's great-grandfather] was Dr Anton
> Rée (1815–91) of whom I saw a good deal; in fact for two years I
> lived in his house ... subsequent to my mother's serious illness. ...
> He spent several years at the University of Kiel where he studied

---

16   This was almost certainly Frederick VI.

philosophy ... and his book on ethics[17] ... enjoyed a considerable measure of appreciation. ... He was a strong adherent of Spinoza.

It is interesting that Harry's son Jonathan would also become a philosopher. And there was yet another in the family: Paul Ludwig Carl Heinrich Rée, a friend of Nietzsche, was a member of the first German parliament. His second wife was Emma Howard, of Melbourne, Yorkshire, a founder of one of the first technical schools for women in Germany. He died by falling into the Charnadüra Gorge near Celerina in Switzerland.

Anton Rée founded a school, and was its headmaster for nearly 40 years:

> [T]he children of all classes were educated together, that is to say the children of the well-to-do as well as the poorest classes and also children of every religious denomination. The esteem in which he was held ... may perhaps be illustrated by mentioning that some 30 years after his death, the Hamburg City Council, of which for many years he was also a member, decided to alter the name of an important street in Hamburg named after Field-Marshall Moltke[18] to the name of Dr Anton Rée.[19]

Anton Rée, it turns out, was the son of a banker to the King of Denmark. He worked from 1838 until his death at the Israelitische Freischule (Jewish Free School) in Hamburg, becoming its Director in 1848. H. Baar wrote, in 1903:

> It was a hard blow for him to learn one day that his father had lost his whole fortune, and that necessity would compel him to accept any position that was offered him.

Baar continued:

> Dr Ree was quite different. He could stoop to a child, could speak to it in its own peculiar language and knew how to condescend to its level of thought. ... In short, he was a real teacher.

The school's wealthy founders were associated with the Jewish Reform movement; and although it was initially created for poor Jewish children, it admitted Christian pupils. By 1869, these would outnumber the Jewish

---

17 *Wanderungen eines Zeitgenossen auf dem Gebiete der Ethik*, Hamburg, 1857.
18 The most prominent figure in the Franco-Prussian War of 1870–1.
19 This document was found in the possession of Helen (Rée) Fairclough [Harry's sister]. It is assumed to have been written by her father, Dr Alfred Rée, husband of Lavinia Dimmick Rée.

pupils. Anton Rée created a scholarship for Christian and other non-Jewish pupils in memory of his only daughter, who died at an early age.

By 1907, the proportion of Jewish students had dropped to just over ten per cent, and in 1920 the school became a *Realschule* (i.e. not a *Gymnasium*).[20]

From 1881 to 1884, Rée sat in the Reichstag as a member of the Deutsche Fortschrittspartei (German Progress Party), the first modern political party in Germany.[21]

What might Anton Rée have thought of Harry's mere decade as a headmaster?

Harry did not describe himself as Jewish or, for that matter, as Christian. I did find one place where he was described as Jewish: in a 2010 obituary of Professor John Orr in *The Scotsman*, Orr is described as having been educated at 'Watford Grammar School, where he was strongly influenced by Harry Rée, the Jewish wartime Resistance hero'.

There are five Rées in the *Jewish Encyclopedia*, including Anton Rée (1820–86) and a Danish priest who was a student of Chopin.

There is Anita (Clara) Rée (1885–1933), a noted Hamburg painter: Harry would have been in his late teens when she died, so he almost certainly knew of her and may even have known her. She is described as coming from a long-established Jewish merchant family, but she and her sister Emily were both baptized and confirmed Lutherans. Anita's Venezuelan mother was half-Jewish, with Indian ancestry; her father, Eduard Israel Rée, began as a businessman, but retired young and lived on his earnings. She studied painting in Germany, and spent six months in Paris taking lessons from Fernand Léger, who has been described by some as a forerunner of pop art.

Anita Rée, very aware of the Nazis' views of her Jewish background and in despair, left Hamburg for the small town of Kampen on the Island of Sylt[22] in the summer of 1932. She lived alone, without money, in unheated rooms. She committed suicide in December 1933, having written to a friend:

> I can no longer live in such a world and have no other wish than to depart that to which I no longer belong.

---

20 It closed in 1933, ostensibly because of lack of enrolment. It is now the Anna Siemsen School.
21 Founded in Prussia in 1861 in strict opposition to Otto von Bismarck, it ended in a merger with the Liberal Union in 1884.
22 Ironically, this island, population around 20,000, is now described as a haven for tourists, with a large number of gay and lesbian residents.

Earlier in 1933, according to her biographer, Maike Bruhns, she had visited Oxford with Valerie Alport, an art collector and patron.[23] They contemplated emigration, but to Italy or Spain rather than England.[24] There is an Anita-Rée-Strasse in Bergedorf, the largest of the seven boroughs of Hamburg, as well as Anton-Rée-Weg just over ten miles away.

Harry visited Hamburg at least once before the War. Marcus Binney wrote:

> His first venture in journalism was an article on Hamburg in the *Yorkshire Post* in about 1937, a big middle-page spread headed 'Where Hitler has German critics.'

Binney probably got the 1937 date from Harry, who recalled 1937 in an interview almost 50 years later.[25] Actually, the piece appeared on 21 May, 1935, headlined 'WHERE HITLER HAS GERMAN CRITICS, Hamburg Retains Her Love of Freedom', by Henry A. Rée: 'Today Hitler will address the German nation on the wireless.' This was the only time that Harry called himself Henry, or perhaps the paper did so. His optimism was apparent:

> Hamburg understood the democratic system. ... In one section of the Hamburg community the feeling of sanity and justice is very much alive, that is, among the cultured people who remember the War [i.e., the First World War], and these in Hamburg are not only important, but are numerous. ... They naturally are not allowed to voice their opinions in public, but this has had the effect of bringing them together, informally, in private.

Harry quoted a joke he had brought back to England:

> Have you heard that the Government offices in Berlin have been broken into, and the only things the thieves took were the results of the next election?

---

23 Maike Bruhns (1986) *Anita Ree: Leben und Werk einer Hamburger Malerin 1885–1933*. Hamburg: Verein für Hamburgische Geschichte.
24 In 1937, Valerie Alport did emigrate to England with her son Eric, who later became Stephen Spender's partner.
25 Marcus Binney (2005) *Secret War Heroes, Men of the Special Operations Executive*, London: Hodder and Stoughton, refers to the 1983 and 1985 Rée interviews at the Imperial War Museum sound archives.

The 20-year-old's article ended thus:

> Poor Germany! Can the culture and sanity of Hamburg bring her
> to her senses? 'Men are we, and must grieve when even the shade
> of that which once was great is pass'd away.'

The quotation is from Wordsworth, which the *Yorkshire Post* of the mid-1930s must have assumed its readers would have recognized.

Chapter 2

Early life and schooling

As Harry described his life as a child in Manchester to Liz Peretz, it seems to have been very Victorian. It was not cruel at all, but old-fashioned even by the standards of the time. Harry described in 1988 how there were three maids, who all slept in one large room at the top of the house:

> There was a terrible smell. And they had to use one particular bathroom, the maids' bathroom. It was horrible really. And yet they were very happy.
>
> …
>
> Just only the other day, I had a letter from a former maid, saying what a wonderful time she'd had as a maid in the house and what a wonderful person my mother was to work for and so on. Extraordinary.
>
> …
>
> It was a very regulated household and life was remarkably secure. It was really a lovely background to be brought up in. There were no real worries.

('Lovely' was one of Harry's favourite words.) He was a teenager during the worst of the Depression. Like all of his siblings, he went to:

> a little school next door, which was a sort of progressive day school. Very well known in Manchester. … starting at the age of six.

Lady Barn House School was founded in 1873.[26] Harry thought 'the teachers were rather good', and when you consider how critical he could be of people in education, this was a noteworthy judgement, rendered almost 70 years after he had been taught to read. He liked *slöjd*, a Swedish method of teaching woodwork, and disliked 'eurhythmics', a method of teaching music. 'I was, I suppose, fairly meek and mild', he reflected in 1988, 'I wasn't a very adventurous little boy', and he mentioned both a nanny and an Irish governess.

---

26   It moved to 57a Schools Hill, Cheadle, Cheshire, in the 1950s.

I find it hard, at this distance, to imagine Harry, whose father's family were non-practising Jews, walking two miles every Sunday to an Anglican church where the Rées had their own pew, and celebrating Christmas Eve like Queen Victoria and Prince Albert. I do not know whether he was baptized. No one seemed to notice that Alfred Rée did not go to church, 'except perhaps on Christmas Day'. His wife was a pillar of the church, 'a very sincere believing Christian'. Bible every night, and God bless every member of the family by name.

Harry was sent to The Craig, a boys' preparatory school in Windermere.[27] The headmaster was William Snow: 'a fine person, very keen on Wordsworth'. There were 40 little boys and the fees were £40 a year;[28] 'a terrible place in many ways ... very traditional and uninteresting'. Windermere is 85 miles from Manchester: one wonders how long it took little Harry to get to and fro, especially since his father did not own a car. The school owner was interested in boys' health, which was well and good; but he made them drink a foul, cold concoction before breakfast that included currants, figs, prunes and raisins. 'We had to drink this obviously, for our bowels.' For a while, Snow was intrigued by the Parents' National Education Union (PNEU).[29]

I quote from a contemporary advertisement:

Craig Preparatory School. W. Snow, M.A., late scholar of Worcester College, Oxford. ... Indian pupils received.

When Harry was just 13 years old, he appeared in several sketches in the *Craig Revue 1927*. The stage manager was 'T.W. Snow, Esq.', presumably the owner's son. Harry appeared in at least four of the 15 scenes: 'Yours to hand'; 'Nigger Minstrels';[30] 'Willow Waly, Duet Song'; and 'Black Chango blues'. What can 13-year-old Harry have been thinking when asked to sing W.S. Gilbert's words:

Prithee, pretty maiden – prithee, tell me true

(Hey, but I'm doleful, willow, willow waly!)

---

27 Founded in 1899 and closed in 1966.
28 About £1,200+ in 2016: economical for a boarding school.
29 Founded in 1888 by Charlotte Mason.
30 It should be pointed out that, today, the N-word is so uniquely unacceptable that *Huckleberry Finn* (discussed below), which first came out in 1885, is hugely controversial. In 1927, the use of that word in rural England was probably thoughtless rather than intentionally racist, but one wonders whether Harry was ever retrospectively embarrassed. As late as 1949, the BBC still used the N-word in its printed programming. See page 217.

Have you e'er a lover a-dangling after you?

Hey, willow waly O!

In an undated essay entitled *Books are Teachers*, Harry was to write:

> Where are snows of yesteryear? William Snow, a residual
> Victorian, ran a small undistinguished prep school in the Lake
> District between the wars. He was old and skinny and ill-dressed,
> but from him we caught poetry – and it stuck. 'All shod with
> steel' we hissed along the polished ice of Derwent Water, as
> Wordsworth had done, and as we lifted up our eyes unto the hills
> above Grasmere, our hearts danced with the daffodils. 'Stone
> walls do not a prison make, nor iron bars a cage', he would
> quote, and a dozen years later before taking off for France, where
> I knew I might end up in prison, I tried to learn the whole poem
> by heart, 'just in case'. ... William Snow was the first to introduce
> me to two valuable assets – sensitivity to poetry, and how to chop
> wood with a big axe!

Harry described in 1988 how William Snow's son came back from the First
World War:

> a sort of dashing captain, who was married and had two
> children. But he fell in love with me, and I can remember it was
> very embarrassing because going out of his study into the main
> school, sort of wiping the kisses off my mouth, I didn't quite
> understand what was happening.

And, for sure, you didn't go telling people about this kind of thing.

Harry was soon to follow his brothers to Shrewsbury School, a well-
known 'public' school[31] some 90 miles from the family home. Founded by
Royal Charter in 1552, Shrewsbury is one of the original and best-known
of the top-tier public schools, along with Eton and Winchester. Even the
imperturbable Harry Rée might be both surprised and quizzically amused
to learn that the school began to admit girls in 2008.

A 1933 handwritten report from Shrewsbury states, and I quote
verbatim:

> (His father died Feb. 27.) (Fine Rugger player.)

---

31 Those unfamiliar with England may be surprised to learn that the most prestigious and
exclusive private schools are called 'public schools'.

(I think, by the way, that he died a day later.) The same one-pager tells us that Harry won the Bentley German prize and speaks of his 'invincible good humour'. We also read:

> 'He develops on lively and attractive lines, making a better monitor and companion, perhaps, than an actual scholar.'

> 'Far less slapdash; v. keen all-round.'

> 'I beg him to beware of casualness of manner.'

He did not become a prefect.[32] And less than 20 years later, having been a genuine war hero, he was one of England's leading headmasters, appointing prefects.

When Harry was about to leave Shrewsbury, the school magazine, *The Salopian*, printed the following paragraph that only a member of the English elite could fully comprehend:

> *Valete*. H.A. Rée. Mod VI1. House Monitor. 2nd XI Cricket Colours. House cricket colours (Capt.) 3rd XI and House Football Colours. Committee of the Debating and Dramatic Societies. Sgt. In O.T.C. Cer. 'A.'[33]

Since much of Harry Rée's thinking about education was shaped in contrast to his experiences at Shrewsbury, it seems important to retrieve as much as one can. Unfortunately, there's little more than his memory, the one-page report referenced above, and quotations from *The Salopian*, mostly concerning the Debating Society, where young men, knowingly or not, rehearsed for adult roles. We should not, of course, assume that the reporters' styles met with Harry's approval at the time. Herewith are most of the mentions of H.A. Rée, between 1931 and 1933:

> Mr Rée (maiden), after treating us to a suspiciously 'debating society-joke', put a ruthless end to the blissful inspirations the chairman might be acquiring ... he flickered dauntlessly on his dais.

> Mr Rée, after deprecating the religious references of the previous speaker ... Optimists were thoughtless people who spent their time in a spirit of jingoistic self-elation ...

---

32 Traditionally, in British schools, a prefect would be given authority over other students including the ability, until relatively recently, to cane.

33 *Valete*: 'goodbye, farewell, be well'; OTC: Officer Training Corps, for learning at an early age to be effortless leaders, at a time when a quarter of the world's population and a fifth of its landmass were within the British Empire.

Mr H.A. Rée revealed himself a Free Trader, and talked about potatoes. ... We had been told that the Liberals were rats, but let the house remember that rats leave a sinking ship. An energetic and sound speech.

Mr Rée ... individualism is a muddle and cannot save the world.

Mr H.A. Rée moved 'That crime cannot be killed by kindness.' The hon. mover, with magnificent alliterations, told the House that crime is the curse as it was the child of civilization ... it is youth that is responsible for all crimes at the present moment. And no kind old lady can stop it; the cat and the birch are the only effective correctives. After a dissertation on yo-yo's ... The House must not let England follow the USA, but must follow Canada and France, and smash crime by severity.[34]

After a thoughtful silence, Mr H.A. Rée rose with a swirl, and subjected the House to a stream of alliteration which was almost endless. Amidst the hiss of his sibilants, he informed us that he was convinced that the films 'drugged the lower classes'.

Mr H.A. Rée wanted us all to return to our infancy and yell at each other.

Mr H.A. Rée stormed at the foolishness of the debate ... He apparently disapproved of professionalism.

Harry took a fairly major part in Galsworthy's *Loyalties*. Published in 1922, this was one of the first plays to deal honestly and openly with the problem of anti-Semitism. According to *The Salopian*:

H.A. Rée, far from military in appearance as Captain Ronald Dancy, wore an air of guilt from the beginning; he has acquired the present-day stage habit of staccato bursts of speech. He was at his best in the final scene with Mabel.

In 1988 he spoke about how he was a 'fag' for his first two years at Shrewsbury.[35] He accepted being beaten by prefects as being part of the culture; as he remembered it, 'you were rather proud of the marks on your

---

34 One assumes that none of his audience would have had any idea of his American heritage.

35 A 'fag' was a junior boy who acted as a kind of servant to a senior boy at a British boarding school, doing minor chores. Salopians, i.e. Shrewsbury School boys, used the word 'scum' for 'fag', thereby earning a place in Eric Partridge's *A Dictionary of Slang and Unconventional English*, which was first published in 1937.

bottom after being beaten'. In fact, he also beat boys, but very rarely. Years later, he would be outspoken against corporal punishment, but I can still recall the name of the poor lad in my class at Watford Grammar School who got caned by the headmaster, though the fact that I can remember his name suggests how infrequent this had become. Harry's thinking on this issue evolved: Alasdair Brown recalled a tutorial at York where Harry argued against corporal punishment, but added that he didn't believe in absolutes.

Harry's son Jonathan writes:

> I was certainly never beaten by Harry. I seem to remember Harry look back on it with complete embarrassment … having been, as he would say, a BF. ['Bloody fool'.]

He wrote poetry, some of which appeared in the school magazine. (Unfortunately, this poetry was published anonymously.) In the sixth form, he studied French and German, and an enlightened senior English master introduced him to *King Lear*, T.S. Eliot's *The Waste Land* and A.E. Housman's *A Shropshire Lad*. Some of the stiff upper lip characteristics he acquired at Shrewsbury stayed with him, or so he said.

By this time, Harry's life was centred on school rather than home, which was perfectly normal for that social class at that time:

> The main thing was the love affairs between boys, which were part of the culture. Strangely, not unstrictly governed by convention. And of course there was an enormous amount of, what one might call, safe sex. Because they used to meet in lavatories and masturbate. … That was a very important part of one's life.

In *The Essential Grammar School* (1956), Harry was to write:

> Homosexuality at boarding-schools must be accepted as a fairly normal occurrence. It can also be assumed that in the majority of cases no permanent harm is done to the individual. … aberration is temporary.

At this distance, one cannot accuse Harry of having thought through the issues in any depth.

In 2005, almost 15 years after Harry's death, the autobiography of the BBC disc jockey, John Peel, came out under his real name, John Ravenscroft. It was entitled *Margrave of the Marshes*. In the book, Ravenscroft credibly claimed to have been raped while a student at Shrewsbury School; he wrote of 'systematic sexual abuse'. But as his reviewer in *The Observer* wrote, the abuse and the rape were described with 'more of a shrug than a howl.' Born in 1939, Ravenscroft would have been writing about events of the early and middle 1950s, when Harry was already headmastering at Watford; for sure, Harry would have recognized the picture being drawn.

Peel's book not only makes Harry's descriptions that much more credible; it underlines the fact that mindless beatings, forced hand jobs and even rape were the norm at Shrewsbury. When the book came out, the then headmaster of the school declared himself 'greatly disturbed' but assured readers of *The Daily Telegraph* that 'such behaviour had been eradicated from the public school system'. He did not attempt to deny that the events had taken place; nor, it would seem, did the book damage the school's reputation.

Downstart, The Autobiography of Brian Inglis, which came out in 1990, describes the 'licensed bullying at Shrewsbury' and goes on, 'our time was never our own'. No wonder holidays at home seemed uneventful!

Harry's social conscience was awakened by what he saw at the Shrewsbury Mission House in the slums off Scotland Road in Liverpool.[36] Here is what he remembered in the late 1980s:

> There was an amazing thing, I can remember it terribly well. ... In the wall of the street there was a sort of iron machine which was known as the iron cow. And the boys, or the women, would put a penny into this machine and a tap at the bottom would then spout a pennyworth of milk. ... It must have been filthy, absolutely pullulating with germs, I should think.

It was understood at Shrewsbury, as at many 'public' schools of that era, that most of the boys would go into some kind of public service: the colonial civil service, the Sudan civil service, the Indian civil service, for example. It is strange to think how short-lived the empire on which the sun never set turned out to be.[37] Harry remembered a housemaster saying, 'You know, Harry, only the real shits go into the City.' Harry added, 'It's probably the same today.'

There were OTC parades once a week ... very boring ... with rifle and bayonet drill and excessive ceremony; annual inspection by a general. All of this led to his active interest in the Peace Pledge Union, which was founded in the mid-1930s following a letter to the *Manchester Guardian* by Dick Sheppard, Dean of Canterbury. In February 1933, ten days after Adolf Hitler became Chancellor of Germany, students at the Oxford Union voted

---

36 Shrewsbury House was founded by Shrewsbury School in 1903. Now in a different building, it is still in partnership with the school.

37 The Sudan Civil Service, very prestigious in its day, lasted from 1899 until the mid-1950s.

275–153 never to fight for King and country: in a 1985 interview, Harry recalled supporting the 275.

Many of Harry's teachers at Shrewsbury were dullards: Oxbridge graduates for the most part, without any training as teachers. There was very traditional clothing, so Harry the sixth former would have worn a top hat. It is no surprise that he revolted against ties, especially during and after his York years. But Ian Lister, his successor at the University of York, did point out that Harry wore top quality shirts, albeit a bit frayed. Nick Tucker tells the tale of how Harry was 'once refused admission to a posh York hotel for the Xmas lunch because of his shabby attire'. Harry's retort to the doorman on this occasion was 'Flipping arseholes!'

And Tim Brighouse tells how he invited Harry to talk to the Education Committee in Oxfordshire, where he was the chief education officer. It was in the 1980s, when ties were *de rigueur*. Harry showed up cheerfully, in corduroys, sports jacket … and no tie. Tim asked the conservative spokesperson to give her reaction:

> What are you worried about? He is so obviously a gentleman.
> Just look at the meticulous way he has his collar open. You could
> learn a lesson or two from him.

Years later, in 2014, Brighouse would describe Harry as 'poshly dishevelled'.

Nigel Gann says, 'Harry did have an effortless superiority. He was an aristocrat.'

He was always close to his family. He spoke, to me at least, a lot about his three children; not so much about parents or siblings. Until she died, his mother wrote twice a week to each of her children, and that must have helped keep the family together, especially after Dr Rée's death. Even though Harry's values were different from those of many of his family, one never senses any hostility towards any of them; rather, warmth, love and acceptance.

So far, then, Harry comes across as a pleasant and fairly obedient boy from a well-off middle-class family with foreign antecedents. I doubt whether, as he left Shrewsbury, anyone could have foreseen the twists and turns of his life.

Chapter 3

Cambridge

And then, it was off to Cambridge. Let us begin with the aspect of Cambridge in which Harry was least interested: he never claimed to be a scholar. His tutor was Claude W. Guillebaud, MA, Lecturer and then Reader in Economics at the University and Fellow of St John's College.[38] In his first year, he 'read' Economics, for which he got a 'third'.[39] He then switched to Modern and Medieval Languages, ending up with a 2:1 in French and a 2:2 in German. At Oxford and Cambridge, anyone with a BA degree could simply apply for an MA after six or seven years – no further study or examinations were required, and almost everyone did, and presumably still does. I always admired Harry for not going through this phony-baloney exercise. When I first saw his name on a list, it read 'Harry A. Rée, OBE, DSO, BA'. No doubt, some of his colleagues at York disapproved, as did a few of the older masters at Watford.

Throughout his life, Harry had little respect for the letters after people's names. As he wrote one time, encouraging someone who happened not to have academic credentials:

> A degree is often the sign of a clot – and the lack of a degree, in a person like you (not that there are many like you!) is utterly unimportant. – And if anyone takes this lack to be in any way derogating, their opinion isn't worth a cat's fart. You've got a huge lot going for you, my dear, and if next time isn't lucky, never mind – try try try again!

Harry the undergraduate had no financial worries. There was almost no mention of the Depression. His father had left more than enough for him to go to Cambridge, and his mother gave him what he called a 'smallish allowance'. Why did he go to Cambridge? Because that's what you did! As he described those years in 1988, 'There was this damned effortless superiority, which is inculcated, or was inculcated, by the public schools.'

---

38 In those days, and until fairly recently, it would be perfectly normal for such a personage not to have a doctorate; and the UK title 'Reader' might be the equivalent of an associate professor in the United States.

39 In the UK, there were, and still are, three classes of honours degrees: First Class Honours; Second Class Honours, often divided into 'Upper Second' (2:1) and 'Lower Second' (2:2); and Third Class Honours.

Harry was a member of the short-lived Apostles (not to be confused with the famous Cambridge Apostles), which was 'a 12-member club which though ostensibly "for the purpose of debating on any subject", chose to ignore the international scene'.[40]

The teaching was mediocre, and one wonders why he began with what Thomas Carlyle called the 'dismal science', i.e. economics. Maybe it was because St John's College, despite its wealth, did not have a single tutor in French or German. He played some squash, having slipped a cartilage during his first rugger game.

I do not know how influenced Harry was by the anti-Franco elements or the Communists: he must have been aware of them. He joined the ADC, the Amateur Dramatic Club, becoming its secretary. At some point, he took part in a one-act play called *Easy Death*, which he described much later as being about euthanasia; he wondered in 1988 whether his strong interest in euthanasia began on Newmarket Road. The mention of this play in his recorded interview for the British Library led me to a fascinating and ultimately successful chase that, it turns out, was possible only in the computer age.

Professor Şükrü Hanioğlu of Princeton University reports that Mustafa Hilmi, the author of the play, was a well-known figure of the Ottoman Tanzimât (Reform) era, whose heyday was from 1839 to 1876. The play's title should be translated as *Affect of Love* or *Effortless Death*. The play was not translated into any other language, so one assumes that the ADC had an unpublished version provided by one of its members. It is in three acts, so not as Harry remembered it, though it is possible that only part of it may have been staged.

İsmet Hanim is Kenan'Bey's lover:

İsmet Hanim: May God Almighty save you for my sake. If not, I hope He will take my life as soon as possible … Because death is a thousand times preferable to living without you.

Kenan'Bey: Physical health does not mean anything to me while İsmet is ill.

---

40   A footnote in P. Linehan's *St John's College Cambridge: A History* (2011) continues:
    Established in November 1934 and surviving for just over two years, it debated such urgent issues as whether it preferred moonlight to sunlight and the proposition 'that pessimism is justifiable in the present age', otherwise concentrating on sex, religion and the royal family. It folded … after thirteen meetings. … Amongst its leading lights was Harry Rée.

İsmet: The utmost aim of lovers is to die for the sake
                  of their beloved ones and pass away before
                  their eyes. Look, I have achieved this aim. I am
                  breathing my final breaths before you. ... I am
                  dying for you. ... How easy is dying! ...

Kenan'Bey: I was living for you in this world. What kind
                  of attachment would I have to life while you
                  are gone?

[*He pulls out his revolver and shoots himself in the mouth.
He falls.*]

Professor Hanioğlu concludes:

> So there is no direct reference to euthanasia. In other words,
> there is no deliberate intervention with the express intention
> of ending İsmet's life. However, the fact that she is brought to
> Kenan's mansion to die without pain might be considered a loose
> reference to euthanasia. Her mother could have taken her to a
> hospital or called a medical doctor to rescue her daughter. Instead
> İsmet is brought to the mansion to die in peace while looking at
> her lover's face.

My conclusion? This is not a play I am aching to see. As for Harry: his
recollection, after about half a century, is more important than what we
read. Clearly, he was thinking about issues of suicide and euthanasia at an
early age.

He became involved with the St John's College Mission in Hoxton,
East London. The somewhat ponderous 757-page history of the college
reports that:

> Harry Rée asked if he might call to discuss a scheme for
> stimulating interest in the College club at Hoxton 'and generally
> of fostering the College spirit'.

Hoxton was historically an impoverished part of inner London, now part
of the London Borough of Hackney, and it is ironic that, years later, Harry
would be teaching at Woodberry Down School, minutes from Hoxton,
and serving on a governing board in the same general area. Harry told
a delightful tale about how, just before Christmas one year, he wrote to
dons in various colleges and their wives, with the result that the pavement
for about half a mile outside St John's College was covered with toys of

all kinds, which Harry sent down to Hoxton on a lorry. One can readily imagine being persuaded to do one's bit by his insistent charm.

In a letter to Maureen Thomas, Harry recalled his first visit to France:

> It was my first experience of France – at age 8 – in 1924!!!![41] I can recall now my fears as the ship rolled through the night in thick fog, blowing its horrible foghorn, and me with my mother in a cabin, worrying because we were below the waterline, and my mother trying to divert my attention by showing me that the bath water was green and *salty* because it came directly from the sea!

He would later write:

> I'm off to Dieppe with my 30 14-year-olds next weekend – cooking for them – the Youth Hostel – it should be hilarious if I don't poison them.

Thus he visited France before the War. His nephew Hugo, now a doctor living near Brisbane, Australia, recounts how his father Eric Lionel (1905–1943) owned a farm in the Dordogne which Harry visited around 1936–7. He spoke later of delivering milk to the village with a donkey. Hugo's French mother, who died in 2005 shortly before her ninety-first birthday, described how Harry 'arrived (by train) with an apology for not having brought any presents, claiming he had no money. He then presented mum with two toilet rolls which he had stolen off the train!'

Hugo describes how his mother, a French widow later living in England, did not have an easy time and was treated with indifference by the Rée family. However:

> Harry was different. Once he was back in civilian life, he took an interest in her family; I think he occasionally provided financial support (we were in dire straits); he visited as often as his busy schedule allowed, and we certainly visited him and Hetty in Bradford, then in Watford. ... He gave me a list of books to read, asking me to write a commentary on each ... which he would read and in turn comment on. The first book was William Golding's *Lord of the Flies*,[42] which opened my eyes and started an interest which has continued to this day. For that I will be eternally grateful.

---

41   If it was 1924, he must in fact have been nine or ten.
42   First published in 1954.

Back to pre-War Cambridge: Harry was also involved with the Universities' Council for Unemployed camps, which had been founded by Richard Sims-Williams and in which six universities participated. In his second year at Cambridge, he went to a camp in Helmsley, North Yorkshire, and helped dig a new bed for a river on land belonging to Charles William Slingsby 'Sim' Duncombe, Third Earl of Feversham. He was an Etonian and a Conservative member of the House of Lords; awarded a Distinguished Service Order (DSO), after the War. The next year, 1936, he said: 'I ran the damn camp myself. I was only 21.'

In his article, 'Service learning in Britain between the wars: University students and unemployed camps', written over half a century later, John Field was to document some of this, but in lingo that Harry would have found almost unintelligible.[43] What, he might have asked, is 'service learning'? And, he would have argued, you cannot possibly document what he had learned; at the same time, passionately demonstrating what he had, in fact, learned.

One wonders: would he have described himself as a socialist at that time? He did visit Durham and Jarrow. It was on a slagheap in Durham that a miner said to him, 'There's only one thing that can save us … another war.' This was in 1937. Over 50 years later, Harry would say, 'And of course the bugger was right. He knew more than I did with all my economics and all that.'

Harry did not make many friends at Cambridge; certainly few that he kept up with. An exception was Frank Thistlethwaite, a fellow-northerner, born in Burnley, who later became the founding vice-chancellor of the University of East Anglia. When Thistlethwaite's daughter Jane was born in 1942, she later wrote that Harry:

> generously purchased a silver beaker as a christening mug that, it was alleged, he acquired in Switzerland, where he ended up after his legendary SOE exploits in France, and brought it back for me before the end of the War.

> I remember enjoying staying with the family in Watford. … Hetty, the Quaker, was a pretty, dark-haired warm, gentle person whom, as a shy young guest, I particularly liked. My near contemporary was Janet.

---

43   Field, J. (2012) 'Service learning in Britain between the wars: University students and unemployed camps'. *History of Education*, 41 (2), 195–212.

Maybe Harry bought christening mugs in batches. Jill Pellew describes how, while Hetty was her godparent, Harry brought back a silver christening mug from Switzerland in 1944.

At Cambridge he met Henry Morris, probably the single greatest influence on his life. Henry, as we might say today, sucked the oxygen out of those who surrounded him.[44]

Forty years after they first met, Harry would return to Cambridge to write *Educator Extraordinary: The life and achievement of Henry Morris 1889–1961* (1973).

Morris was born in Southport, Lancashire, about 40 miles northwest of Manchester, in 1889, becoming an office boy at *The Southport Visiter* (which still exists) at the age of 14 and, soon after that, a reporter. In 1910, he enrolled at St David's University College, Lampeter,[45] to read for a degree in theology, but went on to Exeter College, Oxford, two years later. He volunteered to serve in the First World War, becoming an officer in the Royal Army Service Corps (RASC). He made the then-unusual switch from Oxon. to Cantab., according to Harry, because 'Oxford reminded him too sharply of friends who didn't survive'. At Cambridge, he studied philosophy, then called 'moral sciences' (as opposed to natural sciences), at King's College. After a year as Assistant Secretary for Education for Cambridgeshire (not the City of Cambridge, but the impoverished county surrounding it), he was appointed Secretary in 1922. As Harry would have pointed out about almost anyone else, and scathingly, he had no teaching experience, none.

Harry recalls that his father, who was on the Manchester Education Committee at the time, had mentioned something to the Chief Education Officer of Manchester who had, in turn, written to Morris. This must have happened shortly before Dr Rée's death and before Harry 'went up'. So Harry visited Shire Hall, home of the Cambridgeshire County Council (up Castle Street and a mere mile-and-a-half from St John's College) for a brief interview.

Nothing much happened until Harry was in his last year at Cambridge. He was going round an art exhibition when a man came up to him and asked, 'Are you still intending to do the same thing as you were?' Harry had no idea who the man was, but, 'ever polite', as he described himself at the time, he said, 'Yes, yes, still intending to, yes,' to which the man said, 'Well, if you're interested, you could come and work in my office during the long

---

44 I am aware that I was about the same age when I first met Harry as he was when he met Morris.
45 Now the University of Wales, Lampeter.

vac term and learn something about educational administration.' The penny dropped, and Harry had a summer job.

Harry went round schools with Morris. They went walking in the Backs and out in the Fens.[46] They stayed in touch, off and on, until Morris's death. When he 'went down' to London he would spend weekends with him. One would, of course, dearly love to ask Henry Morris what he saw in Harry: this was before Harry had taught a single class and before the Second World War.

Morris was very interested in architecture, and persuaded Walter Gropius to design the Village College in Impington (1936). Harry showed Gropius around Cambridgeshire in those years, i.e. after he had left Germany in 1934 and before he went to the United States three years later. It helped that Harry spoke some German, though he confessed that he was not very fluent.

Shortly before the War, Harry's name appeared on a list of over 40 subscriptions received in support of the building of Impington Village College. He gave four guineas.[47] Other donors were Julian Huxley, Frank Pick[48] and Israel Sieff.

Harry still had quite a narrow view of education. 'I hadn't after all taught yet.' Rather than going directly to a 'public' school as a schoolmaster, he decided on a year's training. He could easily have stayed in Cambridge, but 'the reputation of the Cambridge thing was very, very bad'. It was run by 'a man called Fox': this was Charles Fox (1876–1964) MA, of Christ's College, Director of the Training of Teachers and Lecturer in Educational Psychology. I remember, as a small boy, being taken every Saturday morning to the Cambridge Synagogue in Thompson's Lane, which had been built in 1937. I can still see the special chair where a very forbidding, formal-looking gentleman sat in his cap, gown and tallith: it was the aforementioned Charles Fox. No wonder his students were known as 'Fox's martyrs'. This referred to *The Book of Martyrs* by John Foxe, first published in 1563. It was the kind of book that many people had heard of, but no one had read.

---

46   The Backs is the sublimely beautiful area behind seven of the colleges and east of Queen's Road, with the Cam flowing gently through. There are punts and the inevitable tourists. The Fens, or Fenland, is an especially fertile area mostly north of Cambridge, which was drained in the late eighteenth and early nineteenth centuries.

47   Equivalent to about £260 in 2016.

48   Known for the graphic design of the London Underground.

Chapter 4

Teaching, and on to London

So Harry went to the Institute of Education, a constituent college of the University of London,[49] where his papers now reside: 'not,' he hastened to add, 'because the London Institute was all that good, but it was an opportunity to educate myself by getting to know London'. He shared a flat in Warwick Avenue, Maida Vale, with Paul Dehn, the poet, who also hailed from Manchester and had gone to Shrewsbury, so both were Old Salopians. Dehn was born in 1912, so was a bit older than Harry. He began life at 13 Belfield Road, Didsbury, less than half an hour's walk, due south, from Mauldeth Road. They cooked for themselves and had dinner parties, 'which was really great fun'.

Harry and Paul Dehn had many similarities. Dehn's parents were British, of German descent. And during the Second World War, Dehn joined the Special Operations Executive (SOE). He was assigned to Camp X in Oshawa, Ontario, before returning to missions in France and Norway. He was Brian Rée's godfather, and died in 1976.

It is significant that Harry decided to 'train' as a teacher, presumably with Henry Morris's blessing, and not to dive straight in, as had his teachers at Shrewsbury. Teaching practice was two days a week, throughout the year, and he was assigned to St Paul's School, near Hammersmith Bridge; half an hour or so from where he was living. St Paul's (whose headmaster at the time Harry taught there was John Bell, High Master, 1927–38) has no record of Harry ever having been there, but I note that, decades later, Harry had some public arguments with Thomas Howarth, who was High Master from 1962 to 1973. Ian Lister, almost 40 years after his death, describes Howarth as 'a bully; neurotic; anxious; didn't keep his word'.

Harry said he learned 'quite a bit' from teaching practice ('Very clever boys. Easy, easy.'), but not much from the lectures at the Institute. Furthermore, the teacher described by Ernest Raymond spent his life at St Paul's.

The Institute of Education was fairly small in Harry's day, so he must have known much of the staff, which included:

---

49   The Institute of Education is now part of University College London.

Sir Fred Clarke (1880–1952), who was Director from 1936 to 1945, having been a professor in South Africa and Canada;

Dr Percival Gurrey, who was Lecturer in Methods of Teaching English from 1926 to 1946 and Reader from 1946 to 1948. Harry said that at one time he modelled his English lessons on his ideas. Long after Harry's days at the Institute, Gurrey wrote *The Teaching of Written English* (1954) and *Teaching English Grammar* (1961);

Susan Isaacs, who was Head of the Department of Child Development from 1933 to 1943;

Dr Joseph Lauwerys, who was Lecturer in Methods of Teaching Science from 1932 to 1941 and Professor of Comparative Education from 1947 to 1970, and whom I remember as a spellbinding lecturer.

Richard Aldrich, the Institute's historian, said that Harry confessed that he 'was a most undesirable student. I think I must have cut most lectures except those of Dr Gurrey, and I took no part in student activities'.

But he did begin to make friends, more from the Institute than St Paul's, and by May, it was time to look for a job. As Harry put it many years later:

It was just assumed that one would go to a grammar school. Absolutely. A graduate who'd got a degree in modern languages would go and teach in a grammar school, of course. I suppose I could have [taught in a public school]. But I think I'd decided by then. And I think the reason for that was a conversation I'd had at Shrewsbury. ... And I remember – I think he was head boy of the school in whose bedroom I was – very interesting man who's now [1988] a High Court Judge[50] – said to me in the course of a conversation 'you know, the future of education in this country, Harry, is not in these public schools of ours, it's in the grammar schools.' And I can remember being astonished – it just hadn't occurred to me, I didn't know what grammar schools were at all.

As I think about Harry's intentional moves from public to grammar to comprehensive schools, I am puzzled that single-sex schools never seemed

---

50 The archivist at Shrewsbury School, Mike Morrogh, cannot find anyone in the records who fits Harry's description.

to bother him; the fact that his own daughter Janet could never have gained a place at most of the schools where he worked. As far as I can gather, this was never an issue for him, or for her.

When I shared my puzzlement with Mary Evans, author of *A Good School* (1991), a discussion of a girls' grammar school in the 1950s, she wrote:

> I think much of the argument about single/mixed sex schools is related to the evidence, some of it reliable, that girls do much better academically in all girls' schools .. essentially the argument for a long time has been that co-education benefits boys more than girls. This is also not just about the pupils ... it's also about who the Head is and the gendered politics of schools where the women staff might get less promotion/recognition than the men.

> My own view is that these arguments are starting to shift but the successful single sex schools (and sadly much of the culture of schools in the UK today is about performance in what I think are largely meaningless 'tables') are unwilling to change.

Harry did not get the first job for which he applied. He was interviewed at Raynes Park Grammar School, whose headmaster, John Garrett, he already knew slightly. Garrett became the first headmaster of Raynes Park when the school opened in 1935, at the age of 33. He became quite well known as the co-editor, with W.H. Auden, of *The Poet's Tongue: An anthology of verse.*[51] Garrett later moved on to the headship of Bristol Grammar School.

Looking back, Harry was quite glad he didn't get that first job. But he remembered the interview:

> The whole governing body was there. There was the chair – a dear, white-haired, 80-year-old, looked down the table at me and said, 'Do you think you're old enough, Mr Rée, to teach other boys?' I must have looked terribly young.

He then applied for a position at what was then called Beckenham and Penge County School for Boys in Bromley, Kent. ('County school' meant 'grammar school'.) Opened in 1901, the school has gone through a baffling variety of name changes: Beckenham Technical Institute; Technical Day School, Beckenham; Beckenham Secondary School; Beckenham County School

---

51 Another small-world coincidence: I was a student teacher at Raynes Park for one semester during 1957/58, and used the anthology as a young teacher at Watford. Raynes Park became comprehensive in 1969 and co-educational in 1970.

for Boys; Beckenham and Penge County School for Boys; Beckenham and Penge County Grammar School; Beckenham and Penge Grammar School for Boys; and, when the school moved to Eden Park in 1969, Langley Park School for Boys. It is now a boys' comprehensive school, with a mixed gender sixth form.[52]

He got the job, and stayed from 1937 to 1940. The headmaster who offered him the position was Sidney Gammon (1894–1940), who had survived the Battle of the Somme where he was wounded, had become a headmaster in 1930, and was killed in the next war by a bomb that was dropped on his home, killing his wife and his daughter also. In 1988, Harry recalled that 'the head actually was not particularly popular with the older staff, because he'd been through the [Great] War and was an idealist'. Soon after he (i.e. Harry) arrived, he was joined by his good friend from Cambridge, Francis Cammaerts, and they shared a flat. Over 50 years later, after Harry's death, Francis would recall 'the man who introduced me to the pleasures of tasting garlic and of looking at the pictures of Paul Klee ... the man with whom I stood hand in hand and looked at Picasso's *Guernica*'.

In the late 1960s, T.D. Martindale compiled a history of the school (*Beckenham and Penge Grammar School: 1901–1968*) in which there is brief reference to Rée (1937–40) and Cammaerts (1938–40) and their distinguished War records.

The school magazine of the day, *The Beccehamian*, is retrospectively hilarious. We know now that both Cammaerts and Rée, having started off as conscientious objectors, became celebrated War heroes, each earning the DSO.[53] Having reported that Rée left the School to enter 'the Army or the Navy', the magazine continues: 'We send ... our good wishes, as we do also Mr Cammaerts, who, we understand, is now indulging his penchant for agricultural pursuits somewhere in Lincolnshire.' Actually, Cammaerts had joined a group of conscientious-objector farm labourers in Holton cum Beckering, herding sheep.

Harry still hadn't shaken off some of the attitudes he had gleaned from Shrewsbury, Cambridge and Morris. As he put it:

> I was going into teaching very much with a view to finding out what it was like teaching in State education before starting in administration. I thought in a superior way, 'I'd better find out something about these schools before I start in administration.'

---

52 In British parlance, the sixth form refers to the final year or two where pupils prepare for university entrance.

53 Distinguished Service Order, awarded for 'conspicuous gallantry'.

> But my goodness, when I got there ... I hadn't been there I
> suppose for, well, say six weeks, perhaps two months, before I
> realized that I was going to teach and not go into administration.

He didn't seem to mind the 45-minute periods, nor the wearing of gowns.
Asked about how his family felt about his going off to teach in a grammar
school, he responded:

> Well, I was always considered by my family, who were fairly
> traditional and conservative, as a slightly one-off socialist and
> dangerous radical. I'm terribly middle of the road actually.
> But they said, 'Oh, Harry's off his head, give him some rope,
> he'll learn.'

Note – and I will be coming back to this – Harry did see himself as middle
of the road, moderate or centrist. He would later write to Margaret Maden,
'I've decided that Illich, though useful, is too far out.' There are times when
I agree; but, more often, I find myself wanting to ask what kind of road he
had in mind.

George Walker opined, 'Harry was not totally radical; satisfied both
parties.'

Harry had a genuine respect for the staff at Beckenham and Penge.
'There was such a good staff; it really was an exceptionally good staff.' But
then he went on:

> There was a big division between the younger ones and those
> who'd taught there before the War and had come back from the
> War. The old gang. Who in a way dominated the staff room, but
> in fact they were fairly tired. And in a way they were fine old
> people, but they were very traditional teachers. But the young
> staff, we got on very well with each other.

He was, of course, referring to the First World War. When he was describing
Beckenham and Penge as he had experienced it a couple of decades after
the First World War, was he aware that he could just as easily have been
describing the staff at Watford Grammar School 15 or so years after the
Second World War?

Harry made £249 a year,[54] and his mother sent him a small allowance.
He inherited a sister's car, which he promptly ran into a wall. (Years later,
he would be known as a fast and carefree driver who was occasionally 'had'

---

54 Equivalent to about £15,100 in 2016.

for speeding.) He told the man who ran the garage that this was bad luck, to which the man responded, 'There's no such thing as bad luck; there's only stupidity.' Then he shared a car with Francis Cammaerts. At some stage he had a little Morgan Three-Wheeler.

Harry and some of his colleagues made a film that was selected as one of the ten best films in the 'amateur cine world' of 1938. Entitled *County School*, it was a portrait of the school where he was teaching.[55]

Needless to say, there are few of his former Beckenham and Penge pupils still alive at the time of writing. Dr David Rands, a general practitioner, recalls a few lessons from Harry before he left the school around February, 1940: 'I recall him as a smallish, dapper, agile young man.' And he remembers Francis Cammaerts as 'tall and moustached'.

Already in his twenties, Harry seems to have known all kinds of people. From a letter to Nick Tucker:

> I was having lunch with H.G. Wells (shall I repeat that!?) in 1938, in his house in Regent's Park,[56] and he said, jovially munching a steak, 'I told Shaw the other day, that having lived till 80 on vegetables, he should switch now to steak – he'd live for another 40 years!' (True story, in all details – I didn't much like H.G.W. ...).[57]

As early as 1940, Harry was writing for publication. He reviewed *What Do Boys and Girls Read?* by A.J. Jenkinson for the autumn 1940 edition of Cyril Connolly's *Horizon: A review of literature and art*. This was, from 1940 until its demise in 1949, an extraordinarily prestigious publication for a piece written by someone in his mid-twenties. In it he demonstrated knowledge of such magazines as *The Wizard* (1922–78) and, to my delight, used the word 'titivated'. One gets a sense of Harry's views, as expressed a decade and more later, as he approvingly quotes Jenkinson:

> Of course it must be admitted that the objective of the State system, of scholarships, of the educational ladder, is to give education to those who deserve it most, not to those who need it most. The concepts of 'scarcity economics' prevail in education.

---

55 There is no surviving copy at the British Film Institute, but Steve Parsons, current head teacher of Langley Park School for Boys, has found one in his school's archives: it is black and white, silent, and lasts 12 minutes with the start missing.

56 13 Hanover Terrace, NW1.

57 Wells died in 1946 at the age of 79, Shaw in 1950 at 94.

Jonathan M. Daube

Beckenham and Penge before the War, and Bradford Grammar School afterwards, gave Harry a unique feel for teaching that Henry Morris could never have had, and a respect for the craft of teaching. People who knew him in the latter half of his life might be surprised at the extent to which he initially accepted the traditions he walked into.

Chapter 5

Hetty and the War

During the first few months of the Second World War, teaching was a 'reserved occupation'. But Harry was a conscientious objector, and he registered as one.

Around that time, he went to visit a prep school in Dorking, Surrey, which was run by a friend of his older brother Edward. There he met the matron, Kathleen H.E. (Hetty) Vine, and they played poker. She won and he lost! They met two or three times, corresponded, and got engaged. Harry described how he proposed in the Penge Tunnel, which is about a mile and a quarter long, so he had barely three minutes. He bought 'an incredibly cheap engagement ring' and met her family, who lived in Beaconsfield, having moved several times from newly built house to newly built house. Harry continued:

> Her father was a lovely man. He'd been in business in the City in wholesale haberdashery or something. And she had two brothers … They'd been at Bedford School.

So Hetty was the youngest child and only daughter of Kathleen and Eardley Vine. Jack was killed towards the end of the War and the other, Brian, died a week or so before Harry in 1991.[58] Hetty spent some time in a finishing school in Switzerland, and later set up as a milliner in Baker Street. She had grown up as a Methodist, becoming a Quaker some time after her marriage.

Brian Vine's younger daughter Lisa has done considerable research into the Vine family history which she has generously shared with me. She says that 'being a Quaker was Hetty's style. Quiet, but determined.' She has written a background piece:

> Hetty's mother was Kathleen Hayman, born in Hackney (where I have lived for 35 years) in 1881, the daughter of Hetty and Charles Gould Hayman, … ardent Wesleyans. Charles worked for the drapers' warehouse firm William Williams in the City, and ultimately became wealthy. … So Kathleen had grown up as a middle-class Londoner, though the death of her mother when she was six was a life-long sadness to her. … Kathleen

---

58 Hetty and Harry named one of their two sons Brian.

married in 1905 ... Eardley Vine, another Methodist ... and they moved to Hendon from Crouch End. Eardley came from a long line of Wesleyan ministers, including his father, who died when he was three. He went into his step-father's family business of Rushbrooke's, London, when he was about 17 and ... worked there all his life. He was a likeable, fun person to his grandchildren and to others ... though tough-minded. Jack, a bright boy who became a solicitor working for Lord Rank[59] ... was killed at D-Day. The next child was Brian, my father, who worked in the family business of Rushbrooke's in Smithfield all his life. Hetty was the youngest and adored daughter of my grandmother. The family moved to Bedford in about 1916. Hetty went to Bedford High School, leaving in 1931. All this while Eardley commuted to London for work. Round about 1928 my great-grandfather Hayman died in St Albans and the family moved to Hampstead Garden Suburb, where they stayed till about 1937–8 when Eardley and Kathleen moved to Beaconsfield.[60]

I believe Hetty had wanted to go to Oxford but my grandmother thought she would work too hard and make herself ill! ... My grandfather and his sons never had a university education. ... Hetty and a friend were set up in business in Baker Street ... and they ran a dress-making shop. Later she worked in a school as a matron.

Hetty became, I believe, a Quaker and that would be consistent with the staunch Wesleyan Methodism of both her parents. She was such a warm person, and I think Harry recognized that same thing in my own father. ... She was very easy to be around if you were a teenager, and I went to stay with the Rées a few times as she recognized that I was rather lonely at home. ... They both deeply disapproved of private education.

I stayed a few times with Harry in Colt Park though my parents never went there. He was such a vital person, though we often had political disagreements and he never quite understood my generation. ... My own father was very conservative and not given much to thinking deeply about things – he was slightly in awe of Harry but also disagreed with his Labour politics and was

---

59   J. Arthur Rank (1888–1972) was best known as a film industry mogul.
60   Hetty would have been in her mid-twenties then.

bemused by these as he considered that Harry's family had been well off!

In another email, Lisa writes:

> Her great aunt 'Hope' (real name: Annie) Hayman, Kathleen's father's sister, was a staunch Methodist and a member of the West London Mission in Marylebone.[61] Hope must have known Beatrice and Sydney Webb. ... One of her helpers in the 1920s was Donald Soper ... These women frequently had to leave their babies completely unattended in order to work.

Harry and Hetty spent Christmas, 1939, in Manchester, and got married on 18 April or 20 July 1940.[62] Harry was 25 years old. Their marriage was to last almost 21-and-a-half years.[63]

In 1988, Harry was asked, 'What did you hope for from marriage?' His response was:

> Companionship, I think. It's funny, because I've mentioned that my school life was actually sort of vibrating with sex. That's perhaps exaggerated, but it played an important part. But then at Cambridge, no, quiescent. And I suppose I was getting out of the homosexual period and not daring to launch away into the hetero. And this went on at Beckenham too really. Until I met Hetty.

He went on to describe how they had more or less the same tastes and how each contributed to the other's way of thinking and feeling:

> We got on extremely well. I didn't know what it meant to be in love. I'm not sure I still do. And I may have been insensitive. ... We wrote very affectionate letters to each other. And I prized her really, more than loved her. ... It was really a very good companionship.

Harry, then, was ambivalent about love. And yet, he used the word 'lovely' to describe both people and situations. Shortly after his death, Francis Cammaerts put it into words:

> I can only call it a capacity for love. Love based on sex, on family relations, on common interests are fully expressed by all the great

---

61   Founded in 1887.
62   Different sources conflict.
63   Harry's second marriage lasted more than a quarter of a century.

writers, musicians and artists of the world. But there is a form of love that is … a love between two people regardless of sex, age, race, social position, wealth and language. A love which does not wear out with the passage of time … That kind of love which I think we can all recognize is known by people in different quantities, I think. One of the things that I feel most strongly about Harry is that he had this capacity in a very unusual extent. And that he not only gave this kind of love but attracted it.

Keith Emmans opines, I think correctly: 'Hetty was the supportive wife that mercurial Harry needed'. George Walker, who knew Harry as well as anyone, adds:

> She was the ideal consort for Harry – a calm geostationary presence around which Harry rotated in his various orbits. She was a lovely person, always interested in one's activities … always with time to talk, to advise and to encourage. She was a governor of Victoria Girls Secondary Modern and one year presented the prizes at their speech day. My mother, who taught there, said it was the best speech she had ever heard: brief, helpful and to the point.

> Many years later I attended a meeting of one of Harry's many pressure groups (SPLURGE, SPLOSH, SCREECH – I forget!) at the then Beatrice Webb House in Surrey. Harry said, 'this is a very special place for me because I met Hetty here'.

Nephew Hugo writes, 'I loved Hetty; she was a singularly beautiful, kind, gentle and intelligent woman.'

Harry was still not entirely clear what their relationship had meant to him 27-and-a-half years after her death, and perhaps continued to mean. I am sure that his life would have turned out differently, perhaps less turbulent, had she lived.

Their marriage began traditionally, with Hetty staying at home with the children. 'And I was happy about that really, because that was the way things were done.' And, in Harry's words:

> There was no question of having nurses. … Absolutely not. By that time young people in the middle classes didn't have nurses. My older sisters did … But no, we didn't, and my younger sister didn't.

He went on, 'But then of course you didn't know what was going to happen at all. I mean the War had just started and there was quite a good chance that we wouldn't win it.' I wonder whether there was any discussion within Harry's family about their relatives in Hamburg or about the possibility of emigrating to the United States, even if it was summarily rejected. After all, the Dupont connection could have been enlisted to save lives, especially before America entered the War.

Harry and Hetty rented a small flat in Beckenham; they did not go back to the flat Harry had shared with Francis Cammaerts. They spent the summer of 1940 at a work camp in Dorset, where boys helped with the harvest. Hetty, who had little experience cooking, cooked for 40, and 'they ate wonderfully. It was great fun.' They had an oil cooker with two burners, plus a Radiation cook book.

According to Harry in his British Library interview, Hetty did another work camp at the end of that summer, this time in Kent:

> And that was interesting because the Battle of Britain, with the German Air Force attacking London and trying to destroy the British Air Force and British airfields, was going on overhead in Kent and there was this extraordinary business – not many people remember it – of the *Evening Standard* ... coming out every evening with the scores as if it was a test match – how many had been brought down and how many of ours were missing. And this battle was going on overhead throughout most of the days we were in Kent.

Beckenham is only eight miles from Biggin Hill, which was one of the key airports in the Battle of Britain, whose official dates are between 10 July and 31 October 1940. (I had always assumed that Harry's apparent physical fearlessness came from his experience in the SOE, but perhaps it dates, at least in part, from the late summer of 1940.)

M.R.D. Foot, described by *The Independent* as 'the world's expert on SOE', wrote in an email, less than two months before his death at the age of 92:

> He was not I think without fear, but he didn't frighten easily: this must to some extent have been due to what he went through in occupied France. And yet, as he told me once, he spent nine-tenths of his time there in the remote countryside of Franche-Comté, staying with sure friends, never seeing a German uniform

at all; it was only during operations, which were quite rare, that he was in actual danger.

Referring to his friend President John F. Kennedy, David Ormsby-Gore (later Lord Harlech), who was the British Ambassador to the United States from 1961 to 1965, wrote:

> With all human beings, one of the things that gives confidence is to have been in extreme peril and come well out of it, perhaps on some occasions to have been near death and come back from the brink. I have always noticed that people who have had that kind of experience have a sort of calm; not quite a detachment from life, but a calm attitude to anything that life can throw at them, which is rather significant.

In 1939–40, Harry was still a pacifist, a registered conscientious objector. I have come across several glosses on this, and there may be more.

Charles Swallow, son of his older sister Irene, and Harry's godson, thinks it may have had something to do with his wife Hetty, whom he believed had grown up as a Quaker.[64] But he never discussed this theory with Harry.

John Hicks, a pupil at Bradford Grammar School, thought it was Hitler's attack on Norway that changed his thinking.

Harry's brother Edward spent much of the War in a PoW camp. Given the closeness of the family, this must have weighed heavily with him.[65]

After the War, when describing his decision to participate, Harry said, 'My father was part Jewish.' The implication was that though Harry was not Jewish, the Nuremberg Laws of 1935 would have defined him as a 'Mischling'.

Most importantly, son Jonathan writes:

> Harry told me that he abandoned CO status because his contemporaries were getting killed and he couldn't see how he could stand apart.

---

64 In fact she had not grown up a Quaker, but became one during the Watford years, though she may have had a serious interest in becoming one by the time she and Harry met.

65 Two further theories may be discounted: Michael Ludgate, another pupil at Bradford Grammar School, suggested that Harry was influenced by the Lidice massacre, where a village northwest of Prague was completely destroyed on Himmler's orders in reprisal for the assassination of leading Nazi Reinhard Heydrich. But these events did not take place until May and June of 1942. Likewise, Harry's sister Irene Swallow told her son Charles that it was the death in Algeria of her brother Eric that persuaded Harry to join the SOE, but Eric died in November 1943.

I am inclined to take him at his word. Initially, as with many of his generation, the very thought of another war only two decades after the bloodbath that was the First World War was inconceivably horrific; then, as the invasion of the British Isles became a possibility, it became inevitable and therefore, in a sense, tolerable. Albert Einstein, for example, was a committed pacifist until, at some point in the 1930s, he came to the reluctant realization that pacifism could no longer work.

Of the following I am quite sure: fear of the unknown or of death played little part in Harry's decisions. The passion for societal change that he increasingly demonstrated was reinforced by his experience of the War: if things didn't get better for people, if equal opportunity was not seen as a universal good, then all the damage, all the killings, would have been for naught.

Professor Foot, in the same email quoted above, wrote:

> I believe Harry gradually dropped his pacifism, because it seemed to him that nothing but force would ever stop a regime as rotten as Hitler's turned out to be. Most of his and of my generation had pacifism, much as most of us had measles; one overcame it.

Richard Overy, professor of history at Exeter University, writes:

> To be anti-war in the 1920s and 1930s was to acquire membership in a broad church, though scarcely a united front.[66]

For a brief time, he worked for the National Fire Service.[67]

As Harry remembered the early War years, he realized fairly early on that he was not a 'religious consci.'; rather, his pacifism was political. So, very relaxed about the whole business, he changed his mind and joined up in early 1941, later saying that it was the 'concentration camp business and the Jewish business' that forced the change. He volunteered for minesweeping, but was drafted to a Royal Artillery training camp in Exeter, where he remained for about six months. He was immediately identified as officer material: not surprising, given his background and his class. It was there, when he was still a lance corporal, that one of his superiors decided to call Gunner Rée, 'Gonorrhoea'! In a 1985 interview, Harry described his time at Exeter as 'absolute nonsense, very funny'.

It was his brother Eric, who had just returned from France, who suggested security, so he was attached to the wireless section of SOE and trained in field security. When he was training others in England, he

---

66 Richard Overy (2009) *The Twilight Years: The paradox of Britain between the wars*, New York: Penguin.
67 Created in 1941.

used his brothers' and sisters' homes as 'safe houses', thus both ensuring confidentiality and enabling visits to his siblings.

Eventually, he and John Kenneth Macalister, a Canadian Rhodes scholar, were granted their request to move from security services to active services. Macalister, who had married a Frenchwoman, later died in Buchenwald. Initially, it should be noted, the 'man in charge' did not want Harry to go to France, thinking that he knew too much, but he was overruled.

Selwyn Jepson, who was in charge of recruiting for the SOE, singled Harry out when asked in a 1986 interview whom he had an especially high regard for:

> Harry Rée was highly intelligent, witty, amiable. Wasn't he headmaster of Westminster? I liked him very much ... a good chap. He knew instinctively what I was after. Very good indeed.

Harry kept his sense of humour throughout the War. Jane Steedman tells the following wonderful tale:

> They used to cycle round looking for things to sabotage, it wasn't always bridges to blow up – sometimes it was less glamorous. One day he and a young Frenchman, on their bikes, caught up with a petrol tanker. Any petrol was for the Germans. All they had to do was follow it without being noticed till it was going up hill and open the taps at the back to drain the petrol out on the road. They managed it, cycling fit to bust, lungs bursting, opened the taps ... and were covered in slurry from a manure tank. They fell off their bikes into the ditch, overcome with shit and laughter.

Harry stressed in later years that there was no fuss about his having been a conscientious objector, especially as he had not got as far as appearing before a tribunal. Hetty thought she would be visiting a husband in prison, so she was a trifle disappointed when he deprived her of that pleasure! By the time he was barely 31 years old, Harry was a war hero: DSO, OBE, Croix de Guerre, Médaille de la Resistance, Médaille commemorative des services volontaires dans la France libre,[68] and star of a film whose script he had helped put together. An experienced teacher, he was also a broadcaster. He understood the power of the effective teacher, and he also understood the power of radio and, later, television.[69] Married, he already

---

68 The first Médaille was created by the De Gaulle French in wartime, the second was established after the War.

69 Eric Midwinter reminded me in 2012 of William Beveridge's famous question to Michael Young: 'do you want power or influence?'

had two children. Asked in 1963 about the OBE and the DSO, he explained, 'They sent for one decoration, and as it was such a long time coming they sent for another.'[70]

By 1944, when he was flown home from Gibraltar, Harry was hankering for home life and getting back to teaching. Predictably, some people expected him to want to get back into the action, but he had had enough and was relieved when the higher-ups told him he was far too well known to return to France. His daughter Janet was a little over one year old and, understandably, wanted nothing to do with him when he first returned.[71]

There were long periods during the War when boredom set in: not unusual or atypical. While waiting to come home to England, Harry wrote a schoolbook about the Resistance that came out after the War. The day after he got home, still in uniform, he reported to HQ and was given a desk job: 'looking after' southwestern France, receiving messages, etc. Years later, he recalled receiving a message concerning his friend Francis Cammaerts, who had remained a conscientious objector longer than him. Francis had been working on a farm when his brother Pieter was killed in the Royal Air Force. Understandably, this served to change his mind, and he told Harry, over a drink some time in 1942, that he was going to join the RAF. 'Francis, my dear,' Harry said, 'if you really want to get killed, I know a much better way to go,' and he promptly recruited him. The rest, of course, is history: 'he had a brilliant war.' The message Harry got suggested that Francis had been arrested, which made him feel guilty, since he, after all, had recruited him. But a few days later, Francis escaped.[72]

Harry's War years are well documented, which is why I say little about them. But, perhaps inevitably, myths grew up after the War. For example, in a 1985 interview, he was asked whether the SOE was a 'hotbed of left-wing activists.' On the contrary, Harry responded, it was conservative and 'linked to the City'. And the code name he was given, 'Stockbroker', was a tease. In that year he also broadcast a short talk on the radio that paid tribute to the bravery of the ordinary French families who had risked their lives to give him and his fellow SOE operatives shelter.[73]

---

70 He was awarded the OBE on 15 June 1944 and the DSO on 15 November 1945.

71 While in France, Harry knew that his first child, a daughter, had been born when the BBC announced, 'Clemence ressemble à sa grand-mère.'

72 See Ray Jenkins, *A Pacifist at War: The silence of Francis Cammaerts*, 2009, and numerous other accounts.

73 'Quietly Resisting', BBC Radio 4, broadcast 30 June 1985. Available online at www.iwm.org.uk/collections/item/object/80012787

Jonathan M. Daube

Any student of his life should, of course, be intrigued by the influence the SOE years may have had on his post-War life. His apparent self-confidence and his ability to think for himself did, I think, have something to do with his War experiences. As M.R.D. Foot put it:

> *Dubito, ergo sum* – I doubt therefore I survive – must be the motto of every successful secret agent.[74]

Even Harry's first drop into France only worked at the third attempt, when he was dropped near Tarbes; he had already said goodbye to Hetty twice and then reappeared.

Harry internalized the principle of 'universal scepticism' at an early age. After the War, he would say, with pride:

> Any mistake I made I would suffer from, but I would probably not suffer from the mistake of a superior officer.

As his son Jonathan has pointed out, he loved the word 'bolshie', which became a term of approval.

Harry's War began only two decades after the end of the Great War, and the lesson he must have carried with him was to trust one's own judgement rather than that of some 'superior officer'.

From ten to 15 years after the War, the staff at Watford Grammar School, myself included, would discuss endlessly the extent to which Harry had been influenced by the War … or had put it behind him. And the more I think about it, the more it remains a conundrum.

In December 1944, the BBC Home Service broadcast an interview with 'Capt. H.R.' entitled 'Schoolmaster into saboteur'. Harry described the France he had got to know so well:

> The industrial area there is very countrified – it's extraordinary. Everyone has their goats and rabbits and little bit of garden. …

> The Englishman, when he's called up to do his duty for his country – he will never feel quite what a man of the French Resistance Movement felt, that in doing what he considered his duty he was endangering the life of his mother and his wife and his children. On the contrary, the Englishman can feel that if anything happened to him they would be looked after. But the French, who are much more family-minded than we are and

---

74 M.R.D. Foot (1968) *SOE in France: An account of the work of the British Special Operations Executive in France 1940–1944*, London: HMSO.

who seek even more after security than we do – for them it was dreadful.

The women had far the worst time of it. ... Nearly everybody I knew and worked with was caught in the end.

I remember an awfully nice industrialist I used to go and see a lot saying to me, 'You won't like going back to being a schoolmaster after this!' And I said, 'On the contrary, to get back to something constructive instead of blowing things up all the time will be a joy!' To come back now to my home, to what was normal ... it's given me a terrific desire to see the continuity of the things one hoped would continue.

Five days before VE Day, *The Listener* printed a talk that Harry had given on the BBC Home Service entitled 'I didn't enjoy it: A British secret agent revisits France'. His name does not appear. In a beautifully crafted piece, Harry began, 'I didn't enjoy my visit. There were too many gaps in the families I went to see.' He spoke about the role of several exceptional women, the feeling of unity between Britain and France and the total commitment of the people amongst whom he had been working, who risked everything, including being taken to concentration camps.

For sure, Harry had a deep love for the ordinary people of France. In a broadcast in French, shortly after the War, entitled 'Teacher to Saboteur', he said:

Since I came back from France I've done nothing but sing the praises of the French Resistance. The other evening I had the opportunity of speaking to the English people over the BBC. I didn't just tell them about the adventures we had. I felt it was more important to explain what daily life was like under the Occupation and what a great debt we owe to you.

He spoke of ordinary people who did extraordinary things:

There was the village butcher who hid explosives in his abattoir. There was the schoolmistress who was in charge of distributing orders to a group of saboteurs. There was the priest who put his whole network at my disposal, even though I was a newcomer ...

He spoke of deaths, but also of fun they had. Of course he was a different man afterwards from what he had been before. 'I could never put into words all that the life I had among you means to me.'

In another broadcast talk, he said:

> Like most of my fellow agents I've not talked much about it since, especially not in public. Why? It isn't thro' modesty; it's because there's a sense in which I've never found it possible to convey to people what that experience meant, not only to me, but to the whole army of supporters ... I realize that it's possibly my fault that I can't get the right message across. ...

> Perhaps because we're getting old and, (I suppose) increasingly rare (!) we've begun to weaken when asked to recall our 'resistance' experience.

He then went on eloquently to describe the 'heroism and moral strength' of 'two women, neither of whom ever held a gun. They are both dead now.'

In 1965, he spoke in Manchester, and his talk appeared as a chapter ('Experiences of an SOE agent in France') in *The Fourth Dimension of Warfare*, edited by Michael Elliott-Bateman:

> This is the first time for twenty years that I have spoken about the Resistance in public. ... I am unwilling to romanticize this business.[75]

Clearly, Harry was still ambivalent about talking in public: he used the pseudonym 'Henri Raymond', even though everyone in the audience must have known who he was.

Almost 30 years after the War, when he was in his late fifties, he gave a talk entitled *Agents, Resisters and the Local Population*. Much of what he said then gives us an insight into his long-term thinking:

> I don't normally talk in public about the resistance.

> ... being something of a softie ...

> ... *the complete and crushing ordinariness* of the people I worked with in France.

> What I want to honour is not these people's superiority ... I want to honour their common humanity.

> We weren't a band of brothers ... we weren't spies.

---

75 Elliott-Bateman, M. (ed.) (1970) *The Fourth Dimension of Warfare: Vol. 1. Intelligence, subversion, resistance*. Manchester: Manchester University Press, 111–26.

Of those of us who survived the war, very few of us met afterwards.

I never carried a gun with me, never.

Harry, then, spoke of the 'complete and crushing ordinariness' of the people with whom he interacted in France; his lifelong friend Francis Cammaerts, on the other hand, according to his obituary in *The Daily Telegraph*, described the French fighters he knew as 'no ordinary men'. Maybe, coming from totally different directions, each was trying to say the same thing, deflecting credit from himself. In May 1961, the *Sunday Times* wrote:

> What still moves, even haunts both men is the memory of individual acts of courage by ordinary French people.

Over 40 years later, Bronwyn Hipkin, describing stays with her five children at Colt Park, would write:

> The boys especially remember his very special take on courage, a particular interest for them as they were very much aware of his SOE experiences. He put it into the context of 'ordinariness' ... and stressed how human reactions should always be remembered, fear, wanting to run away, etc. ... 'Remember that "going over the top, getting the VC" was sometimes the act of suicidal madmen', he would tell them.

Harry had been involved in film-making at Beckenham and Penge, so persuaded one Wing Commander Edward Baird to release him for about 18 months to help write and then act in *Now It Can Be Told*. Made by the RAF Film Production Unit and released through the Central Office of Information in 1946, filming began in 1944.[76] The two-hour-long film was originally shown under the title *School for Danger*. It is unusual in that the main parts were played by the real secret agents, not by actors. Harry's co-star, Jacqueline Nearne, who was only a couple of years younger than him, lived in London with her sister after the War and then moved to New York City to work in the Protocol Department of the United Nations. She died in 1982.

As indicated elsewhere, Harry was ambivalent about discussing his wartime experiences; usually but not always reluctant. However, he must have been open to the public recounting of War stories at least once: in September 1984, the BBC put together an eight-part documentary on the 'SOE's chequered history of heroic successes and catastrophic failures',

---

76   It can now be bought online from the Imperial War Museum and elsewhere.

as *The Times* put it, and one of the programmes featured Harry. Sir John Keegan previewed it, along with a picture of Harry, then about 70, in a highly unusual swaggering pose, holding a Colt .32 automatic at Wanborough Manor in Surrey, where he was trained 'the SOE way with a gun'.

Harry's post-war broadcasting career began with an admirable demonstration of humility. The tabloids were, he thought, full of 'anti-French stuff', so he wrote to the BBC asking to be allowed 'to do a broadcast about what the French had done for us'. Nephew Hugo, whose mother was French, confirms that 'anti-French feeling continued for a long time after the War'.

Brendan Bracken (1901–1958), who was Winston Churchill's Minister of Information from 1941 to 1945, gave permission, and Harry sent a draft of a talk to a producer who said the talk might be fine as a piece of writing for the *New Statesman* or the *Spectator*, but it would not do for radio. She offered to coach him; he allowed himself to be taught; and he then did about six more broadcasts. He did not use his own name, calling himself a 'British secret agent'. This would not have been unusual in those days, when most BBC announcers would not think of using their own names, simply enunciating, 'This is the BBC.' When he was at Watford, he would initially write for newspapers as 'A Headmaster', only later using his own name.

Throughout his life, Harry understood the media. When he had finished the film, he became involved with Forces' Educational Broadcasts, which began in the autumn of 1945, doing mainly current affairs. He became, as he said, 'a sort of BBC producer still in uniform'. He was paid by the Army, not by the BBC.

Harry and his family lived at that time in Hetty's family's home in Beaconsfield. As the children came along, they would call their parents 'mother' and 'father'. Harry sometimes became 'Dad', but more often 'Harry'.

He would go into Broadcasting House on the train, still wearing his uniform.

I spent a full day at the BBC's Written Archives Centre in Caversham, Reading, a comfortable house full of unimaginable treasures, and was impressed by the quality of the records stored there. From the files there, I learned that Harry could certainly have decided after the War to become a full-time broadcaster. I found not only numerous scripts and recordings, broadcasts on the War, broadcasts on educational topics, but also far more from the 1950s and 1960s than I had expected. Harry broadcast to France and North America as well as the British Isles. There was evidence of very careful writing and editing, but not of censorship. No wonder that the BBC of the mid-twentieth century was hugely respected throughout the world.

In a file dating from 1947–9, I found evidence of a positive but careful relationship between the Harry and the BBC. Examples of exchanges are:

'I believe it *should* be scripted.' (An editor to Harry, March 1947)

'Your last letter to me was so wittily rude.' (Harry, of course, August 1947)

'I'm afraid we can't use this, attractive as much of it is. At the end it is a little too tough physically even for this unpleasant age.' (Another editor, December 1947)

'The programme is not sufficiently good to be broadcast.' (February 1948)

On one occasion, in mid-May, 1949, someone with the BBC 'booked a studio at Leeds for you to rehearse down the line to me in London'.

In April, 1950, someone wrote:

Harry Rée is a talented but highly personal broadcaster who should be used where these talents are appropriate but should not be used where the emergence of his own viewpoint would be out of place, e.g. in Current Affairs programmes of the impartial type.

And two years later, Richmond Postgate, Controller of Educational Broadcasting, wrote:

One gets a definite impression of boyish enthusiasm, of the capacity to be fired by an idea, but also, particularly in the first years, a great willingness to take advice from the producer. [Quoting Vincent Alford] Distinguished for some remarkably immature judgements. Listeners' Association[77] alleged that Rée was a Communist. All this suggests to me that Rée is not the kind of person who can be relied upon to be objective and impersonal, though there seems to me little evidence that he is unwilling to take editing or briefing when it is put to him.

In mid-1945, 'Captain Rée' spoke at his old school, Shrewsbury, as reported by 'C.B.C.':

---

77   Chaired by Norman Fisher; not to be confused with Mary Whitehouse's later group.

The most significant thing about the German occupation [of France] was the almost exemplary behaviour of the Germans; had they been able to use a bit more tact, they would now in all probability be masters of all Europe. ...

Captain Rée then spoke of some of the families with whom he had operated, ranging from an old lady of 80 to a village butcher.

He went on to discuss sabotage:

In a football match between the saboteurs and the SS a bomb had fallen out of one man's pocket, whereupon an SS man had quite calmly returned the article without suspecting anything!

The only safe way of travelling was by cycle. ... France ... is deeply grateful to England for all she has done in the occupation; don't judge the French, go for yourselves and see them, then you will realize their full worth.

The lecture was very well received ... especially because Captain Rée spoke with such charming intimacy that he easily succeeded in holding his audience from beginning to end, in a talk where grim facts were excellently blended with humorous anecdotes.

At Reading I found the much-edited script of a November 1945, talk entitled 'TO-NIGHT'S TALK: TRAITORS MUST DIE': By a British Secret Agent, a compelling 15-minute tale that began, 'It was a beautiful morning for a murder.'

In 1946, Basil Blackwell, the Oxford bookseller, published a 76-page book by Marcel Pavigny entitled *Jours de Gloire*. Written in French, it was a primer for children based on stories of the French Resistance. And Marcel Pavigny was none other than Harry Rée. His use of a pseudonym and the very existence of this book remained a well-kept secret.

Not quite so secret, but hardly known was that in 1949, Nicholson and Watson published *Six Friends Arrive Tonight*, Harry's translation of *Six Amis Viendront Ce Soir* by the Belgian Gilbert Sadi Kirschen.

Until he died almost 50 years after the War, Harry was, understandably, conflicted about how to reflect back on his experience in France and how, or even whether, to talk about it. In early 1968, the *Sunday Times* quoted him as follows:

There's nothing romantic or James Bondish about spying. It's not even patriotic, or at least I wasn't being patriotic. I did it to prove myself, I think.

Around Christmas-time, 1946, he had a lucky break. He was asked to go to Russia, representing the Army, as part of a 20-person youth delegation. Representing the Navy was a young Member of Parliament called James Callaghan, who had first been elected to Parliament in the 1945 landslide, representing Cardiff South. 'Sunny Jim' and Harry were about the same age (Callaghan was about two years older), and both were pining for their wives. Callaghan, who was to become prime minister about 30 years later, was then vice-chairman of the Parliamentary Defence and Services Committee. The group was led by the MP for Finsbury, a former New Zealander who later became a leading barrister and who rejoiced in the name of John Faithful Fortescue Platts-Mills.

The Russians thought that Harry was a spy. Both Harry and Jim Callaghan recalled an enormous amount of drinking during the six weeks they spent travelling round the USSR. Platts-Mills certainly flirted with communism, having been expelled from the Labour Party in the late 1940s; Harry and Callaghan did not.

Nick Tucker writes:

I met Callaghan after he retired and he remembered Harry vividly – as I'm sure most people did who had ever been in his company for a time.

Chapter 6

After the War: Teaching

By the time Harry returned from the Soviet Union, it was time to be demobbed. He had choices. He could have credibly gone into film acting or directing; he could have strengthened his BBC ties and become a full-time broadcaster; or he could have gone back to Beckenham and Penge, where his position had been left open.

But Harry decided to apply for a position at Bradford Grammar School. As noted above, his grandfather Isidor had moved his business to Bradford in the early 1870s and his father had gone to that school. Was this background part of the decision? He'd be 50 miles or so from his own Mancunian roots. Harry was still at the stage in his life when he believed that it was grammar schools that provided the 'essential' (his word) avenues of opportunities for people of all incomes, stations and backgrounds. And BGS was one of the very best. Founded in 1548 and granted its charter in 1662 by King Charles II, the Merrie Monarch, its headmaster was the renowned classicist Richard B. Graham and its reputation unquestioned. (Even today, every pupil there is required to take at least two years of Latin, and the fees are around £12,300 per annum.) One of his former pupils at BGS (and I heard from over 20) noted:

> It is interesting to speculate why he chose to teach at what must have been one of the most selective schools in the country.

Ian Wilson, now living in Australia, says:

> What intrigues me is why, if his general outlook on life was from a socialist perspective, did he choose to become a master at the fee-paying BGS?

The fees at BGS ranged between £52 and £62 per annum.[78] About 30 per cent of the fee-payers could claim some kind of relief, and at least a quarter of the total school population would have had a scholarship from the Bradford or the West Riding local authority.

The Bradfordian, 'The Magazine of the Bradford Grammar School', welcomed five new masters, including Harry, with the words, 'We hope they

---

78   Equivalent to £1,963–£2,340 in 2016.

will enjoy their work here, and find relaxations to their taste in this grim Northern city.' Only five months later, *The Bradfordian* wrote:

> Mr H. Rée has been much in the public eye since joining us; his talks on Current Affairs in the Northern Children's Hour, and his chairmanship of BBC Public Enquiries, have brought his name into prominence in the local press; and the national press has said some very kind things about his acting in the recently released film 'School for Danger'. We shall look forward to seeing this story of anti-Nazi activity in France when it comes to Bradford.

In 1946, the year Harry joined the staff, Douglas Hamilton, chair of the school governors and after whom a room has been named, stated, very publicly:

> The BGS must not let inadequate means of a parent stand in the way of his boy's education. We must educate rich and poor alike, not merely for the sake of the boys themselves, but because as a community we simply cannot afford to wrap our talents in a napkin. Democracy can only work if we make the most of the rich human material we have available.

From a letter to me dated February 1961, i.e. only about 15 years after he first taught at BGS:

> I find I am wedded to the cause of the underprivileged, probably for sentimental reasons, but it is in my gut. It struck me the other day how strange it is that in the 30s I went into grammar school teaching because I wanted to boost the products whom I felt were getting a raw deal – and that now in the 1960s I am finding myself uneasy in the G.S. world because I am rather ashamed of the g.s. products! ... The logical place for me to go would be a sec. mod. but I'm not good enough to do this.

Around the same time, Harry wrote to his nephew, Charles Swallow:

> I'm crying for the moon, of course, and I shall never see a society where 'excessive' privilege is banned.

When Harry was settling in at York, Peter Waymark was to report:

> He now likes to be described as an egalitarian. 'I am keener on equality than liberty, but this does not mean I am not keen on liberty. ... The accent must be on trying to give people equal

opportunities to do what they want. This will naturally involve some interference with liberty and it's a question of finding a balance.'

Harry got his BGS job through the University of Cambridge Appointments Board. Today, he would, I think, have gone to the Institute of Education in London rather than Cambridge for assistance. Bradford probably had little interest in his teacher-training year. 'I wasn't a scholar'; but he was to be not just a teacher (they would probably have called him a 'master'); he was to be head of the modern language department. He was competent in both French and German; today the school offers French and German, of course, plus Chinese, Japanese, Russian and Spanish.

'The staff were very good,' Harry said later, 'keen on getting open scholarships to Oxbridge'. He 'took over the literature stuff' and organized the department, trusting two colleagues with French proses.

He probably got the job, at least in part, because of his War record, but he soon proved his worth.[79] When he left, 'R.P.' of the School magazine opined:

> Mr Rée came to us nearly five years ago, and very quickly showed that his approach to Modern Languages followed a new track. New ideas and unusual methods indicated that for him French was not a subject to be picked up from books but rather an adventure.
>
> Mr Rée has always been something more than a schoolmaster. … The cinema, the radio, both modern media, have been his instruments.
>
> We shall always remember the spontaneous outburst of laughter that greeted any touch of the ridiculous.[80] We shall remember, too, that it was Mr Rée who took on the organization of cross-country running.
>
> … We say 'Thank you' for helping us …

He may not have been a sportsman, but an Old Bradfordian recalls his introducing hurdling to the school in 1953 or 1954, having enthusiastically demonstrated the art in the gymnasium of the old school on Manor Row.

---

79 More than 40 years later, Harry said, 'I'd never have got it if I hadn't been in the War.'
80 Many years later, Bill Bailey, who knew Harry at Watford, would speak about the 'sound of laughter, banter and easy relationships'.

In the summer of 2007, *The Old Bradfordian* ran a full-page piece entitled 'Fond Memories of a French Trip':

> What amazes me now is that we made our way from Bradford to the Golden Arrow[81] platform, only there meeting up with all the party ... how the whole venture had come about: a notice from the newly appointed French master, the celebrated Harry Rée, that he was able to offer the opportunity for boys ... to have exchange visits with boys attending the lycée at Tourcoing, a textile town on the Belgian border.[82] ... one thing had to be done immediately: the visit to the Hôtel de Ville to obtain a ration card.
>
> ...
>
> Another fascinating snapshot in time is the memory of that charismatic teacher, Harry Rée, a slim, distinguished man who spoke our language in quite an impressive way. ... Subsequently I came to appreciate the aura with which his pupils surrounded him. For them, it seemed he was far more than a school master: a hero.

I began serious work on the life of Harry Rée fully 60 years after he left Bradford Grammar School. As the reader can well imagine, I doubted whether I could find anyone with recollections of someone who had taught them between 60 and 65 years previously. Full credit, above all, to Roger P. Bland, who helped gather memories from over 20 individuals. One gets a sense from what follows of an extraordinarily effective and charismatic teacher. Clearly, much in Harry's background came together in the four-and-a-half years he spent at Bradford Grammar School; clearly, by the time he became a headmaster, he had a vision of education as it should be and the experience to make things happen. One also gets a sense of a group with enviably sharp powers of recall.

All of the men who responded to Roger Bland must have been in their late seventies or eighties when they wrote, and, as he pointed out to me:

> The duplication in the texts adds a great deal to the veracity of what has been portrayed, particularly as none of the writers knew anything about the thoughts and memories being offered by other contemporaries.

---

81 From 1926 until 1972, the Golden Arrow from Victoria Station was the most prestigious London–Paris train.

82 Harry had been there during the War.

I might add that none of them knows me, so none can have been influenced by me.

Let us begin, then, with Roger Bland:

> Harry started teaching at BGS in September, 1946, and left at the end of the January term, 1951. It was soon known that he had been in the Resistance Movement in France ... which afforded him a kudos not available to other members of staff. This knowledge did not come from Harry himself ... he was quite reticent about it. Perhaps we were the more prepared, however, not to be surprised when his behaviour or dress or values seemed at odds with the rather traditional staff attitudes we had got used to. He was a master who was easy to get on with but one just wondered whether he was at that time feeling his feet as a new teacher.
>
> We were doing a cross-country run ... to my surprise there was Harry ... puffing and panting like us, his strides were as wearisome as ours, and yet there he was giving us some audible encouragement.
>
> His gift of empathizing with us may have been his most distinguishing characteristic ... and it was spread across our school life from sport to academic studies and to extra-mural activities. To us all this was a phenomenon we were not used to.

John Seekings has no doubts:

> Harry Rée was the most memorable teacher I ever had. French lessons were always a delight with this charismatic man keeping consistent order with a class of boisterous boys without ever having to raise his voice. ... I credit him with imbuing in me my love of the French language and the country. We did not know then of his wartime heroics.

David R. Watson writes:

> Naturally, we were all very impressed by this hero of the Resistance. ... He never talked about his War experience. I remember two classroom discussions. One was on French colonialism, compared with British. He explained the French aim of assimilation, and certainly left me with the idea that this meant that the French Empire was a good thing while the British was

bad. This would I suppose have been the standard left-wing view at that time, though it has not stood the test of time very well. The second was on the subject of our favourite films. One boy insisted on *Tarzan*, which made Rée very cross. He was trying to give us the French idea that films could be part of 'high culture', just as much as literature. ... That one year played a part in getting me involved in all things French, which has been the backbone of my academic career.[83]

Denis M. Foster remembers Harry and the War somewhat differently:

He told us many tales of his War experiences, and showed us *School for Danger*. ... He was an inspiring teacher and personality and we were all in awe of him and probably worked much harder for knowing something about his wartime background. ... We were sorry to lose him but thrilled that he was going to Watford as headmaster. ... Harry Rée's influence may have suggested a life of service to others, though I was not conscious of it at the time.[84]

Peter White remembers 'his style of teaching, and, because his approach was new, one of his classes was given in the BBC (radio) studios at Leeds'.
    Ian Wilson adds:

I remember the trip to the BBC studios in Leeds where we had a 'typical school French lesson' to be broadcast in France. Of course, it wasn't typical. ... Apart from the general 'fun' of the lessons with Harry Rée what I do remember is his insistence that only French was spoken. Others have noted that he was known to have socialist views when he was at BGS.

John Cureton writes:

Harry Rée stood out as a pupil-friendly master with a gift for communicating his subjects to us Yorkshire tykes. ... I can say without doubt that he was one of the select few whose name still resonates in my memory. He was without doubt an inspiration to a young lad who had come from the inner city and had been given a scholarship by the city fathers. Whilst the entry to BGS was a daunting experience, it was made easier by some of the

---

83 Watson taught French history at the University of Dundee until he retired; his *Georges Clemenceau: France: Makers of the Modern World*, came out in 2009.

84 Foster now lives in New South Wales, after about 15 years in the military and eight years as Manager of Cranbrook School, Sydney.

new fresh blood in the common room, who recognized what the new post-War crop of young boys needed, and Harry was the foremost of the new breed. His tales of his Wartime exploits mesmerized us, and by osmosis taught French, sowed a seed that one day got me on the road to my career.[85]

Peter J.M. Bell became a Governor of BGS in 1970; he retired in 2002 after a career in the wool business, and writes:

> Mr Rée lived at 303 Toller Lane, Heaton, in a rather large dilapidated stone-built semi-detached house. Despite my problems with French, I was good at art and secretary of the art society, with David Hockney as a member. ... I recall several visits to his [Harry's] home to discuss art. ... Harry Rée founded and organized the European Society, which held joint meetings between BGS (boys only in those days) and Bradford Girls' Grammar School. This is how I met my wife.

It should not surprise anyone that Harry would sponsor a European Society. As early as 1947, *The Bradfordian* wrote:

> We are indebted to Mr Rée for his assistance in forming this new School Society, the aim of which is to stimulate interest in the affairs of our neighbours on the continent of Europe.

Three months later:

> Looking back upon the work of the past year, one is struck by the unqualified success of the new Society. It is only fitting that we should here express our thanks to Mr Rée, the Society's founder, without whose work this success would not have been possible.

Harry already knew how to garner publicity . The December 1950 issue of *The Bradfordian* reports on the sudden illness of a speaker:

> Mr Rée kindly flung himself into the breach and gave a highly interesting talk on 'Eating and Drinking Your Way Through France.'

> Mr Rée began by describing a novel competition organized by the French railways, whereby railway restaurants competed to see which one could produce the best meals. Each meal was to

---

85 Cureton and his wife left England in 1957 to work in Africa. He spent 25 years working for Qantas, and they now live in Adelaide.

contain at least one regional dish, and the winning stations were to be marked in a special leaflet for travellers. This, said Mr Rée, would not work in England because English people over the age of 21 lose interest in food and regard eating as a disgusting necessity. The French agree that it is disgusting, but their resultant attitude differs considerably from that of the English. The English resign themselves to it, and it is bad manners to talk too much about it. The French, on the other hand, have turned it into an art, to be discussed and criticized like all other arts. Mr Rée told us that the best way to eat in France is to give time to enjoy the food, and not to snatch hasty snacks at intervals in a car journey. This point made, he described the specialties, alcoholic or otherwise, of various French provinces and ended with a story of the origin of Gruyère cheese.

The March 1951 edition reports:

A debate was held at Belle Vue Girls' G.S. Mr Rée was in the chair, and the motion before the House was 'That we favour the establishment of the United States of Europe, comprising a European democratic government which would have power to act in economic, military and social matters common to member states.' ... The motion was declared defeated by the overwhelming majority of 76 votes to 13, perhaps not surprisingly, since this was, after all, less than six years after end of the War.

John Hicks wrote from Surrey, where he has lived for half a century:

His teaching style was rather unconventional and a breath of fresh air; very relaxed in approach, though nonetheless thorough and insightful. He was very approachable and unstuffy, though still keeping the master/pupil stance, but more informally than many other masters. And poles apart from R.B. Graham.[86] Charismatic.

I remember being invited to tea, with two other form members ... It was a most enjoyable experience, completely informal and relaxed, and plenty of laughter. And Hetty was absolutely charming.

He was instrumental in my going to Christ's.[87] ... He wrote to his own former tutor, Dr Guillebaud.

---

86 The headmaster.
87 Christ's College, Cambridge.

He was a big influence on my young life, for the better. He was pretty left-wing, of course, and was a pacifist until Germany attacked Norway.[88]

He would arrive at BGS on a scooter-type motor bike, dressed in his army greatcoat. An abiding memory for me. ... Harry Rée brought a breath of fresh air to the school ... His style of teaching was refreshing and unorthodox, and he certainly aroused our interest in e.g. Racine, Corneille and Molière. ... He certainly opened our eyes and minds in new ways ... I don't think he was too popular with some of the other masters – too innovational for them, I think.

David Finney adds:

He was a new type of teacher; he readily disclosed his age (he was much younger than all the others who had weathered the War) and he was the first to treat us like contemporaries. He swore and became angry when we sniggered over the German 'Fahrt'; his continuing reference thereafter to farting took away all the schoolboy enjoyment of the word and in the process made us grow up a little.

He was not a sportsman, but he regularly attended first eleven cricket matches on Saturdays, always in the exclusive company of two or more stylish ladies.[89]

Brother Peter writes:

Harry Rée was like a breath of fresh air after the rather sclerotic old guard whom we had been lumbered with for the War years. ... He organized ... a 'Treasure Hunt' to Normandy. ... We had a limit of £5 to spend in France and had 23 'treasures' to locate ... and bring home some evidence to confirm what we had achieved. Examples of 'treasure' ... were rubbings from certain gravestones ... and two post cards sent *post-restante* from one town to another.

When they got home first, Finney and another BGS pupil had their pictures in the *Telegraph and Argus* and were featured on radio.

---

88 April 1940.

89 Finney emigrated to Sydney in 1968. At the time of writing, he was studying for a modern history degree at Macquarie University. His older brother Peter, he says, beat him to tertiary education by 58 years.

In 1951, shortly after Harry had moved to Watford, Harrap published his *Normandy Treasure Hunt* in its 'good holiday' series. The book, with photos by Harry's niece Pamela Newell (now Lowe), cheerfully tells the tale of how several boys went to Normandy, where they had to locate the following:

(1) A round Camembert cheese box stamped with the Mayor's stamp of the village of Camembert.
(2) An English exercise done by a French schoolboy.
(3) A picture postcard of Alençon lace, posted at Alençon to yourself at Lisieux.
(4) A picture postcard of Le Tour de Beurre at Rouen – explaining in French why it is called Tour de Beurre.
(5) A picture of the inside of Chartres Cathedral, together with a newspaper published in Chartres during April.
(6) A Scout badge, showing the coat of arms of Normandy.
(7) A proof of a visit to the petrol refineries at Le Havre.
(8) A picture postcard of the church where William the Conqueror was buried, posted to yourself at Dieppe.
(9) Entry ticket to the Bayeux Tapestry.
(10) Souvenir of a visit to the Trappist Monastery at Soligny la Trappe.

In a recent letter, Mrs Lowe writes, 'Harry was of course responsible for my education.'

Present-day readers may be struck by the seeming lack of concern for the safety of adolescent boys hitchhiking or cycling in France by themselves or in twos, five or so years after the War, sleeping in fields and relying on the kindnesses of the local population.

Roger M. Charnley remembers Harry's beret 'of course'. (He must have given that up by the time he moved to Watford.) He writes:

I vividly recall … at this particular Scout meeting … he not only described life in occupied France … but gave us a real insight into the workings of the French Resistance.

Harry demonstrated … some never-to-be-forgotten basics of unarmed combat, using a bemused patrol-leader as his enemy dummy. … We were also treated to an impressive display of knife-throwing at a distance of several feet and given some very useful 'professional' tips on the art of camouflage.

I could claim that Harry Rée and myself had, in addition to our love of France, at least one other thing in common – the headmaster certainly disliked both of us. Richard Brocksbank Graham was an ardent Quaker and a pacifist – hence his reluctance to embrace Harry and to recognize his wartime exploits!

His teaching approach could be said in today's parlance 'to be somewhat laid-back' … 'laconic' … I can visualize him now, mid-lesson, leaning well back in his chair with his feet propped up on his desk!

I seem to recall, back circa 1949/50, the now world-famous artist David Hockney[90] … doing a brilliant chalk-on-blackboard cartoon of Harry Rée – complete with his war-time beret, carrying a hand-grenade or similar weapon and looking very menacing – and not at all his usual classroom friendly self.

The thought of a Hockney cartoon of Harry, carelessly erased well over sixty years ago, reminded my wife Linda of a very short story by Ray Bradbury entitled *In a Season of Calm Weather*. George Smith is on holiday with his wife. At the beach, he sees a man drawing pictures in the sand. He recognizes Pablo Picasso and is dominated by the thought of the incoming tide.

John Hill remembers 'a teacher like no other at BGS.' He goes on:

Harry Rée was always something of a mystery, the speculation of his role in the Second World War was rife, accurate knowledge was missing, but imagination more than made up for that. His classroom style was extraordinarily laid back, comfy seat, feet on desk, casually flicking the hair back to see us better. There was rarely any anger, just a hint of frustration and sorrow if someone was wasting precious time. His accurate distribution of marked homework books from a single point was occasionally accompanied by an apology for those which, sadly, had accidentally slipped into the bath.

There's a wonderful line in *Butley*, a play that Harry especially liked, by Simon Gray. Ben, played by Alan Bates in the original 1971 production: 'He brought around 17 exercise books, of which I dropped a mere three into the bath.'

Hill continues:

My own interest in learning French was certainly stimulated by my respect for this very different style of teaching. … I have very

---

90   Born July 1937.

fond memories of a remarkable man, who probably more than any other helped me to respect, appreciate, and enjoy the work of all the teachers on whose efforts our futures depended.

Michael Ludgate recalls:

> He was a subject of hero worship ... because he was young, dashing, with a mellifluous voice, great charm and a splendid and romantic war record. ... I vividly recall my first French lesson with Harry. ... He said, 'Today you are going to listen ... to some French music, and he put records on of Trenet[91] and Sablon[92], the two great stars of French music hall. We learned the words with him of 'Sur le Pont d'Avignon' and 'La Mer'. What a wonderful and clever introduction to that beautiful language! He organized outings for us in school time to French films.

> Racing home after school to listen to Children's Hour,[93] I was amazed to hear him giving a weekly talk about his adventures in occupied France. ...

> In autumn 1945 he was invited to luncheon by the King. The Queen, later Queen Mother, became a personal friend and every year attended a reunion of surviving Resistance members.

> He was an inspiring, kind and unforgettable teacher. How lucky we kids were!

Ludgate has spent time pottering, as he puts it, on a boat from the Danube delta; then off to Las Palmas. Until his retirement he was a company director in London, moving to the Canary Islands. He wrote:

> Harry ... has had a lasting influence. We kids had admiration and awe – not too strong a word – for this young dashing teacher who broadcast, had high decorations and had made a FILM! Imagine the impression that made on schoolboys whose brothers and parents had fought in the War. We were in a bomb-damaged provincial city in austerity post-war Britain. ... He never talked of his exploits or behaved in any way as a celebrity.

> I was so stung by his remark on my 1947 school report – 'his work is full of the most elementary mistakes' – that I applied

---

91 Charles Trenet 1913–2001.
92 Jean Sablon 1906–1994.
93 BBC radio, 5 p.m. to 6 p.m. every day from 1922 to 1964.

myself sorrowfully but determinedly to French, and French won me my only distinction in School Certificate.

Did he influence me in later life? Yes, of course. ... He showed us what courage and quick wit and guts could accomplish and I had a lasting ambition to achieve what I wanted in life and a lasting admiration for young men recently sent to risk their lives by politicians who have themselves never experienced the horror of war.

He was in a class apart from our other teachers.

My first lesson with Harry is vivid, such was the impression he made on me. ... As I write I am in that room on the ground floor of the old school in Manor Row (long since pulled down), I remember where I sat, Harry is there with his back to the windows facing us ... He is wearing a grey Harris tweed jacket and grey flannels, relaxed and friendly. ... The memory is indelible, such as to have erased all the previous lessons. THAT was the effect Harry Rée had on me. No other teacher ever came close. ... He was a breath of fresh air in an age of deference. ... I wish only that I had written to him to thank him for helping to change my life.

Many years later, Martin Trow, Berkeley professor of public policy, was to write, 'Higher education ... is for society a functional substitute for deference.' And Margaret Maden spoke of the death of dad (i.e. father figures) and deference.

Peter Drumm described Harry as 'one of the few teachers I remember as being in any way inspirational'. Recalling the film *Now It Can Be Told*, he continued:

In one scene, an aircraft ... had become bogged down in a field ... Harry (who played himself in the film) was seen encouraging a group of partisans to shove the aircraft from its muddy trap. They strained away ... while Harry stood back urging them on with cries of 'un, deux, trois, poussez!' ... While Harry was watching a school rugby game, there rose from the BGS scrum an orchestrated chorus of 'un, deux, trois, poussez!'

Drumm has another recollection:

Harry always seemed to be very relaxed, best demonstrated by his habit of teaching from a sitting position. Sooner or later his feet would go up on the desk and the chair tilted back on two legs, at which point his class's concentration on the lesson dipped sharply as every boy tensely waited in eager anticipation for this being the day he would fall right over. To the best of my knowledge he never did.[94]

John A. Grange, a retired educational psychologist, has several memories:

We boys found him a very pleasant person and he was certainly full of life. (Indeed, some mornings he looked a little bit the worse for wear as if he'd had quite a convivial evening the night before!) He also had the endearing quality of being able to admit in a discussion ... that there might be a slightly different interpretation from the one he had proposed – although, of course, any need to do this was rare because he was so knowledgeable, in particular about the French language and culture.

On one occasion he showed me a kind of support that was probably crucial at the time and which he gave with a characteristic lightness of touch. In 1947 my father had died and I felt terribly guilty that my mother was consequently having to spend even more time in our business to support me and pay for my education. On two occasions I tried to leave school and find work. On the second occasion ... I tried to find a role for myself in our music shop as an assistant in the record department. After about a week, my mother refused to have me there and I remained at home, wondering what to do next. After one or two days, Harry rang me and said, 'Isn't it time you came back, Grange?' to which I replied meekly, 'I suppose so'.

During my time in the sixth form, the school was visited by two or three German dignitaries. Harry Rée delegated me to take them round during lunchtime. ... I mentioned this event to Harry's sister Helen Fairclough ... because I had felt at the time that it was a bit unusual to delegate such a task to one of the boys. I had the feeling that Harry was avoiding contact with the Germans. Mrs Fairclough confirmed my feeling, and said at the time he had a strong aversion to Germans in general because of his experience of them during the War.

---

94 Drumm spent most of his post-BGS years in public relations, working for the Scottish Office until he retired in 1992.

Some years back, I met a chap named Barker who had been in the same form as me. ... He was present when R.B. Graham told Harry off in the presence of himself and a few other boys for a lack of courtesy to the Germans. Of course, to do this in the presence of some of the boys was itself hardly appropriate.

In a 1991 letter to Helen Fairclough, shortly after Harry's death, Grange wrote:

Looking back, I don't think it was, for me, Harry's teaching ability in the narrower sense which created a lasting impression, but rather his broader qualities as a human being. He respected those he taught, and in turn they respected him for his abilities and qualities as a person. He helped create an atmosphere in which his pupils could feel that their opinions counted and, furthermore, that they counted as people with rights to their own individuality and to their own opinions – although these should be well grounded and thought out.

I may have caused Harry a bit of anxiety. I had learned from another pupil how to hypnotize and I got enough confidence to start giving demonstrations. ... during the lunch hour, I would hypnotize a volunteer, get him to lose his memory for who he was, where he was, etc. I would bring him round, and on a signal from me he would do some performance. ... This might be something like jumping onto a chair and shouting 'peanuts', or something equally silly, whereupon my volunteer would regain his memory and, hopefully, all would be well. ... I got quite large audiences. However, on one occasion, Harry walked into the room and caught me in the middle of my act. He was obviously quite perturbed and instructed me not to repeat the exercise.

I remember Harry for the sort of person he was. I am sure that he himself would probably never realize what lasting and positive impressions former pupils will have retained. ... It was his qualities as a person, as a human being, which made ... an enduring impression.

Paul Hockney, Lord Mayor of Bradford in 1977, is the eldest brother of David Hockney. It was Paul who funded the large School Theatre. He writes:

I was never taught by Harry, but one incident I remember well. ... In 1947 a film entitled *The Outlaw* starring Jane Russell was being shown at the Regent Cinema in Manningham Lane. ... This film received much publicity and was a breakthrough role for Jane Russell who showed much of her bosom freely exposed and turned the young actress into a sex symbol and Hollywood icon. Many local councils had banned the film, but Bradford did not, and almost every boy from BGS wanted to see this film. Imagine their joy to discover that the supporting film was ... *School for Danger* ... starring our own Captain Harry Rée. The Regent Cinema was full all week with BGS boys wanting to see their Harry (and of course Jane).

He was still publicly referred to as Captain Rée as late as September 1957, more than 12 years after the end of the War.

Barry Hoffbrand adds:

Harry Rée was my French teacher. I remember him as a handsome man with a reputation as a War hero and the subject of a full-length film. I have scanned a school report for that period more distinguished by Harry's elegant initials than my accomplishments in French.[95]

And Victor Hoffbrand remarks:

Harry Rée taught me French. He was very keen to get over to us a feel for the French language, its poetry and other literature and not just learning the vocabulary and grammar. I did query his marking of one of my efforts and as a 'reward' he wrote on my report that 'he must remember to learn French and not just to collect marks.' ... He was an extremely professional teacher ... charismatic.[96]

Pierre Richterich reports:

He always had a pretty relaxed approach to discipline. ... For good work he created the Order of the Meringue.

After mentioning the 'wretched' R.B. Graham, Richterich reports that he did not go on to Oxbridge, although he could have, but joined a wool firm; then served in the Army at Supreme Headquarters Allied Powers Europe

---

95 Barry Hoffbrand was a consulting physician and nephrologist until his retirement early in this century. He edited the *Postgraduate Medical Journal* for 15 years.

96 Victor Hoffbrand was Professor of Haematology at the Royal Free Hospital in Hampstead from 1973 to 1996; since then, he has been Emeritus Professor of Haematology at UCL.

(SHAPE) HQ near Paris, where he used his French to good effect. He started his own business in 1959 with £800, retiring almost 40 years later.

Not everyone rated Harry as tip-top. Alan Langford, for example, writes:

> Harry Rée taught me French ... I remember him as a clever and charming man. ... I had a French and Latin master Mr H.A. Twelves ('Douzey') ... who was a brilliant teacher and probably had more affect on my young life than Harry.

But Michael J.G. Whitaker refers to 'his certainly unusual method of teaching;' he goes on:

> Leaning against the side of the blackboard, he would regale us with thoughts on perhaps women, wine, French manners and mores; all the while permeating French language through a sort of mental osmosis. ... The most remarkable picture of those years was when Harry was presented – in front of most of the school – with the first motor scooter most had ever seen. ... It was a gift ... in gratitude for his wartime activities.

Harry's son Jonathan thinks the scooter was a gift from Rodolphe Peugeot.

During the Bradford years, the Rées became friendly with Richard and Ailsa (Elizabeth) O'Brien, both of whom, over the years, became as close as anyone, both to Harry and to his children. Sir Richard (he was knighted on Margaret Thatcher's recommendation in 1980) was decorated several times during the War (DSO, double MC) and became Field Marshall Bernard Montgomery's personal assistant. In 1976, he was selected by Michael Foot, Secretary of State for Employment in Prime Minister James Callaghan's government, to chair the Manpower Services Commission, a quango[97] from which he was dismissed by Norman Tebbit, almost certainly at the behest of the prime minister who had knighted him. He was appointed by Robert Runcie to chair the Archbishop's Commission on Urban Priority Areas, which produced the influential report entitled *Faith in the City, A Call to Action by Church and Nation* in the autumn of 1985.[98] He died in 2009 at the age of 89. His wife, whom I was privileged to meet, is a child psychiatrist who has seen it all. A Cambridge graduate, she received her medical training in a Leeds hospital. She and her husband met at a Bradford Grammar School dance in 1949; as she put it, 'many of us married

---

97 Quasi-autonomous non-governmental organization.
98 Chelly Halsey, another of Harry's long-time friends, was a member of the Commission.

war heroes'. She took 12 years out, had five children, and returned to her profession in 1965.

Ailsa found Harry 'very glamorous'. But, she says now, she didn't discuss important things with him, being 'too busy cooking, entertaining, reading fluff'. He was 'an open person, not narrow; had convictions and high standards; very sympathetic, but demanding'. He was not big-headed, though Eric James was. And 'never awe-inspiring'. He handled Hetty's death badly, and Ailsa and Harry's daughter Janet meet for lunch at least once a year, around the Christmas season. He was dogmatic about food.

Lady O'Brien writes:

> I remember my first meeting with Harry and Hetty at a Christmas party at the Grahams (headmaster of Bradford Grammar School) who were family friends. Gertrude Graham started the Marriage Guidance Council in Bradford and later helped me to organize a committee in Wakefield which would start one there. I was working for Family Planning when we lived in Wakefield … I remember eating delicious meals in Toller Lane when I was working in Bradford Children's Hospital and watching Hetty sewing super little corduroy trousers for Jonathan (aged 2) with zip pockets.
>
> Hetty wrote a letter to Richard … telling him not to expect me to be a wife like her. Harry told Richard regarding my ignorance of cooking, 'Don't worry about it. She likes her food. She'll learn.'
>
> Richard drove Harry to York to catch the train for his Watford interview and it was a very foggy day but they made it!
>
> One Easter I had rented a house in the Dales from a farmer called Bainbridge and it was Colt Park. Harry and Jonathan came to stay. Jonathan climbed Ingleborough straight from the house. Two or three years later they bought it and we nearly always called in there on our way south from Scottish holidays.

For some reason, her husband 'couldn't stand Francis Cammaerts; thought he was a bad influence; couldn't understand how Harry could like him'. I asked her why, in her opinion, neither Harry nor Francis was offered a knighthood. 'Too individualistic', she replied. Would Harry have accepted one? 'Yes!'

Chapter 7

Watford

Anyone who has read the comments from Bradford Grammar School Old Boys almost certainly knows more about Harry the man and Harry the teacher than the people who were involved in bringing him to the headship of Watford Boys' Grammar School (WBGS). Some BGS boys were quite knowledgeable about his War record … 'mesmerized' … while others were reportedly unaware. Some remember his talking about it; others recall avoidance. More than one mentioned charisma. As Roger Bland suggested, one does get a picture.

I wonder whether anyone at BGS knew that, at one time, Harry was earning more from the BBC than from his teaching job. (Or so he said: his son Jonathan cannot quite believe it.) But he was getting restless … Nigel Gann and others later saw the restlessness in him … and wrote to some chief education officers/directors of education about the possibility of being considered for a headship. He got 'one or two fairly dusty answers'. He remembered getting 'a good brush-off' from Derbyshire: could this have been from (Sir) Jack Longland, who was Director of Education there for 21 years and was best known for chairing the BBC radio panel game *My Word!* from 1957 to 1977?

He was probably more interested in a headship than he let on. In an interview with Dinah Brook in *The Guardian* in the late 1960s, he said:

> I'd never thought of becoming a headmaster. I suppose Eric James first put the idea into my head when I used to go over to Manchester to broadcast for the *Children's Hour*. In 1951 I applied to be head of a school in East Anglia for the sons of officers of the Merchant Navy.[99] And I also put in for Watford Grammar School.

John (later Sir John) Newsom, Chief Education Officer for Hertfordshire from 1940 to 1957, described by someone who knew him as 'ebullient', encouraged him to apply for WBGS, although he warned that his chances

---

99   Might that school have been the Royal Hospital School in Holbrook, near Ipswich? If so, he was beaten by J.H. Babington, GC, OBE, a former Hertfordshire assistant education officer who went on, four years later, to a headship in Berkhamsted. It is interesting to note jobs Harry expressed an interest in throughout his life, but did not get.

were slim, given his 'small amount of experience'. (But then, Newsom himself was only 29 when he became a Chief Education Officer.)

Watford, at the end of the Metropolitan line and the first stop from Euston on the way to Manchester, is about 20 miles northwest of central London; in the southwest corner of Hertfordshire. Depending on how you count, the population is about 80,000 (the town) or over 120,000 (the urban area). When Londoners speak, 'north of Watford' can mean 'provincial' or 'unsophisticated'.

Watford Boys' Grammar School moved to its present site, less than a mile west of the town centre on Rickmansworth Road, in 1907. Headmasters tend to stay a long time: Edward Reynolds (1922–38), Percy Bolton (1938–51), Keith Turner (1963–91). Bolton and Reynolds had both been headmasters previously; Bolton, a physicist, for 14 years at Dean Close School in Cheltenham (all-boarding at the time) and Reynolds at Northampton Town and County Grammar School. Wanting the best of both worlds, WBGS describes itself today as a 'partially selective comprehensive school'.

So Harry applied, and got the job. He was 36 years old: young, but not ridiculously so; experienced, but not as a headmaster. He recalled the interview:

> In the course of it there was a marvellous moment – I think he [Newsom] asked the question – he said, 'You are the only applicant whom we've got in front of us today who hasn't been a headmaster. So we don't know what your standards would be in appointing staff, because you have a great responsibility for appointing staff. What is the main quality you would look for in the appointing of staff?' And I've always said that an angel at that moment came and sat on the tip of my tongue, because I said, 'Generosity, in the widest sense of the term.' That was a wonderful answer. And I was offered the job.

This lovely and revealing story, which Harry told throughout the rest of his life, connects, I think, with a rare moment where Headmaster Rée showed his emotions, as recalled by Commodore Peter Swan many, many years after the incident he describes:

> The remedial French class was taken by Rée. … The classroom allocated was the one behind the school hall and when the stage was set … the door was blocked by the additional staging and scenery. Harry Rée had … tried to insert the basics of French

into the minds of the unwilling; the bell rang for the end of the lesson; and Rée, forgetting the normal door was blocked, opened and saw a small space behind the door beneath the stage. His face turned an ashen colour and he started to cry. 'When I went into Belsen at the end of the War, I saw a space that size with five people crammed in,' he croaked. He then turned and ran out by the other exit.

As I discuss elsewhere, Harry did not speak much of his experiences in the War. But there were occasions when they just came out. Another example, from his time at the University of York: John Langton, a painter, describes how he and Harry spent some time together driving people to the polls. They finished around 9 p.m. and were setting off back to the University for a drink. John suggested that, since it was Bonfire Night,[100] they drive by the City Wall, where there would be bonfires. 'Christ no,' said Harry, 'they will not be bonfires; you should have seen the Peugeot works burn during the War. I'd set it alight and watched its flames light up the sky, lying under a hedge.'

John Newsom appointed daringly. From 1952 to 1961, Harry's close friend, Francis Cammaerts, was headmaster of Alleyne's Grammar School, Stevenage, Hertfordshire, about 20 miles from WBGS.

Newsom told Harry he'd better send a 'very good bottle of sherry' to his referees, Henry Morris and Eric James.[101]

As his Bradford pupils could have foreseen, Harry was a breath of fresh air. 'There is surely no profession', he would write in *The Essential Grammar School*, 'which enjoys more laughs per hour, none where the unexpected so frequently happens'.

He, his wife Hetty, and their three children moved to 58, The Avenue, just over a mile from the school. It was, in Harry's words, 'a really rather lovely house in a nice part of Watford, with a lovely garden ... Janet always says, "the sun was always shining in Watford"'.

About 60 years later, his nephew Philip Rée Mallinson, son of sister Meta, and now himself a teacher at Phillips Exeter Academy in New Hampshire, US, recalled a household where everyone was constantly asking questions.

---

100 Guy Fawkes Day, 5 November.
101 So Harry must have known James at least a decade before he became a professor at York (see chapter 10). To those who would complain that Eric did not put him through the traditional search-and-interview process – and there were some – I would argue that he would have had a full decade to watch Harry in action, so by 1961, he must have known exactly what he was in for.

Harry, an inveterate letter-writer, frequently wrote to Richard and Ailsa O'Brien. In April 1951, he must have been writing from Watford, when he told them that the children had never been so happy; the garden was a perpetual joy; he didn't think that his mother-in-law would be a nuisance, though he found she 'unfailingly' induced a whole trail of unethical thoughts in him. He had also made 'a most excellent English appointment ... a man of considerable dynamism and personality'.[102] He continued:

> The male secretary, Mr Jones, continues to be admirable, though what he thinks of the young whippersnapper in the HM's chair, I can't say.

Only eight days later, he was writing:

> Janet is miserable at school and rapidly becoming the unpopular prig of form 1 – poor child – she can't take it.

Hetty added a note:

> Harry looking very solemn and headmasterish (I'm sure you would approve!) ... How right you are about his competence.

Harry, in turn, shared his notes from his first staff meeting:

- No sweeping changes. You have got the school working too well for me to want to meddle ... [103]
- Hope I may very soon cease to be unknown and unpredictable. Therefore please realize that I am here at your service. What I can usefully do for you I shall do for you.

A week later Mr Jones ... 'very friendly and loyal secretary' ... was warning Harry that his deputy, Mr Merrett, 'was a bit of a chiseller'. 'Mr Jones', as we all called W.J.T. Jones, was a former pupil of one of Harry's predecessors, Edward Reynolds, whom Reynolds had brought with him from Northampton. According to Norman Marrow:

---

102 This must have been Don Taylor, who became the author's boss almost seven years later, and a lifelong friend. He went on to be headmaster of Durrants School.

103 Many years later, Norman Marrow wrote:

> Nothing so much points the contrast between him and PB [Bolton] as their respective attitude to change. When PB held his first staff meeting he told us that he proposed to make no changes for at least 12 months. ... Harry Rée, in contrast, began making changes from the very beginning and one said of him that if a month passed without some major alteration in our arrangements he became restless and miserable. (Marrow, N. (2012) *Avi epistula: A grandfather's letter*. Online: *sine nomine*).

He took a melancholy view of life in general and of education in particular, and would invariably turn down any request that involved expense. But the wily among us came to discover that, if we put our request in the form 'I suppose it wouldn't be possible …', there was more than half a chance that he would say, rather sharply, 'Why not?' and insist on our having what we wanted. … I learned that this redoubtable Mr Jones had been in early days in business in America. He seldom smiled more than fractionally. … When I was collecting from his room a number of new books for the history section of the School library. 'I can't understand', he said 'why the history people keep wanting new books. After all history's history; it can't be changed!'[104]

Harry was in France for Good Friday 1951 or 1952, visiting L'Abbaye du Bec Hellouin in Normandy. He writes to Richard O'Brien:

I read D.H. Lawrence on the journey – *The Rainbow* – but he's not suitable here.

I'm reading Russell's *Western Philosophy* which is excellent and … Simone Weil.

I envy your ability to submit to a faith.

Quite honestly, I have got a reasonably good conscience!

Life is a glorious accident.

Death becomes fairly unimportant.

Hetty again: 'Harry shows no signs of flagging.'

In 1955, Harry wrote to the O'Briens: he was off to Windsor Castle for a conference with professors of education and Eric James on the training of graduate teachers. Clearly, he already had a close relationship with Eric. He had written something, saying, '… I was looking forward to sending it to Eric James for approval …'. He must also have been doing some television: 'The TV has been fun, but it is not very serious. (It has been paying for the van.)'. As always, Harry was reading voraciously and widely: 'I am rediscovering Gide' … 'You must borrow *Such Darling Dodos* by Angus Wilson … it's a wicked attack on *US*!'

Harry's voracious reading, in both English and French, went back to his years at school. For example, Gillian Tindall recalls his recommendation

---

104 Marrow, N. (2012) *Avi epistula: A grandfather's letter*. Online: *sine nomine*.

of Philippe Hériat's *La Famille Boussardel*, which came out in 1944 and won the Grand Prix du Roman D'Académie Française three years later.

Looking back, I wonder whether the staff realized how much their headmaster thought of them. As Harry recounts in his British Library interviews:

> It was an incredibly good school. It was an ordinary state school, of course. But the staff were quite exceptional. ... I've always liked schoolteachers. But they were very conscientious. Very successful. There was a lovely atmosphere in the school. It was very nice for me because the man I was succeeding was pretty old, and he wanted to retire, was very much loved. But he realized, and the staff realized, that it needed a change. So there wasn't any feeling of nastiness ... They realized that it was a good thing to have somebody new.
>
> The teaching was very good, very straight. ... The staff were terrific in the amount of time they gave to the boys.

From what I personally observed (1957–60), Harry was gilding the lily somewhat. For sure, there was enthusiasm for him: deeply felt, but not 100 per cent. I do remember some of the old timers pining for Bolton and/or Reynolds.

For sure, Harry must have profoundly changed the school's culture. Example: Fred Bridgland remembers him 'turning up at school at the time of the 1955 general election campaign in his grey Bradford van plastered with vivid red VOTE LABOUR posters'. Bill Bailey also told me the story of a pre-War boy who was not allowed to swim in the school's pool, which had been built by public subscription, because his parents had not made a contribution.

Clearly, Harry made a huge and lasting difference to Fred Bridgland's life:

> My mother, a Geordie who began her working life as a 14- or 15-year-old school leaver humping sacks of flour during the Great Depression got a passage on a coal boat from the River Tyne to Shoreditch, married a Kent village lad who was a printer machine-minder and became a Coldstream Guard as the Second World War began. ...

My mother, a feisty and occasionally volcanic lady, knew there was only one route out – education, followed by education and yet more education. …

In my first year I performed well in English and geography – far less well in maths and Latin, which were as culturally alien as seal hunting is to a West African. … We had a brilliant French teacher, Harry Rée himself, who rechristened me Pont-terre.

I did well enough to be moved into the top stream in the second year. At some point in that year I began a prolonged sullen revolt against home and school that lasted perhaps three years. I began to behave badly, acting silly and taunting vulnerable masters. On one occasion I drove a particularly fragile French teacher to near-tears. My behaviour was intolerable … The moment I began telling Rée why I was there he twigged what was happening and beat the bejeezus out of me with a cane across the buttocks.

… I was leading the taunting of yet another vulnerable teacher … Our 'triumph' was short-lived. Soon Harry Rée was striding into the classroom, his gown flowing behind him and his right hand sweeping through his combed-back hair … He read the riot act and then turned specifically to me and said witheringly: 'As for you, Bridgland, you're just a fool.' I withered! Hugely.

But that marked a turning point in my life. I would show Harry Rée … I even began to vow that I would go on to university. …

Inspired by Harry Rée's very real qualities John Rigg shepherded me to a prize-winning geography 'A' level result. And another fine teacher, 'Willy' Wiles, got me through 'A' level botany and zoology. But I revelled most in the general studies courses taken by Harry Rée. He challenged us to think widely, far beyond our immediate horizons.

… I worked hard and behaved impeccably. … Rée encouraged me to become one of the pioneers of Voluntary Service Overseas … Borneo. … Harry Rée began an exchange of letters with me, and I was shocked when he told me that if he had the choice he would scrap school examinations altogether. He was obviously far into his conversion to ever-more radical education beliefs, including the necessity for comprehensive education, which led him to the Professorship of Education at York University and finally a return to being a humble schoolteacher at a North London comprehensive school.

I received a letter from him saying I had won a place to study at St Andrews University – WITHOUT the need for an interview. I owe him so, so much for whatever strings he pulled. ...

One of Harry Rée's sterling qualities, apart from his natural leadership abilities, was his innovative thinking – 'outside the box' ...

When I suggested in a letter from Borneo that he should give a Borneo boy a place in the Watford Grammar School sixth form, Rée responded enthusiastically. David Lin Shu Lim arrived, worked hard, went to Sussex University, became Professor of Economics at Monash University in Australia and is now President of Hong Kong's new Technological and Higher Education Institute.[105]

David Lim tells the story himself:

When Fred Bridgland returned to Watford after a period on VSO in British North Borneo, now Sabah, he suggested to Harry that it would be a good idea if a boy from Borneo were to start or continue his sixth form at Watford. Being the adventurous and liberal-minded person that he was, Harry took to the idea immediately and I was the first in the VSO-in-reverse scheme. I gather that he announced the new scheme at school assembly ... and asked the boys to find out if they would be happy to have him on a termly basis. I stayed with the Fitzpatrick family, whose son, Michael, was in Gambia on VSO. ...

I met Harry on my first night in Watford in mid-September 1962, after travelling for over three weeks in a boat from Singapore to Marseilles, and then by train across France, ferry across the English Channel and train to Victoria, and many underground stations on the Bakerloo line to Watford. ... He struck me as a very unpretentious person.

He took me to see the head of the VSO in London one night. ... It was a very foggy night but he drove as if it was a bright clear

---

105 Established in 2012.

day … pretty much driving as he would have been when escaping from the Germans. …

Harry was a great headmaster. I remember the story told of Mr Miller, the rather stuffy maths master, asking a boy caught by him riding illegally through Cassiobury Park to report this to the headmaster, whereupon Harry was heard to have said, 'Not that bloody man again!'

Many years later, Harry was asked about the differences between the three grammar schools where he had worked (Beckenham, Bradford and Watford):

Beckenham was, of its kind, very, very efficient. … But was a straightforward, unquestioning and unquestioned grammar school. Doing the kind of job which grammar schools were supposed to do. That is, be as good as any independent day school aiming to get boys into universities. Bradford, of course, was the epitome of that. In fact, it went, I think, too far. It competed with Manchester Grammar School … to get as many scholarships to Oxbridge as possible. Successfully. We too, at Watford, were in the grammar school race. … The aim of the grammar schools, I felt, was to compete with the public schools.

For Harry, the cup was almost always half full. In a book that he is preparing for publication, Stephen Plaice, a professional writer, discusses 'the pathology of the Victorian schoolmaster replaced by a new breed of sports-jacketed teachers'. He continues:

These two incongruous breeds, under whose tutelage we were placed, worked uneasily alongside each other, until the old guard was safely ushered into retirement in the following decade. But my generation was the one to experience the transition, and the contrast of attitudes and pedagogy it presented.

To say that many of the old guard were War veterans would be to over-dignify them. They had for the most served in Waughian backwaters of the Army. … I don't believe many had seen active service. It was rumoured that Mr [name deleted], my first French master, a very humane and soft-hearted man, had been a POW in Japan, and this story was used to excuse his disciplinary ineffectualness.

I have to disagree with Plaice, knowing the facts of the War service of several of my colleagues from the late 1950s ... but by no means all, I admit. Burma under William Slim, for example, must have been very active service!

Plaice continues:

> But there was a true hero among them, straight out of the pages of *Boy's Own Paper*,[106] the headmaster, Harry Rée. ... Good-looking, patrician, universally admired by masters and boys and parents alike, he had been rewarded by the boys with the simple nickname Harry. But there was another side to the *Boy's Own* hero who became the darling of the establishment. ... Despite his elevated birth and his public school background, his instincts were egalitarian, and this did not sit well with the older reactionary masters who considered his radical educational ideas as subversive.

Overstated perhaps, but strongly felt and clearly remembered:

> When this golden legend came to teach me, the Apollonian god ... cut a remote and melancholic figure. His wife had died the previous Christmas, and he had already announced his intention to take up a professorship of education in York. There was no vitality, just an inscrutable and unengaging manner that seemed to border on *ennui*. Perhaps it was grief that he was concealing ... but the Harry Rée I encountered as an 11-year-old was a rather weary man.

Martin Cartwright writes:

> Harry Rée seemed to us younger boys as rather a patrician figure, perhaps a bit remote. ... Although Harry's patrician air gave the impression that he was perhaps a bit too relaxed ... he managed ... through a mixture of firmness and understanding ... without bending the rules or relaxing standards.

Mike Wilson, a retired biology professor at the University of Essex, wrote:

> He was an excellent Head, although at the time I did not fully appreciate this.

---

106 Published 1879–1967.

When I asked him why he didn't recognize Harry's qualities, he responded:

> Although I respected Harry and knew everyone else did too I think I was less aware of how good and caring a head he was for two reasons. Firstly he was not a character in the way that, say, Fanny Lister and others were ... He also bought in less, or so it seemed, to the sport ethos. ... Secondly, I was not very aware in general.
>
> As I know now, but did not then, he was strongly supportive of non-selective education and so I suppose he didn't engage in much of the self-congratulation that we all, consciously or unconsciously, engaged [in].

Professor Wilson went on to tell the following story:

> I received a message soon after to ring Harry ... He was kind enough to have thought about me and wanted me to go to University, something that was new to my immediate family, and he told me about the University of East Anglia. ... The years that followed were some of the happiest of my life ...

Years later, Harry said:

> That was a lovely ten years. Not only the staff were good, but the boys were very good. Watford was a prosperous town. The working class of Watford were, many of them, printers, with pretty intelligent boys.

In 2006, Peter Hennessy wrote:

> The slump of the 1930s saw a *worsening* of the proportion of working-class children in grammar schools as economic hardship left fewer working-class families able to let their children take up the few scholarship places available to them. ... This partly explains why many in the interwar Labour generation of local councillors were so keen on getting more grammar schools built in working-class areas. As [Ross] McKibbin puts it, 'The conquest of the grammar school, not its abolition, was thus their aspiration.'[107]

---

107 Peter Hennessy (2006) *Having It So Good: Britain in the fifties*, London: Allen Lane, 75

Chris Anthony, professor of biochemistry at the University of Southampton until his retirement in 2005, has many memories:

> My father was a labourer in Benskins Brewery and neither of my parents was educated beyond age 13. They were amused when I told them that the head teacher came into hall in the morning out of his office wearing a mortar board. They did not know that such things existed outside comic books. At the start of morning assembly the prefects marched up the side of the hall. The Head's door flung open and Rée shot out into the hall in black gown and mortar board which he swept off as he reached the lectern. My memory of his appearance becomes slightly confused with that of Sir Malcolm Sargent.[108] Rée's way of sweeping it off and brushing back his hair told me that he thought privately that it was slightly archaic and comical.
>
> My father ... remained very sceptical about education, always asking when I was leaving school; the last time he asked was at my PhD graduation.

In due course, Janet went to Watford Girls' Grammar School[109] and the boys went to Merchant Taylors' School[110] in Moor Park, Northwood, three-plus miles from the house.

It is extraordinary that Harry was able to run a school with over 40 teachers, teach both first-formers and sixth-formers and, increasingly, write and broadcast ... all with just one secretary, the unsmiling but always helpful Mr W.T.J. Jones. Once a week, he taught every incoming class: language, and everything else, including sex education. (There was the famous time when a small boy said, 'You mean, Sir, nine months before I was born, my father and my mother ... o yuck!') And he introduced 'essay sets' to the sixth form, a period or two a week when all sixth forms had to discuss topics of general interest and write essays.

David Lim writes:

> I do recall that Harry was an extremely impressive person. ...
> In our first year, he had one class per week with us newcomers and talked about procreation and – spare our blushes – sex! He must have started the first lesson by asking who knew how

---

108 The great conductor known as 'Flash Harry', 1895–1967.
109 The headmistress was Jessie Tennet during the latter half of Harry's time at WBGS.
110 Their website confidently describes themselves as 'one of the great nine schools of England'. This refers back to the Public Schools Act of 1868.

babies were born ... sniggers of embarrassment all round. But eventually, I suppose he managed to impart some smattering of natural knowledge ... rounded off, when we were about to leave the school ... by the stern instruction: 'For God's sake, use a contraceptive!'

Michael Gray, who now lives in Pinner (not far from Watford), was a pupil at the school when Harry arrived:

Percy Bolton ... was a traditional headmaster. The use of the cane was not politically incorrect, and I remember waiting outside his study for punishment for some relatively minor offence. He had an electric bell outside his door, operated from a buzzer on his desk: when it rang, you went into the room and took what was coming. A very different style of headship occurred with the arrival of Harry Rée.

David Harman described how his first class was just next to the Headmaster's study:

You can imagine the impact on our young minds hearing the muffled thwack of someone being caned by Percy.

One sports afternoon I was cycling through the park [Cassiobury] and also had a classmate (John Gurney) on the crossbar. ... Then an old man stopped me and gently told me it was illegal to ride a bicycle in the park and that it was dangerous to carry people on the crossbar. It was not until the next day ... Percy spoke about the dangers of riding bicycles in the park ... that I realized the old man had been our headmaster. ... I had not recognized him because he was not wearing his gown.

Later ... John was caned for reading a book under his desk during a French lesson.

Harry must have seemed extraordinarily different. Gray described a prank involving him and two others. There were some exposed but insulated fire alarm cables adjacent to the chemistry and physics labs. The boys placed a pin through the insulation of each cable so that the alarm would be activated when the pins touched each other. Naturally, the alarm went off as planned, and people had to leave the building. The next day, Harry asked the perpetrators to own up and report to his study, which they did. Their punishment?

We were set the task of updating and rewriting the procedure for the evacuation of the building in case of fire or any other emergency, which of course we duly undertook.

Headmaster Harry treated the boys as adults ... to the extent he could and to the amazement of young and old. An example mentioned by David Harman:

Harry had to handle the mocking of Mr Merrett ... a (very) aged deputy headmaster [before Lister] who had a habit of muttering in public. His nickname was 'Dreamy', which just about sums him up. A very gentle, kind man. Occasionally Mr Merrett took morning assembly in place of Harry. ... The boys in the hall used to audibly mimic Mr Merrett. This got so bad that Harry had to ... address this issue. (Mr Merrett was somehow diverted.) ... He mentioned Mr Merrett's long service and that the mocking was rather cruel. I was most impressed with how the Headmaster handled it – certainly the public mocking of Mr Merrett stopped.

Fred Bridgland has a similar recollection:

The ageing deputy headmaster ... was facing terrible torture from the whole school at morning assembly. Every boy was mumbling, creating a loud collective humming noise which the deputy could not silence. But the moment Harry Rée opened his study door ... the communal murmuring stopped immediately, as though a switch had been flicked.

Rumour had it that 'Dreamy' acquired his nickname because he seemed to be dropping off to sleep. It is possible he had suffered from shell shock in the First World War. One of his pupils, who later became a doctor, diagnosed him as having suffered from idiopathic senile head tremor. 'Dreamy' had taught geography before he became deputy head.

David Harman continues:

Being a bit of a tearaway, I had a habit of collecting detentions from both masters and prefects, particularly the Head Boy. Eventually I was asked to go and see the Headmaster and expected ... to be reprimanded if not whacked so I was pretty apprehensive. ... Harry did not reprimand me in any way. He explained the difficulties of being a Head Boy and that it was up to me to help him. Basically, he treated me like a sensible being and I responded in kind. ... That was the end of my detentions. Eventually I became a university academic [in Australia] and

I'm sure that incident and Harry's general demeanour had a big impact on my later relations with students.

Stephen Plaice saw things a little differently:

> I was never 'prefect material'. [Nor was Harry.] Each morning, these school-appointed lictors marched into the school hall for assembly like a military platoon. Wearing double badges on their breast pockets. ... During assembly, they stood at the side of the body of the school scouring the ranks for pranksters, talkers or even smirkers to punish. They were invested with the power to award detentions for misbehaviour. ... The criteria by which they were chosen were essentially two-fold, deference to authority and sporting prowess.

> Perhaps Harry Rée did champion liberal *ideas* of education. He certainly did come into conflict with the old guard of masters who had been used to a more disciplinarian approach, and especially with his second master, the fulminating boy-beater Herbert Lister. But it would be a misconception to imagine that on Harry Rée's watch an atmosphere of liberalism pervaded the school. He too was a caner.

Ian Ashcroft has an illuminating anecdote entitled *Harry's Operating Style*:

> Harry was the first of the 'new breed' of headmasters to be appointed at WBGS. He 'inherited' the old brigade of masters who were used to strict and unquestioning discipline – no matter where in the school you sat, and whatever age the boy. Thus senior boys were treated in exactly the same way as junior boys.

> The story is told of the sixth form boy who was sent to the Headmaster to be disciplined. He had been misbehaving in class and this had, in the past, been punished by 'six of the best'. The boy duly presented himself at the door of the School Secretary in order that he would then be admitted to the 'Headmaster's sanctum', which duly happened. Harry questioned why the boy was there.

> 'To be punished, Sir,' came the reply.

> 'What for?' asked Harry.

'Misbehaving in class, Sir,' to which Harry's response was along the lines of 'Do you think that kind of behaviour is befitting of a senior boy at this school?' and then got the boy to sit and discuss his actions, the reason for them, and what his behaviour should be in the future. No beating! Apparently, after half-an-hour or so, the master who had instigated the punishment sent another boy to find the miscreant as he had been away so long he was afraid he had absconded!

Another anecdote, from the same source, entitled *How to Exercise Discipline*:

When reaching the fifth form, one was allowed to remain in classroom at lunchtime should the weather be wet. My classroom was diagonally across the School Hall from the headmaster's study and … we were all in class. There was a 'battle' going on. Desk lids up as 'shields', and anything that could be thrown was being thrown – gym shoes, books, pencils, etc., etc. I sat two desks up, along the wall that also had the doorway into the room.

Battle raged and the noise was horrendous to the extent that it obviously wended its way … into Harry's study. I continued to participate fully in 'aerial warfare' sending missiles with great accuracy to the other side of the room, until suddenly I became aware that the intended recipients were not returning fire. Rather, they were straightening their desks and reading a book, or preparing some written work. Turning to the doorway, I discovered Harry – just standing there. He said not a word; he didn't need to. Within a couple of minutes, we had all returned to a state of 'quiet normality'. He shut the door and went back to his study.

By his sheer presence, he had admonished us far more severely than if he had screamed and yelled …

Nick Tucker would say, years later, that 'Harry was basically an authoritarian liberal'. It is important, I think, to acknowledge that not everyone saw the Harry I saw. Returning to David Harman, Harry's socialist leanings, he wrote, had a big impact on his brother Chris who later became a leading Marxist in the UK.[111]

---

111 Chris Harman (1942–2009) was a journalist and a member of the Central Committee of the Socialist Workers Party. Michael Rosen's obituary in the *Guardian* refers to WBGS, which was then being 'run by the maverick leftward-moving Harry Rée'.

More recently, Michael Rosen spoke with the *Watford Observer* about his years at WBGS (1962–4):

> Going to Watford Boys was an extraordinary break. … It was very much about tradition and it all seemed very grand and rather formal when I arrived. I was quite surprised and rather destabilized by it, and didn't behave very well I'm afraid, which I regret bitterly. … I think I couldn't cope emotionally with the sort of teasing that boys do of each other. I couldn't take what I'd given out at my previous school [Harrow Weald County Grammar School]. So I did some silly things, drawing on desks and things.

He was 'taken to one side' by Harry, who:

> happened to be a friend of my dad's. I remember him saying, 'Rosen, you've made a bloody bad start'. In those days teachers didn't swear, you didn't hear them say 'bloody', but he did, it was quite funny.

For sure, Harry voted Labour all his life; he had campaigned for Herbert Morrison in the mid-1930s, when Morrison became Labour leader of the London County Council.

Occasionally, of course, he would get frustrated. Example, from a letter to Nick Tucker:

> Foot[112] is fine, but he's not had a constructive political idea in his life, and if we're going to face the years after 2000, by god we've got to have some vision – vision about what work is, and service is, and production is, but who? Kinnock? He can just make jokes about Thatcher – not enough.

Stuart Field, retired Professor of Radiological Sciences at the University of Kent, recalls Harry's single lesson a week with various classes:

> His 'remit' was to introduce us to the wonders of 'language'. However, this was a guise for sex education – prior to this most of us had had none. We were impressed by his informal approach to a subject which to many was still 'taboo' and his willingness to discuss quite intimate details of sexual intercourse and masturbation without any of the usual embarrassment or smut.

---

112 Michael Foot, Labour leader from 1980 to 1983.

At the 2014 celebration of the centenary of Harry's birth, Field added that Harry listened to everyone who had something to say: most unusual in the 1950s. This was a lifelong quality: Peter Renshaw described him as 'respecting the voices of other people,' and Jon Nixon spoke of his 'capacity for conversation' and 'belief in thinking together'.

Harry asked Field to be head boy for 1962/63:

> In his typical manner this was done very informally during a 'stroll' across the school playing fields. ... Harry warned me that joining me in the prefects' room would be a number of ... controversial choices. He implied that he had made these decisions against the advice of his more conventional masters. ... He explained that he wanted a mixed bag of prefects with all views and perspectives represented rather than the traditional 'right of centre' view which was typical at Watford at the time. ... Having accepted the invitation to become head boy, Harry invited me to his house for dinner. ... He introduced me to 'sherry'. ... Subsequently I was often asked to visit the off-licence to purchase a bottle of 'South African medium dry sherry' for his cupboard in the headmaster's room at the same time as going to the bank to pay in school cheques.[113]

In another email, he writes:

> Harry Rée's influence on me all my adult life both as a parent and as a teacher was to encourage me to encourage others to pursue as wide a range of interests as possible, and to take nothing at face value – always have an open mind and question even the apparently obvious – if you have any doubts.

Keith Emmans, who taught at Watford and then at York, has interesting memories:

> One of the first amazing things happened to me on my first Friday lunchtime. The Latin master escorted me to Harry's room, and about six masters including Harry stood round in a circle drinking wine. All of them were language teachers.[114] The routine was that in turn each of us chose a crate of wine and we then tasted two bottles ... before going off to the dining room. The

---

113 The drinking age was 18, and Field confirms that he was indeed 18.
114 Language must have included English as the senior English master, in whose department I was a very junior master, was part of the circle.

wine came from the Schoolmasters' Wine Club.[115] Each bottle not to cost more than ten shillings. Originally Harry had had lunch sent over. ... The other non-attending staff members saw this as a clique – so the wine tasting continued but we joined the other staff a little later for lunch.

I suppose I owe the Schoolmasters' Wine Club something. It was early 1959, and one of Her Majesty's Inspectors was to visit my class so that I could be fully certified as a teacher. Mervyn W. Pritchard, a very senior inspector, came and sat down ... I still remember which room. My lesson was mediocre. Mr Pritchard left early, and I thought I was finished. In fact, he was hurrying towards Harry's room, not wanting to miss his glass, and I passed muster. About ten years later, I bumped into him at Francis Cammaerts's house in Nairobi, and he did recall the incident.

Commodore Peter Swan (Royal Navy) writes:

He was the antithesis of the conventional Headmaster. He dressed in a most casual attire; he built a sixth form common room where we were allowed to smoke and on occasions have a drink. He encouraged us to partake in the Aldermaston Peace marches.[116] The conventional parents were deeply concerned that this socialist, pacifist man would corrupt their precious offspring but were won over by the quite exceptional results that the school achieved.

As pupils we considered ourselves privileged to have such an unusual and exceptional Head. After the exams were completed we were encouraged to do a school swap with a week at a top public school followed by a week at a London comprehensive ... He was a powerful advocate for Voluntary Service Overseas.[117]

Stuart Field again:

I became aware that there were real tensions between some of the staff and Harry Rée. Although the school was considered to be 'outstanding' ... it was really held together by the more conventional staff. Harry had a very positive and good influence at Watford by introducing lateral and left-wing thinking. However,

---

115 This was started by Francis Cammaerts, and there were soon thousands of members. I remember buying Yugoslav Riesling in those years.
116 1958–63.
117 Founded in 1958.

he was a poor disciplinarian. ... It fell to the more conventional masters to maintain school discipline, in particular the Second Master, Herbert Lister. On several occasions Herbert (known as 'Fanny' Lister) called me to one side to consult with me as to how he and senior staff should handle the head! Less frequently Harry would ask me how he could handle his rigid senior staff! I was the 'go-between'.

Chris Mullen wrote, 'Rée was urbane and kind, Lister sadistic and fearsome'. Chris Anthony:

Squadron Leader Fanny Lister never taught me – except to stop us running or talking in corridors when we heard his metal-shod shoes marching. ... When Wiles[118] heard the approaching Lister he quickly moved to one end of the room and marched with swinging arms parallel to Lister in the corridor. He said nothing but it was a comfort to know that this bully did not have the support of the whole school staff. ... When ... I published my first book it was dedicated to him. [Wiles]

In a personal conversation, Professor Field spoke lovingly of Willy, whose life sadly ended with Alzheimer's.

Back to Field:

Harry's left-wing views were well known and I think this had a profound influence. ... He would discuss the headline contents of the previous week's *Sunday Times*. ... This introduced us to a balanced discussion of topical subjects and allowed us to hear viewpoints and ideas to which ordinarily we would not have been exposed in our own homes. ... [It provided an] ability to respect others' views ... I ... briefly joined the Campaign for Nuclear Disarmament.[119]

One of Harry's great ideas was to arrange sixth form 'exchanges' with boys at different types of school. I think this was really a ploy to get us to see and be influenced by the 'comprehensive schools'.

Field recalls an exchange with Charterhouse School, a well-known public school in Surrey. Forty-five years later, he spoke at the same conference in

---

118 Willy Wiles, the wonderfully eccentric biology teacher.
119 Founded by Canon John Collins and others in 1957.

Cambridge as his Charterhouse counterpart, Sir Bruce Ponder. By this time, both were distinguished medics.

John Law wrote:

> WBGS had an exchange arrangement with a comprehensive school somewhere, but also with Winchester. As a lefty I wanted, of course, to go to the comprehensive. No. That wasn't going to happen. It would be good to see Winchester, and I was sent off there, which turned out to be a fascinating learning experience.

Harry had a huge and lifelong influence on and friendship with several Old Fullerians from his years at Watford Grammar School. Jack Altman writes:

> He spent a weekend sleeping on my sofa in Paris a couple of weeks before he died. He was looking for French bookshops for children.[120]

Altman has lived in Paris since 1972, as a freelance writer specializing in travel. He begins a powerful email with, 'I truly loved that man', and continues:

> He had an amazing immediate impact. His predecessor, Percy Bolton, was a worthy, dignified representative of the Old School, a traditionalist. Harry respected that – and systematically overturned it. He made little effort to conceal his own atheism and after a while turned over the reading of prayers to the Second Master, Herbert Lister, a fierce defender of the Old School. More importantly, he allowed prefects to deliver the 'lesson' from texts other than the Bible. As a Jew (though progressively atheistic myself), I had been exempted from the Religion class until Harry suggested I should participate to provide another perspective ... That was fundamental to Harry's teaching – teaching us that there was always 'another perspective'.

At one point, Altman had to choose between German and Greek:

> Harry suggested ... just six years after the War ... it would be a good idea, as he put it, for the little Jewish kid ... to go for German. 'That way,' he said (his words have remained indelibly with me) 'you can get to know this people, the best and the worst of them, how both are possible, in all of us. And when you grow

---

120 He was also speaking at a dedication at Valençay (see pp. 220–1).

90

up, you'll know the Germans well enough to be able to say what you like about them, good or bad, without people saying, "What do *you* know?" I'll help you.' He kept his promise, four years later he sent me off for six months to Mainz, to work in a factory and to audit classes at the local university.

In a later email, Altman wrote about Don Taylor (later headmaster of Durrants School), senior English master and one of the teachers Harry gathered around him:

> An unrelenting sceptic who taught me long before my contact with some Talmudic modernists, that the question is always more important than the answer.
>
> …
>
> I am convinced that the education I received at Watford Grammar School proved ultimately much more valuable for the life I have led since then than the undeniably good years I spent at Cambridge.

Chris Anthony again:

> In 1952 a scheme was announced that aimed to promote reconciliation between England and Germany. Poor boys from slums of German cities would come here and live in English families for a month or so. I went home enthusiastic that we should invite a boy but my mother said we could not afford another mouth to feed.[121] It was later announced that there was one boy with no family to stay with. So my mother wrote a note to Rée to say that we could have him if a small amount of money could somehow be provided for food. Rée asked how much and then told her that the amount she suggested was not nearly enough to feed a boy and that she could have three times as much. She then sent him her whole budget proving that the amount he proposed for one boy would be enough to feed all her four children. He then sent an apologetic and very humble letter apologizing for his lack of understanding.

And then there were the famous lorry trips. Harry's wartime boss, Colonel Maurice J. Buckmaster, had been corporate manager of the French branch

---

121 Food rationing did not end in the UK until July 1954.

of the Ford Motor Company before the War and became Director of Public Affairs for Ford in Dagenham when the War ended. Through him, Harry managed to get a lorry – David Green describes it as 'an open-topped truck with a canvas roll-over cover – for several summers, and this was long before the age of low-cost air travel. Altman again:

> This was for me perhaps the most inspired piece of education I ever experienced … the idea of travelling in a lorry, 12 sixth-formers and four teachers, from Watford to Naples … via Belgium, France, Switzerland and the length of the Italian peninsula, made me a European for life. Quite apart from the experience of roughing it in fields, barns and under tarpaulins (no tents, hostels or hotels), we got to know strange food in Burgundy, wonderful architecture, Caravaggio in Rome, classical antiquity in Pompeii and Paestum, along with first impressions of boring Belgians and Swiss, sexy French, crazy Italians.

Altman makes the key point that there's little here of Harry's articulated educational philosophy; 'only a few benefits from the practice.'

Keith Emmans recalls:

> It was the tradition after school on a Friday to stay until about 6 p.m. for the staff to discuss with Harry the progress of boys – form by form – the lower forms one week, upper forms the next … but not every week. Getting staff to stay late seemed no problem. … The staff were a committed team.

David Pinchin has had a varied and distinguished career. He left his NHS District General Manager job in 1991, joining the Civil Service as Director of Investigations for the Parliamentary and Health Service Ombudsman, retiring in 2005. He is presently chairing the Independent Monitoring Board at Isis, a prison that opened in 2010. In an email, he said:

> … I was struggling to know what to do with my life and not sure about the prospect of university away from all my theatre and music in Watford, and also my Dad was dying. What I can remember vividly now is the calming influence Harry had on me at that time – he welcomed long chats and was so totally understanding and helpful. He told me all about the pitfalls of university and that it was not for everybody and that I should not feel bad or lacking ambition if I didn't go. He pointed me in

several career directions, one of which I eventually went down. ... He gave me the confidence to take an alternative route.

He also welcomed me regularly into his house. ... I was never made to feel awkward. ... I bumped into Harry several times in later years and he without fail always remembered what I had been doing and was interested in what the future held. ... I also looked him up at York University ... and he entertained me for a couple of hours rather than the few minutes I had expected. ... He was a brilliant headmaster, a man ahead of his times. Even the toughest of kids respected him – and Herbert Lister too! He had a real understanding of young people, he wasn't dictatorial or judgemental, just a thoroughly sensible human being with a mass of experience. He was held in exceptionally high regard.

Yes: sensible, and trusting. I don't think he ever watched me teach, and yet somehow he knew what was going on in my classroom and was constantly encouraging. For example: my degree was in English, but I had taken two years of mathematics at college level. I asked whether I could take the same class for both subjects, i.e. at least twice a day. Not only was Harry supportive; the eldest son of my immediate boss, the head of the English department, somehow made it into that class. (He is now a distinguished academic, so I can't have done too much damage.)

Discussing the comprehensive school where she was headmistress, Margaret Maden put into words a concept that Harry might not have verbalized during his Watford years but certainly practised:

The solitary teacher who sees teaching as an activity discharged once the classroom door is closed cannot operate successfully.

Peter 'Tub' Andrews recounts a delightful tale. He was in his first (probationary) year, and knew that the Head would have to make some kind of report on him. When Harry showed up one day, he immediately made him comfortable and taught the lesson. He wrote:

I ... dismissed the class. Harry came up and said, 'Peter, that was a very interesting lesson but I only popped in to tell you that the Friends have agreed some extra money for the Scouts!' I never did get a proper inspection ...

Everyone ... including me ... has memories of Fanny Lister; it's hard not to keep mentioning him when discussing Harry Rée. Norman Jarritt remembers him as 'strict and always fair,' encouraging cross-country runners.

> He was of a special breed of schoolmasters and mistresses and, typically, my lasting memory before we left Watford ... is of him cycling purposefully around the Cassiobury Park Estate exuding interest and enthusiasm.

Mike Benton, who taught English in the early 1960s, replaced someone

> who, it turned out, had been hounded by a fifth year class to the point of nervous exhaustion. In the weeks up to Xmas, every lesson I had with the fifth form class was accompanied at some point by the sound of clicking toecaps along the corridor outside the room. We all knew these belonged to the Deputy Headmaster, a man of military bearing – sharply sculpted features, toothbrush moustache, brisk in walk and talk, slipper in the armpit under the gown – who believed in military discipline and upon whom Harry relied to keep the school in order. Harry's strengths lay elsewhere ...

Bill Bailey writes:

> Herbert Lister taught us Certificate French with a thoroughness and attention to detail that saw us get outstanding results. Outside the classroom he was a martinet and very disloyal to Harry whom he would occasionally rail against. We thought he [i.e. Harry] deserved better.

> I last met Harry at Herbert Lister's 80th birthday celebration. [1984.] ... In HL's speech he made reference to all the heads he had worked with. He spoke of Harry as someone who during his time at the school had tried desperately hard to look like a headmaster but had failed miserably. Harry, who attended in an open-necked shirt, with the collar turned up in typical fashion, and set off with toed sandals, roared with laughter. Despite the barb he appeared very warm to Herbert which impressed the attendees enormously.[122]

A couple of years earlier, when Harry's tieless portrait was unveiled, there were, according to a contemporary press report, 'some raised eyebrows'. Harry explained that his dress suit and gown and mortarboard had long

---

122 The point I would make is that Harry made the effort to attend, an effort that would have involved several hours' driving.

since found their way 'into the children's dressing-up box'. But he did describe the portraitist as a:

> lovely young lady. She made me look quizzical, friendly, slightly uncertain but yet knowing ... Recognize me?

Second master Herbert Lister was quoted as saying, 'Although our views were often diametrically opposed, we never had a cross word.' They complemented each other, as Lister noted:

> He was good for me when I was too rigid, and I think occasionally I was good for him when he was too free and easy in his approach to a problem.

David Harman writes:

> Many years after Harry had left Watford, I asked how he could possibly have worked with 'Fanny'. Very sweetly, he told me of their mutual respect: Lister, of course, respected Harry for his War service, and Harry recognized that he probably couldn't have done what he did had it not been for Lister's rampaging through the halls. It would be so different today!

Fred Bridgland writes:

> I recall Tony Wilson telling me about an occasion when Fanny Lister sent Tony to the headmaster's study because he was caught wearing a red waistcoat, which was a contravention of the school dress rules. Tony was a prefect ... at the time. He knocked at the headmaster's door and was invited to enter. As he walked in, Rée looked up and said, 'Oh, hello Wilson – nice waistcoat!' Tony explained why he was there and they had a civilized discussion about trying not to annoy Mr Lister.

There were two Herbert Listers. There was the Lister with gym shoe in hand ... to slipper boys routinely and frequently ... and steel-tipped shoes ... at least one knew when he was coming. And there was the Herbert who helped old ladies at St Mary's Church, an Anglican church in the centre of Watford, and who took on the old boys' register when he retired. Stuart Field, who knew him well, surmised that his wife had no idea that there were two sides to her devoted husband; I am sure Harry did.

In the archives at Watford Grammar School, I found a piece from the *Times Educational Supplement* of 28 October 1960, entitled 'Continuity Man: The second master's role'. Annoyingly, as was the custom in those days, it was 'From a Correspondent', but I would bet that the author was Herbert Lister. With less confidence, I would bet that Harry set him up to write it.

The author, then, points out how little had been written about the role of the second master. Needless to say, everyone in the article is male; there was no thought that there might have been 'second mistresses'.

It is nonetheless a balanced account with nothing in it that one might not have expected:

> To the boys, he is a remote figure who takes prayers when the headmaster is ill; to the staff, he is the man who robs them of their free periods; to the parents, he is the head's deputy; to the old boys, he is often a sort of Mr Chips. ...
>
> He is not the headmaster's private secretary, although he must be a remembrancer of sorts. ...
>
> It will be readily understood that the second master's duties vary considerably from school to school. ... It is always, of necessity, a post of great delicacy, involving ... close personal relationships with both headmaster and staff, and demanding the necessity of retaining the confidence of both. ...
>
> Above all, he must watch his own peculiarities, and try to avoid mannerisms that may irritate or incense others.

Was 'Fanny' somehow indicating here that some of his behaviours were, to say the least, subject to criticism? The main point of the article, stressed a number of times, was that the second master is crucial in the relationships between headmaster and staff. Nothing about the governors or the broader community; nothing about being a master teacher; nothing about societal change.

> He has ... much of the responsibility for school discipline, particularly when the school is assembled before the arrival of the headmaster. ...
>
> He is, in whatever type of school he may find himself, a safety-valve through whom both headmaster and staff may relieve their pent-up feelings by discharging their grumbles and complaints into his patient ear.

In over two years, I don't think I ever saw the safety-valve in action!

Back to Bill Bailey:

> ... Keith Turner [Harry's successor] was totally out of his depth when he arrived ... and was obviously horrified by what he saw. Regrettably there were no more haircuts for the staff at lunchtime, no days off for staff or students to take a driving test, no smoking in the newly established sixth form common room, and a reintroduction of severe floggings!

Turner, said Bailey, couldn't handle disagreement. And yet, he asked head boy Stuart Field for advice on how to handle Fanny Lister, just as Harry had done.

Norman Marrow wrote that Turner:

> put their backs up the first few days by uttering *ex cathedra* a number of vague but terrible sounding threats in rather unconvincingly portentous tones. Thus he conveyed the impression that he was going to put back, as it were, in terms of autocratic domination, the clock of progress which Harry Rée had kept consistently fast! When the aforesaid threats seemed not to have amounted to much, this, paradoxically, didn't seem to help a lot![123]

George Walker was a close and lifelong friend of Harry's; and yet he wrote:

> By his retirement, Turner had become one of the most respected heads in the UK.[124] By that time I was a colleague and friend and he gave me much encouragement and advice as a fellow Hertfordshire head. Keith judged the political climate much better than I did ... and I am bound to say today WBGS (which is a very popular, successful school) bears his hallmark, not Harry's.

Keith Turner, like Harry, came from Bradford Grammar School, where he had been senior mathematics master for nine years and was highly praised for 'his lively teaching and constant care for the individual' as well as his 'unfailing cheerfulness and modesty'.

Chris Anthony writes:

> I think perhaps I owe my subsequent career to Rée's acquired appreciation of my family finances. ... I had previously intended to do maths, physics and chemistry at 'A' level and then to try

---

123 Marrow, N. (2012) *Avi epistula: A grandfather's letter*. Online: *sine nomine*.
124 He was awarded an OBE.

to join the Air Force. I was in the Combined Cadet Force (CCF) and influenced strongly by Biggles.[125] At Dale Fort, Wales[126], I became friends with the biologists there and was amazed at their enthusiasm for the subject.

Anthony explained how Harry and John Rigg[127] had found some money for him to go. He learned from his roommate that:

it was possible to go to university on a full grant and that it was not necessary to have Latin. He was going to Reading University to study zoology. On my return I horrified Knight[128] when I told him I … would do biology instead of maths. 'The only careers in biology are in medicine or agriculture.'

And by 1963 he had a PhD in biochemistry from the University of Reading, becoming a full professor in 1986. He continued:

Rée was very keen that those studying science should not be 'narrow minded scientists'.[129] … he instituted a system of education for us in the sixth form for which I continue to feel grateful. We had lectures on art history, literature (doing the War poets – as does every boy now), and music. I still surprise my family by my ability to distinguish Monet from Manet, etc.

One lesson on literature was taken by Rée in which he read us a short story and asked us to criticize it. It concerned a boy in occupied France who wanted to see fireworks to celebrate something. A strange man who was staying with the family arranged to blow up an ammunition dump for the boy. We all said it was absurdly unlikely, only to be told it was true. (Rée was the strange man.)

Alfred Bradley lists 'a few thoughts':

1. The grand entry for morning assembly, gown, mortarboard, grandeur and suitable fear.

---

125 Invented by W.E. Johns, about 100 Biggles books have appeared since 1932.
126 A Field Studies Council Centre since 1947.
127 A wonderful geography master who was a passionate supporter of the CND.
128 'Inky' Knight, the chemistry teacher.
129 C.P. Snow delivered his famous Rede Lecture, entitled *The Two Cultures*, at Cambridge in May 1959.

2. Advice to those of us going off to University: 'for God's sake use a johnnie.'[130]

3. Serious advice about books to read and the reading habit, which has filled my life.

4. For a working class boy, opening the door to learning, music, Sunday night play readings at Harry's house ... and an open, humorous view of life ... laced with a total respect for always learning more.

5. Wonderful stern response to my cheating ... I held out for a week, 'no, sir, not me, sir.' ... Harry suddenly lost it and thwacked me several times across the arse with a cane. I sulked for several weeks, or was it years? But Harry and I became very close as I got to know his children very well and much later, when I was teaching, I would take groups of students to stay at his Yorkshire home and walk from there.

6. One of the last times I saw him, he was teaching at Hackney Downs and fairly shell-shocked. But the measure of the man was that he was doing this when he could have not gone near education again.

I asked Alfred about the caning, in view of Harry's later role in the Society of Teachers Opposed to Physical Punishment (STOPP). His response rings true:

> Yes, the thwacking was odd, but Harry was also a man of his time and I really think he thought a spot of toughening up was good. ... It was the 1950s. I think with the War only a decade gone, a lot of men had gone through some terrible things and pewling schoolboys were going to get short shrift. We all accepted it, parents too.

David Lim:

> Harry ... assisted gently in our cultural education by providing a room in his house for monthly play readings – organized for a select group of sixth formers and with links to the Girls' Grammar School so that there was mixing of the sexes.

Anthony Priddis, Bishop of Warwick from 1996 until he became Bishop of Hereford in 2004, recently wrote in an email:

> Clearly he was hugely respected and demonstrated the importance for a school of a really able head teacher. That is as true now as then. I suspect that he would not have cared for a culture of targets, bureaucracy and risk-aversion.

---

130 Michael Fitzpatrick recalls 'the stern instruction' as, 'for God's sake, use a contraceptive!'

Bishop Priddis lauded Harry's practice of deliberately making sure that he taught all new classes every year, thus getting to know all the boys. He went on to tell the following tale: one year, they had unusual difficulty finding someone to teach religious education (RE), and 'presumably someone very unsuitable was allocated'. A mother buttonholed Harry: even though he knew exactly what the problem was, he said, 'Madam, in this school we are particularly fortunate with the number of gifted RE teachers that we have.'

Harry could be funny in a schoolboyish way. Marcus Binney begins his chapter on Harry in the SOE thus: 'Harry Rée was an agent with a sense of humour that shines through all his exploits.' Before his adventures in France, he:

> found himself with Michael Wharton, author of the famous Peter Simple column in *The Daily Telegraph*.[131] Satirically they invented the Royal Army Tram Corps, 'where I was drilled by Sergeant Cesspit who called me Gonorrhoea'.

When I applied for a job at Eric James's Manchester Grammar School, Harry's letter of reference began, 'Jonathan Daube, pronounced Cow Pee ...'. Robin Atfield, Emeritus Professor of Philosophy at Cardiff University, recalled:

> He once came to a French class and asked whether we knew what was really meant by the French saying 'Tant pis, tant mieux'. The answer ... 'aunt goes to the lavatory; aunt feels better'.

He encouraged laughter. For example: at a staff meeting in the late 1950s, he announced that, since the Hall was being repainted, form masters would be conducting mini-assemblies in their own classrooms for a week or two. Toppy[132] shouted at his colleagues: 'All right. Stand up. Bless me. Fuck you. Sit down.' Bill Bailey talks about the 'sound of laughter, banter, easy relationships'. Many people associate Harry with laughter.

One of the two masters' common rooms was next to the Hall where Harry conducted daily assemblies. One day, a note appeared on the notice board, in his inimitable handwriting: 'Gentlemen of the common room are asked to conduct their devotions more quietly, as the boys are having

---

131 It's a small world: Wharton (1913–2006) went to Bradford Grammar School as a boy. Wharton published a short story, 'The Bitter Lozenge', in the same issue of Connolly's *Horizon* as Harry's 1940 book review.
132 E.F. Topsfield, senior modern languages master; later to succeed Fanny Lister as Second Master.

difficulty concentrating on either performance.' I wish I had stealthily removed the note and kept it.

Neil Hart told of how 'an irate and pompous don' wrote to Harry when a group of Watford boys and their French exchange partners misbehaved during a coach outing to Cambridge. Harry's reply was short:

'Dear Dr. X,

Dear, dear, dear.

Yours sincerely,

Harry Rée.'

And at his last Watford Grammar School speech day, he said:

I remember a famous cartoon on the staff room notice board before speech day one year, drawn by Mr Greenwell showing the staff sitting behind me at Speech Day, and one is turning to his sleeping neighbour and saying, 'Look out, this is where he starts trouncing the parents'.

I wish I had a copy of that one, especially since I both loved and respected George Greenwell.

Atfield went on:

I remember the late Norman Marrow[133] ... breaking the unspoken code that members of staff never talked about each other to boys ... and acknowledging that Harry Rée was a complete enigma, and that one could never tell what he wanted.

Former head boy Stuart Field described Harry as 'hard to predict'. Not necessarily a bad thing, I would add.

Keith Emmans: 'Harry seemed not to give credit to the rather staid head of classics – who year after year had pupils get Oxbridge entrance.'

Poor Norman. Unlike some of the Old Guard, he really did want to do the right thing. He was a Quaker, and Atfield recollects that Harry would occasionally go to the Quaker Meeting House, which was ten minutes' walk from the family home: not surprising, given Hetty's background. Marrow could be quite droll. For example, when Sir David Eccles, who had been Minister of Education 1954–7, was brought back to the same ministry in 1959, quoth Marrow: 'He has failed before, I believe.'

---

133 Senior classics master; 1907–1998; retired in 1967.

Ben Foley, a superb teacher of mathematics, which he calls 'sums', and lifelong friend, writes:

> My memories of Harry are mostly through the things that happened (often funny) that affected me. These are still remarkably fresh.[134] It is much harder to describe his influence. I know that some of it came directly through conversations, meetings and occasional parties, pubs and dinners. In all of these I felt it was worth trying to say what I thought. But maybe it was that he made it easier for nearly all of us to talk to each other, and to hold very different opinions, and argue our cases without falling out. ... There really was life outside of school.

After leaving Watford, Ben spent most of his teaching life at his old school, St George's in Harpenden.

Keith Emmans adds:

> One of the pleasant things about working with Harry was the social aspect. The day after we broke up at Christmas staff plus wives were invited ... for mulled wine and nibbles at Harry's house where we met his wife Hetty and his children. There were also social events in the evening. I remember one where Harry suggested we all come with a university don. ... Harry seemed to know everybody.

> Harry had a cheeky sense of humour. My wife was a teacher at a girls' grammar school and was coming up to 30. ... Harry asked her if we had any children ... she said no ... he offered to lend her his first year's film strip on sex education.

> Harry used to referee rugby ... his long trousers tucked into his socks.

> One interviewee for a job[135] arrived at the main door of WBGS and noticed that the gardener was pruning roses. He went over and had a chat ... asked the man about the head – what his opinion was – what he thought of him. Imagine the interviewee's surprise on walking into the head's study to meet the gardener – now Headmaster!

---

134 Ben was reflecting on events 50 or more years in the past.
135 I think this was John Collins, an Australian geographer, who became a close friend of Harry's, and mine. He lived near Melbourne until his death in 2017.

David Bentley put Harry in context:

> We were, I suppose, fairly conservative boys. … So Rée's informal style was unsettling. (I seem to remember he sat in his study in shirt sleeves and braces.) I suspect he found us pupils a bit stuffy. I remember his reaction when I said I'd been reading Lord Chesterfield's *Letters to his Son*: Chesterfield was a second-rate snob. I stopped reading them. I think of him with raised eyebrows and a slightly amused air.
>
> He could certainly be tough. You may remember James, the master who ran the school play. I'd become a sub-prefect, and one evening a number of us were in a pub. James and a girl friend were there as well. We started whispering and giggling. Next day Rée came to the prefects' room and demoted me and the other offenders on the spot.
>
> Rée spoke very little about his War. … He never glorified war.

In his early years at Watford, Harry really did believe in the grammar school. In his novel *Donkey Work*, published in 1983, Edward Blishen described 'Maurice' (i.e. Harry):

> Maurice … that ardent man who was a sort of educational Hermes. A winged messenger. He came from a long line of public-spirited intellectuals. … He was then a grammar school headmaster who was totally and eloquently in favour of the grammar school: on the grounds that the post-war arrangement of education in England and Wales (based on the idea that humanity, at the age of 11 and with a minimum of complaint, divided itself naturally into the high-flying and the low-flying) was splendidly sensible: good men and women at both ends, in the grammar school and the secondary modern, being bound to provide the very best for their own kind of child.

Bill Bailey, whom I taught in 1959/60, remembers being door monitor! About 55 years later, he wrote:

> Every class in the Lower School had a form monitor and a door monitor. The job of the latter was to stand by the classroom door and close it once the master had entered. The job of the former was to stand on the dais at the front when no master was present and write the name of any miscreant on the board. Those so

identified were given a detention by the incoming teacher. Pretty progressive, eh? As our form master you organized a democratic vote. I came second so held the prestigious position of door monitor so escaping the embarrassment of being labelled the class sneak!

I cannot remember any of this!

Bill further embarrassed me recently by sending me a copy of a report I had written at the time: I accused him of 'cheerful idleness', and he gallantly thanked me for the 'effective bollocking' I gave him. He spent about 20 years as a comprehensive school headmaster, first in Wales, then in Leeds. He said, 'I would not have had the passion for education that has driven my career and absorbed my interests if it wasn't for Harry.'

Chris Price, a Queen's College, Oxford, graduate who stayed on for a year to train to become a teacher, had the good fortune to spend a term at WBGS; fortuitously, his parents had moved from Leeds to Hertfordshire.[136] Harry Rée, he said:

was an anarchic saboteur. ... He was one of a clutch of idealist heads, handpicked by John Newsom ... to influence the post-War generation of teachers and students. ... One of the classics masters fell very ill and for the whole of the term I taught a full timetable with virtually no supervision and no one to tell me how to teach. The contrast between Watford and Leeds could not have been more stark. Harry's Watford Grammar School was a relaxed and informal place. He put sympathy and energy into encouraging his student teachers to think for themselves and create their own teaching style. ... He never saw the object of education as that of grading or pigeonholing individuals.

We should not be surprised that Harry was asked by the well-known and respected publisher George G. Harrap and Co. to write a book. The result was *The Essential Grammar School*, published in 1956. The volume was indeed slim: 86 pages with no index. It came out about the same time as *Secondary Modern* by Harold Loukes,[137] Reader in Education at the University of Oxford: 127 pages with an index.

---

136 Price was to become a Member of Parliament for almost 12 years and then Director of Leeds Polytechnic, his title changing to Vice-Chancellor when that institution became Leeds Metropolitan University. He died in early 2015.
137 1912–1980.

The blurb says:

> Though a progressive in politics, Mr Rée believes that the Grammar School offers the best education for certain types of children and one, moreover, that will help in building and sustaining the moral fibre of the nation. ... As one who loves his fellow men and gets the best out of them, he is to be commended ...

Since Harry's views were to change so dramatically in the second half of his life, it makes sense, I think, to take a look at what he said in the early 1950s:

> This book is offered hopefully. ... If the Grammar Schools did not exist, they would have to be invented. ... The aim of the grammar school is to produce good people who are broad-minded, inquisitive specialists, who are sensitive, intelligent, tolerant, and tough, who are both civilized and natural, and who work hard with their minds ... so devoted to their work that they are prepared for plenty of drudgery before they get to the interesting part of it.

Harry saw the grammar school as offering a leg up. And he did not hide his feelings about schools like Shrewsbury and their ilk:

> For many years people have been wondering how long the Public Schools could last; they are very expensive, and their inevitable exclusiveness is neither socially nor educationally desirable. ... The power and the attraction of the Public School will tend gradually to diminish.

Well, he was wrong: almost all of the public schools in England of his day still thrive, charging the proverbial arm and leg. Annual tuition and board at Shrewsbury School, the last time I looked, was £11,250. The Sutton Trust reports that:

> Over one-third of MPs elected in the 2010 General Election attended independent schools, which educate just 7 per cent of the school population.

With hindsight, it is amusing to read Harry on comprehensive schools:

> The case against the Comprehensive School, as put by the Grammar School masters, is not concerned with politics; it is an educational argument. ... The Grammar School must remain

selective. ... The Comprehensive School is too comprehensive to be efficient and humane.

Is he being defensive already? He quoted the powerful General Secretary of the Labour Party, Morgan Phillips[138] when he declared, 'We are pledged to abolish the 11-plus examination ... to provide a system of comprehensive secondary education.' Harry went on to pontificate:

> The LCC [London County Council] ... marches blindly forward under the comprehensive banner, undeterred by criticism from the profession or by the anguish of parents.[139]

In the last 35 years of his life, he was eating his words on a daily basis. And he became rhetorically more careful.

Some of Harry's stated views seem quaintly Victorian ... and I think he would agree. For example, 'Some children are much more intelligent than others. ... The intelligence test is a remarkably reliable guide to a child's mental ability.'[140] Not so many years after writing *The Essential Grammar School*, Harry would have agreed with Professor Clyde Chitty when he wrote about 'the fallacy of fixed potential in education'.

Harry was 'spot-on' on the issue of headmasterly independence:

> No first-rate school is without a good measure of independence. ... No Head ... should have to undergo the faintly humiliating experience of 'sharing' an interview with a Governor or a committee of councillors; when Local Authorities insist on this happening, they are gratuitously lowering the prestige of the profession and of their schools in the eyes of candidates for jobs, and in the eyes of the public.[141]

Harry was right in describing WBGS as an 'incredibly good school'; one hopes it still is. 30 per cent of his staff could, in my totally subjective view, have been described as outstanding.

---

138 1902–1963.

139 The London County Council was created in 1889 and became a very powerful entity. Its responsibility for education was taken by the Inner London Education Authority during the reorganization of local government in 1965.

140 Harry must have been acquainted with the work of Sir Cyril Burt, the educational psychologist, who died in 1971. Shortly after his death, Burt was credibly accused of falsifying data.

141 Benn, C. and Chitty, C., (1997) *Thirty Years On: Is comprehensive education alive and well or struggling to survive?* London: Penguin.

George Walker, former head boy, is tougher:

> The vast majority were rather dull, inflexible and not very good at explaining complex issues. On a 1–10 scale of teacher quality[142] I would rate the WBGS average during that period as around 5, disappointingly low for one of the country's most prestigious grammar schools. ... At the start of Harry's reign (1951) the school was still suffering from Second World War teacher appointments. ... Grateful grammar school parents didn't complain; nor did grateful grammar school pupils.

At the 2014 Harry celebration, George went further; opining that Harry was not, in fact, a great teacher; that he taught by the seat of his pants and did not have a coherent theory of pedagogy; that he may have heard of the likes of Bruner and Piaget, but hadn't read them.

I still remember three or four masters – they were all men – who were disasters: we all knew they were disasters, but no one seemed to do anything about it. Perhaps surprisingly, Harry wrote in his book:

> The actual executive power to turn a man out on to the street, without a job, is not a weapon that should be placed in the hands of the Head. ... Each staff (and each Head) must carry their share of less good teachers.

Of course, this has nothing to do with grammar schools *per se*, but I wish I could argue the point with Harry. Why should children be required to sit through classes that are stultifyingly boring and/or plain nasty? Why should the taxpayer pay for people, however few, who can be guaranteed to turn a youngster away from a language or a science? Yes, I know the schoolmasterly argument: life is not a bed of roses, and we need to get used to the idea that pain is part of human existence. Perhaps Harry's generation, having been through the War, accepted mindless boredom in a way we do not: Graves and Hodge, in *The Long Week-End*, write, 'School subjects were usually taught in a way that bored and repelled.' And the ability to dismiss, if it is used from time to time, does serve to distance the head teacher from the troops.

George Walker continues:

> I guess Harry simply didn't perceive intervention ... as part of his job. He never had much to say about curricular structures,

---

142 When he wrote this, George had been a headmaster himself.

> styles of teaching, the choice of resources, i.e. the art and craft
> of teaching. ... That might have been avoided if there had been
> a strong team of heads of department, curriculum co-ordinators,
> etc., but there wasn't.

George confirms my doubt whether Harry spent much time trying to improve the performance of teachers who were less than first-rate. Thus the boys in his school did have to endure some mediocrities as well as the superstars. (Exactly the same held true for Eric James's Manchester Grammar School. A large minority of the staff were surprisingly mediocre, and that minority tended to stay, while the high flyers moved on.)

George Walker again:

> There was a powerful assumption in Harry's time that you were
> born to be a teacher and all you needed to get started was a
> sound knowledge of your subject and a desire to impart it.

It was assumed that good teachers are born and not made. Bill Bailey, over 50 years after observing them, described the very worst:

> The first prize must go to [name deleted]: arrogant, humourless
> and totally useless with few redeeming features. His lessons were
> characterized by a scarcely disguised malevolence towards us.
> Second prize goes to [name deleted], a tragic man with no class
> control whatsoever. The sad reality is he had such a miserable
> time that he never knew that we did actually like him not least
> because as a man he had no malice whatsoever.

Harry must have known. And if any of the mediocrities had bothered to read his book, they would have known that they were safe.

As early as 1952, however, Harry was arguing on the BBC for the right of a headmaster to appoint his own staff.

During a sabbatical in 2002, I spent a day at Watford Grammar School, over 40 years after I had taught there, and a day at Manchester Grammar School, almost four decades after I had left. I got the strong impression, in both places, that the contemporary equivalents of the very worst teachers were gone; they couldn't have survived. But I also sensed that the very best, by any standards, those who changed lives just by being there, were gone too. When I recently shared this perception with Chris Husbands, the Director of the Institute of Education, University of London (now Vice-Chancellor of Sheffield Hallam University), he responded:

I think over the last 25 years we have lowered the ceiling and raised the floor. The question is whether that is a necessary or even a worthwhile trade-off. I started teaching much later than you but some people around in the early 1980s were dire. One doesn't see them now, but one doesn't see the brilliant individualist.

Harry seemed singularly unconcerned by the separation of males and females into separate institutions. 'If ... there is a choice,' he wrote, 'between two day-schools, one co-educational and the other not, then the decision should depend upon which is the better school.' And at the very beginning of the book, as if to explain to headmistresses, schoolgirls and others why they were not uppermost in his thoughts, he wrote, 'I am no anti-feminist.'

The book, then, is thin. It tells us more about Harry as a young and beginning headmaster than about grammar schools. In a 1957 review in the *British Journal of Educational Studies*, J.J.B. Dempster, Chief Education Officer, Southampton, called it 'rather pedestrian':

> There is little constructive thinking. ... Mr Rée appears just a little self-satisfied. ... 'Homosexuality at boarding schools must be accepted as a fairly normal occurrence.' Accepted by whom? Surely not by the parents who send their children there, nor by the staff of the schools.

When his successor at York, Ian Lister, wrote an obituary, he mentioned *The Essential Grammar School* and how Harry had totally changed his views within a few years of its publication:

> The story was going round that Harry was buying up copies of his own book in order to destroy them.

I might add that Harry never touted his book as having Shakespearean qualities. *Educator Extraordinary*, which came out almost two decades later, is far better written, and stands the test of time; *The Essential Grammar School* does not.

Harry would often write for the *Times Educational Supplement*. Or he would write for *The Manchester Guardian*. Or he would write for ephemeral, usually left-wing publications. In the late 1950s, he would write anonymously, as was the practice in those days; by the 1960s, he was writing under his own name.

And yet, I found a note in the BBC archives, written by Duncan Taylor of the Schools Broadcasting Department in January 1960:

He is anxious to maintain this anonymity because he is headmaster of Watford Grammar School and most anxious to avoid anything which might look in the least like self-glorification.

In a file dated 1962, someone wrote, 'He is a distinguished chap and a very experienced broadcaster'.

In 1958, 'A Headmaster' wrote 'State and public schools: The myth of superiority' and 'Future of public schools: No case for state support' for *The Manchester Guardian*. Harry differentiated between the major and the minor public schools:

> Often the minor public school is a cheerful community of energetic teenage boys ... they are cut off from the normal community, from girls of their own age, and from family life, and they are not discouraged from thinking that they are born and trained to occupy a privileged position. ... Interest in academic subjects is seldom strong, and the masters have not usually followed a course of training between leaving their university and starting teaching. ... Often these schools succeed in turning out young men with good manners, a sense of fair play and decency in their everyday relationships.
>
> ...
>
> It is often a delusion of parents when they think that by sending their children away they are in fact getting a better education ... than they would get at the local school.

And taking one issue after another, he patiently and skilfully showed how the advantages of a public school education are few and far between, ending up thus:

> Whatever the independent boarding-school may provide, it is hardly something which the taxpayer should be asked to pay for.

In 1934, when Harry was at Cambridge, Michael Foot had written in *Young Oxford & War*:

> The public school system as at present existing, would no doubt provide an admirable equipment for a person entering life at the beginning of the nineteenth century ... The aim of almost every public school is to turn out persons who will be loyal members of their class and willing adherents of the world order as they find it.

Back to 1958. Within a couple of weeks, there were several letters to the Editor. Peter Ure[143] criticized a proposal to skim off the best brains for the public schools:

> The grammar schools automatically become second-class institutions ... a system closely resembling the system of discrimination now obtaining between Oxford and Cambridge ... and most other universities.' (However, he was commenting on a proposal that Harry had not made.)

D.D. Aldridge of Oxford described the dormitories in his school days as 'unnatural'. Bruno Watkins described the school Alec Waugh attended:

> I was subjected to so much compulsory chapel, rugger, battle training, porridge oats, and slavish morality that I was too exhausted to absorb much of the excellent tuition. ... I was accused of laziness, immorality, letting the side down, and conduct unbefitting a gentleman. I was shown sympathy by no one and caned each term. It was for me a grotesque beginning to a happy life and I would not have missed it for worlds. ... But I am not sure that I would wish my own child to receive the same treatment.

There is a piece in the *News Chronicle* entitled 'Is homework really a menace?' by Robert Milne-Tyte, according to whom Harry's stated views at that time were those of a traditional headmaster:

> Homework is necessary and highly desirable. It's necessary in order to fix in a pupil's mind the facts he has been handed out during a lesson. And it is extremely desirable for a youngster to have to discipline himself to learn on his own. ... Homework means far more work for teachers. Everything has to be marked, usually in a teacher's own time.

---

143 Cowen Professor of English Language and Literature at the University of Newcastle upon Tyne from 1960 until his death in 1969.

Chapter 8

The man who changed his mind and comprehensive schools

I had never thought of Harry as being 'data driven'. *Au contraire*, he would, I am sure, be laughing uproariously at the mention of the phrase 'evidence-based management', wondering how I had been hoodwinked by bureaucrats who had rarely if ever stood in front of a class. He might be surprised to learn that George Walker, over 20 years after his death, described him as 'demanding of information and rational explanations'. And yet: in the early 1950s, three scholars from the Department of Sociological and Demographic Research of the London School of Economics, supported by Professor D.V. Glass,[144] conducted the famous study that led to the book *Social Class and Educational Opportunity*, which was first published in 1956. J.E. Floud, A.H. (Chelly) Halsey and F.M. Martin set out to investigate whether the observed differences between social classes in measured intelligence are more likely to be explained by environmental than genetic factors. J.W. Thompson, in a review at the time, described their book as 'ingeniously planned and shrewdly written'.

The two areas they chose to study were Middlesbrough (North Yorkshire; Teesside) and South-West Hertfordshire (i.e. Watford). The three authors got to know Harry pretty well, and many years later one of them, Chelly Halsey, wrote about Harry for the *Oxford Dictionary of National Biography*.

As Floud and Halsey put it in 1956:

> In the inter-war years the use of intelligence tests was widely regarded as a guarantee of the objectivity of the selection procedure; the results of the tests were held to be as nearly as possible free of bias from environmental influences, so that by giving them an important place in the selection procedure, social discrimination in the award of grammar school places could be reduced to a minimum. More recently, the reputation of the tests

---

144 1911–1978.

as an objective and administratively convenient instrument for the diagnosis of potential educability has been seriously undermined. ... The campaign against the tests has been strongly supported, if not actually led, by egalitarian reformers in education ...

Harry was taken aback when faced with the evidence that (a) a youngster's life chances are very heavily dependent on conditions in the home and that (b) the 11-plus examination, which he had been defending and administering, was unreliable. To an extent of which he had been unaware, social factors influenced educational selection. Never again did Harry claim that 'the intelligence test is a remarkably reliable guide to a child's mental ability.' The mantra was now 'I became the man who changed his mind'. There was still a leap to be made: from querying the entrance tests to questioning the very existence of grammar and secondary modern schools.

Perhaps Harry took what he was learning from Halsey and his colleagues so seriously because he had already internalized what Auden and Worsley had written in 1939:

> Since education can never be much better than the social system within which it functions, the improvement of the latter must take precedence over everything else. Until every child has the same educational opportunities, until equal social value is put upon all forms of employment, all suggestions for educational reform, except on quite minor points, must seem highbrow and unreal.[145]

By 2006, Hennessy, in *Having It So Good*, was able to say:

> It is certainly true that God or Nature (depending on one's position in the spectrum of faith/disbelief) does not distribute intellectual curiosity according to the socioeconomic status of the loins that deliver us into this world. But, as Michael Young's magnificent satirical warning *The Rise of the Meritocracy*[146] showed, an unmoderated meritocracy, while righting some of the wrongs of past centuries, can bring with it new inequalities of even greater rigidity ...

Fully 55 years after Harry 'changed his mind', the researchers were still at it; clearly, many people were still not convinced. According to *The Guardian*:

---

145 W.H. Auden and T.C. Worsley (1939) *Education Today and Tomorrow*. London: Hogarth Press, 41.
146 First published 1958.

Thousands of UK primary schools are locking their pupils into a cycle of disadvantage by separating them into ability groups, a major international study has warned. The Organization for Economic Co-operation and Development (OECD), a Paris-based think tank ... found that countries that divided pupils into ability groups at an early age tended to have higher numbers of school drop-outs and lower levels of achievement. In the UK one in six pupils are divided according to their academic ability by the age of seven, according to a study conducted last year by the London University's Institute of Education.[147]

Dividing pupils into ability groups was commonplace in the UK in the 1940s and early 1950s. By the early 1990s it had virtually disappeared. ... It is gradually being re-introduced into UK schools. ...

A spokesman from the Department for Education said it was for schools to decide how and when to group and set pupils by ability.

One can imagine how that last sentence, from an unnamed person, would have driven Harry to distraction. And as recently as 2012, a cross-party committee of MPs reported that:

Britain is far behind the rest of the developed world in terms of social mobility and studies show that today's 40-somethings have even less mobility than those who were born in the 1950s.

Harry would note, with controlled anger, that not much has changed. His friend Edward Blishen had written, as early as 1958:

Tripartism is quite the most stupid and frustrating concept that education has ever stumbled upon.[148]

In 1976, Peter Wilby, writing in *The Observer*, asked:

What led to his conversion? 'We found there was an enormous increase in measured IQ after a year at Watford. There was nobody who didn't increase and the best went up by 20 points. Meanwhile in the secondary modern school, we found that there were some whose IQ actually went down.'

---

147 *The* Guardian, 9 February 2012.
148 Blishen, E. (1966) *Minus Eleven Plus*. London: Council for Children's Welfare.

What about the very bright pupils? 'Maybe they won't achieve the old grammar school standards. They won't be as good at French verbs. But we've overrated those things in the past: they were badges of culture, like the bays and capes and books of the Bible that people had to learn by heart.'

Whatever the rights and wrongs, one has to be impressed by Harry's willingness to go where the facts led him and his willingness thoughtfully to change his mind.[149] Besides, his three children must all have been taking the 11-plus around the time Harry was confronting the issue.

I have no idea whether Harry ever read Machiavelli. But I am sure he would have understood this quotation from *The Prince*, which was written about 500 years ago:

> There is nothing more difficult to carry out, nor more doubtful of success, nor more dangerous to handle, than to initiate a new order of things.

Perhaps one should not be surprised that many of the supporters of the essentiality of the grammar school accused him of betrayal. He was not alone. W.H.G. Armytage, describing the 1944 Education Act, writes, 'It was ... approved by those educational sociologists who were later to become its vehement critics.' Maybe it's OK for academics to change their minds, but not for headmasters.

Around that time, the American journalist Martin Mayer, now a Fellow of the Brookings Institution, was swanning around England. He confronted Harry with research that suggested that while less than one in five of children from managerial or professional families were 'early leavers' from grammar schools, two-thirds of the children of unskilled workers dropped out. In his book *The Schools*, which came out in 1961, he wrote:

> Harry Rée says that these statistics are wildly out of date, and that 80 per cent of his entrants now move on to the sixth form with little discrimination by social class. Without for a moment doubting the word of this lively, ardent, wholly charming gentleman, it must be said that Rée protested publicly in 1954 against the findings of the Early Leaving Commission, writing in a letter to the *Times Educational Supplement* that 'the huge majority' of the 60-odd per cent reporting as departing before

---

149 He once gave a talk to the Leeds Association for Advancement of State Education entitled 'The man who changed his mind'.

sixth form 'have approached their academic ceiling, and to ask them to continue would be a waste of time.' The grounds for Rée's complacency were interestingly expressed in his book *The Essential Grammar School*, where he wrote of 'many ... who qualify for a Grammar School education but who – because of some strain of natural modesty, or perhaps honesty – will never become leaders.'

By the mid- to late-1950s, then, it was clear that Harry was struggling with some of his core beliefs, sometimes wanting to have it both ways. Dinah Brooke, Educational Correspondent for *The Observer* wrote:

> A fighting speech was made by Mr Harry Rée ... He advised his colleagues to abandon the defensive position they had taken up about a comprehensive system of education. They had adopted, he said, a schoolmasters' Maginot Line, from behind which the guns had boomed, 'No, No, No.' He thought the time had come to attack. 'We should say, 'Yes.' We accept a comprehensive system of education, but on our own terms. ... Inside that system we must maintain the principle of selection.'[150]

I wish I could embarrass Harry by telling him that WBGS describes itself, today, as a 'partially selective comprehensive school'. He'd be squirming, I think, getting what he asked for: 'a comprehensive system of education' with 'the principle of selection'.

In an aptly titled book, *A Mythology of British Education* (1974), Robert Bell and Nigel Grant write:

> We have the supreme illogicality, the simultaneous entertaining of mutually contradictory elements ... One often hears Government spokesmen, for instance, declaring in favour of comprehensive schooling *and* the retention of selective grammar schools. (Even the late Iain Macleod stated that the two types could 'flourish together' – *Times Educational Supplement*, January 1966.) It must be obvious that if comprehensive schools have to coexist to any great extent, they cannot be comprehensive; whatever they are called, they can hardly be more than 'secondary modern' schools under another, and possibly less unattractive, title.

---

150 *The Observer*, 4 January 1959.

Back to the conference: the *Sunday Times* Education Correspondent wrote:

> Mr Rée rebuked the conference and especially the platform, and hoped its like would never happen again. He thought its lamentations were out of date. … He asked why teachers had not got the courage to refuse to teach for the 11-plus examination.

The 11-plus in the UK was an examination administered in primary schools that would determine what kind of secondary school a child would go to. It became extremely controversial and, while it still exists in some localities, far fewer children now take it. In the mid-1950s, Richard Gross, visiting from Stanford University, was in no doubt:

> This division of children starting with the invidious *11-plus separation* seems to be the real curse of British education.

> Harry regretted the assumption that the less able children were relegated to mediocre teachers. 'It should be an honour,' he said, 'to teach a 'C' stream. Don't you agree?' The audience murmured doubtful assent.

In the late 1950s, then, Harry was going through a period when he wanted it both ways: he still opposed comprehensive schools, but he also opposed streaming (tracking) and pointless exams. It took him a while to get to the point where he would agree with Eric Midwinter when he said:

> a community school must always be comprehensive. … There must be internal comprehension without streaming or setting.

The issue of streaming was sensitively and sensibly discussed by Margaret Maden when she was headmistress of Islington Green Comprehensive School in a piece entitled *Thoughts on Comprehensive Developments*.

Mid-century, everyone on the left must have been reading Tony Crosland's *The Future of Socialism*. Just over 50 years after its publication, Shirley Williams wrote:

> In one respect Tony was bounded by his times. He had little feeling for diversity, and neither gender nor race equality imbued him with the passion that class discrimination engendered. He hardly noticed the discrimination against girls and women that undoubtedly thrived in educational circles.[151]

---

151 Williams, S. (2009) *Climbing the Bookshelves*. London: Virago.

Two of Crosland's assertions stand out:

- The school system in Britain remains the most divisive, unjust and wasteful of all the aspects of social inequality.
- Division into streams, according to ability, remains essential.

The second point is confirmed in Anthony Sampson's *Anatomy of Britain*, which first came out in 1962, i.e. shortly after Harry had arrived in York:

> Children ... were *not*, as in America, to be all in one stream: the comprehensives have their own 'grammar school' classes, leading on to university, and their own technical and modern classes ... They allow children to change streams after eleven, and also to mix out of class with other children cleverer or stupider than themselves.

It is amazing that Sampson, who fought inequality all his life and was Nelson Mandela's authorized biographer, should use the word 'stupid' so casually.

I quote from papers edited by Edward Blishen, from a conference organized by the Council for Children's Welfare and the National Federation of Parent–Teacher Associations in January 1959. Harry's paper was entitled *The Advantages of Selection*:

> ... I want to be fairly rude, because I want to say that I hope this is the last time that a Conference like this has to be called. I think this Conference is out of date; I think that many people who five years ago, ten years ago, were convinced that Comprehensive Schools were the only answer, are beginning already to change their minds.

> There has been a terrible lack of respect for the primary schools. ... Some primary school teachers have got the courage to say, 'To hell with you, as far as your exam is concerned' – that they are teaching English not merely to do these nonsensical I.Q. tests. ... In many decent schools the best teachers are put on the most difficult children. ... There has been a terrible lack of respect for the secondary modern schools. It has been assumed that the secondary modern school is bound to be something worse than the grammar school. ... There are areas where a secondary modern school is doing a much better job, as far as general education is concerned, than are many grammar schools.

If I had been there, I would have been tempted to shout out, 'Name one!'

And he went on to sing the praises of 'no streaming in primary schools' and of professional teachers making decisions about who goes where without interference:

> There has been the acceptance of streaming. We should not have accepted it. I do not agree at all that to remove a child from an 'A' stream to a 'B' stream is something which you approach with anxiety and you do not like doing; I think it is one of the most fascinating things you have to do.

Harry had used the word 'tripe'. How can you oppose streaming and, at the same time, enjoy moving someone from one stream to another? Harry went on to describe the four or five transfers per year from WBGS to a secondary modern school: I doubt whether these transfers or their parents would have shared his joy! In a book published in 1965, Donald Taylor wrote:

> There is a border-line, a substantial border-line, some of whom just get in to a grammar school, others go to a secondary modern. To call the one set bottom of the grammar school and the other set top of the modern school, is too easy a generalization. There must be an easy and sympathetic transfer for all those who, after careful observation, appear to have been placed in the wrong kind of school. We have transferred from the grammar school perhaps two or three a year though in recent years the practice has almost ceased as has the practice of transfer from secondary modern to grammar school.[152]

Harry again:

> You need different schools for different types of children. If we were a better school, and if we had angels on the staff, and I myself were an archangel, then perhaps we might be able to do it; but I am not; and they are not; we are human beings. I am in favour of selection then.

And he dug himself further in, describing a secondary modern head who 'finds that a child is doing particularly well' and promptly rings up the local grammar school head and suggests a transfer. For sure, I never heard of it happening at Watford.

---

152 Donald J. Taylor, 'Watford Grammar School'. In Gross, R.E. (ed.) *British Secondary Education: Overview and appraisal.* Oxford: Oxford University Press, 1965, 166–208.

Addressing Raymond King, Headmaster of Wandsworth Comprehensive School for over 30 years, Harry went on to say:

> I do not want to be patronizing to Mr King, but I do honestly admire what the London comprehensives are doing. I certainly would not like Mr King's job myself – he is an archangel.

Less than two years later, Harry was writing to me:

> I want to get away from Watford, of course, and, I agree, a comprehensive school is probably the place.

Was Harry aware of the contradictions in his thinking? Was the speech quoted above so strong because, in fact, he wasn't so sure any more?

Once again, Harry was gilding the lily. David Harman, who was a pupil at Watford, recalled:

> There was a lot of resentment among the parents of those children who did not pass. My mother used to tell a story, when we three brothers passed ... about how peeved she was when a friend of hers said she did not know where we got our brains to pass the 11-plus.

In the years before he publicly changed his mind, Harry did try to humanize the notorious 11-plus. Peter Taylor-Gooby, FBA, now a distinguished professor of social policy at the University of Kent, writes:

> When I came for interview as a nervous and rather tubby 11-year-old, we were shown into a classroom with much battered wooden desks. An energetic and wiry man appeared and proceeded to talk to us about the rules of etymological derivation as they related to Latin, German, French and English. He was completely captivating, and I remember thinking how really interesting this is. Then (because it was actually the test to decide which class you went in, though I didn't realize this) he produced paper, pencils and asked us a series of questions.

> Looking back I am impressed by his activity and charm and also the civilized and effective way he carried out the test. It could have been stressful ... As it was it was pleasant and also a learning experience. Now I know something of Grimm's Laws! Harry Rée was certainly a notable educationalist.

Harman went on to discuss streaming, in some detail:

> This streaming was very powerful because a couple of people each year were exchanged between the A stream and the C stream but I cannot remember anyone changing between the A stream and the B stream. ... When Harry arrived he found a very rigid system.

Bill Bailey did claim that, under Harry, the C stream 'felt valued and got a fair deal'.

And Harman described how Harry made some changes, but these changes were somewhat superficial, and the stereotypes remained.

I sometimes wonder whether Harry's wider audiences knew that he would frequently practise what he preached. Did the staff know how much he valued them? Did they believe him when he said the following at his last Speech Day in 1962?

> I leave the school very proud to have served here and deeply grateful for all kindnesses, aware of an unpayable debt to all I've learned, and profoundly confident that the school will send out, into Watford and the world, increasingly greater numbers of whom we can all be proud.

In his 1988 interview, he said:

> What was very good at Watford was the attention that was paid to the boys who were nowhere near getting successful 'O' levels.[153] I used to teach myself the bottom French set. And it was lovely. We got on terribly well. And I knew the tricks for getting them through 'O' level, and they mostly did quite well. And the master who was in charge of the lower forms [George Greenwell] was a great person. He was no scholar. But the work he did with those boys was just as important as the work of the lovely man who ran the classical sixth [Norman Marrow], who was a Quaker and a real scholar. A wonderful person. There was this overall concern with the totality of the boys. ... I was approached by a publisher [Harrap] to write a book about the grammar school, and I was very pleased to do so. ... I believed that the job of the grammar school – as I'd said about Beckenham – was to

---

153 The General Certificate of Education lasted in England and Wales from 1951, when it replaced the School Certificate, until 1987, when it gave way to the General Certificate of Secondary Education. There were two levels: 'O', Ordinary, and 'A', Advanced.

> compete successfully with the public schools. And indeed we
> were beginning to do so at Watford.
>
> After a bit I began to wonder about the secondary modern
> schools, which were quite good in Watford. And I used to go and
> visit them. I used to visit the primary schools too.

He rarely if ever took anyone with him on these visits. He recalled getting
'this wonderful brass band' from a secondary modern school to play at WGS:

> And I got that wonderful man Edward Blishen to come and talk
> to the sixth about the joys of teaching in a secondary modern
> school, after he'd written … *Roaring Boys*.

Blishen was described in an obituary as 'one of the wittiest writers and best
conversationalists of his day'.

Harry was constantly bringing interesting people to the school. Just
one example: Kurt Hahn, founder of Gordonstoun School in Scotland,
visited WBGS in October, 1956. Not surprisingly, Hahn, in his thank-you
letter, asked, 'Has the story of what happened to you in France ever been
printed? I should love to have a copy.' Harry's reply was: 'I do not trust
myself to write about the War – one is too easily misunderstood.'

1959 saw the publication of a major report sponsored by the British
government: *Fifteen to Eighteen* (The Crowther Report). Not surprisingly,
Harry weighed in: his piece in *The Guardian* (no longer the *Manchester
Guardian*) was entitled 'Crowther on the sixth form: Proposals lacking in
bite'. And this time the author was not 'A Headmaster', but Harry Rée. It is
hard to think back to the days when far, far fewer people went to university
than today. Harry, damning with exceedingly faint praise:

> The labour of bringing forth the 200 pages which the Crowther
> Report devotes to the sixth form was not entirely wasted. …
> Good to see that it comes down strongly against the requirement
> of Latin as an inevitable entrance qualification for Oxbridge,
> dubbing it as 'antiquated and serving little real purpose'. … One
> is pleased to see the affirmation: 'The job of a sixth form is above
> all to teach a boy to think, not just to memorize facts.'

Harry, Crowther: what about the sixth form girls?

Overall, Harry admitted that the Crowther Committee had mentioned
all the major questions of the day, but accused them of super-cautious
gradualism. 'The smooth pens', he said, were 'lamentably lacking in bite'.

The sheer scale of schooling increased hugely during Harry's professional life. In 1946, there were 175,275 teachers in England and Wales; 30 years later, there were 448,034.

In October 1960, Atticus of the *Sunday Times* met some modern headmasters at St John's College, Cambridge, Harry's former college. He (I am assuming that Atticus was male) interviewed, among others, Sir Desmond Lee of Winchester College, Dr Robert Birley of Eton College, Lord James of Rusholme of The Manchester Grammar School, and Harry. By now, he was amongst the best-known headmasters in the country. Watford Grammar School was not a member of the Headmasters' Conference[154] so his invitation should be seen as a very personal compliment:

> Rée believes that the grammar school boy is much freer than his opposite number in a public school and it is not just a question of being able to go to the Expresso Bar or have girl friends. 'Here', he says, 'it's much more like a university.' He is extremely keen on a scheme called Voluntary Service Overseas, under which his boys go abroad for a year, between school and university, to Africa or the Far East, to teach or serve however they can.

Today we'd call it a Gap Year; in 1960 it was still unusual, as it is today in the United States. VSO was founded by Alec Dickson in 1958, thus preceding the Peace Corps by about three years. Both organizations operate today in about 140 countries; VSO has had 42,000 volunteers over the years; the Peace Corps has had 200,000. They are now officially partnered.

Chris Manning remembers Harry vividly. Not everyone would agree with the words 'laid back' in what follows:

> He was a laid back, informal person. He was very reluctant to have his portrait painted and hung in the School Hall. One look at his portrait supports the concept of his informality in *total* contrast to the portraits around him. ... He was interested in his pupils and staff as individuals. He believed in listening to people and trying to understand misbehaviour. Mr Herbert Lister was the disciplinarian par excellence, but that is another story. ... I remain very grateful for his gentle and adult approach. ... He was a most remarkable man.

---

154 Renamed the Headmasters' and Headmistresses' Conference around 1996.

John Hinds, Bishop Emeritus of Chichester, writes:

> Such feelings as I can recall are reasonably positive, so I imagine that as a fairly pious teenager I was not offended! ... he taught me to think and to think independently.

Manning recalls a 'gentle and adult approach'. Michael Harloe, Vice-Chancellor of the University of Salford from 1997 to 2009, says he

> first met him, as a pretty terrified 11-year-old trying to find answers to a simple intelligence test which he gave me to determine which stream I went into ... his patience in getting me to respond coherently was one sign ... that he wasn't only a fine head but a fine teacher ...

> Leadership is hard to define but whatever it is, Harry had it. He transformed WBGS into a school where we were taught to think for and express ourselves and where we were treated as responsible young adults not children. ... this shaped my subsequent career profoundly.

As I have said already, George Walker knew Harry as well as anyone. They first met when George was ten years old and Harry interviewed him for a place at Watford Grammar School. From his Harry Rée Lecture, delivered at Settle High School in Yorkshire, where Harry had been a governor:

> Our final contact was an exchange of letters just a few weeks before he died. Those 40 years of Harry's advice, encouragement and friendship provided the greatest unearned bonus of my life which, I have no doubt, made me a different person.

In an email about 15 years after the lecture, George wrote:

> Quite simply, I owe the way I think to Harry and ... few days pass without his coming to mind.

Chapter 9

Hetty's death, and moving on

Hetty was, I think, absolutely crucial to Harry's success and
stability.

George Walker

I can still see her quizzical look, querying one of Harry's wilder statements.
Many years after her death, Harry recalled:

In a way I think, and I've been told, that I wasn't a very good
father. Particularly to Janet I think. That I may have been a bit
distant. ... We used to have staff parties, great staff parties. We
had wonderful parties for the staff and children. Ice cream and
things. And Hetty involved herself a little in the school. I mean
not in any active way that required any decisions. But she would
come along and watch matches with me, and that sort of thing.
So she was known to the staff. ... She rescued me, I can remember
once or twice, from rather stupid things. ... Hetty worked,
obviously, very hard. It was a big house. ... In the later years
at Watford ... she became more and more involved in marriage
guidance. And was 'passed' as a marriage guidance counsellor.[155]
And she was marvellous, because she was a terribly good listener.
And she used to do a lot of the guidance in the house. ... And
people would come round. And the children used to get a bit
fed-up ... 'Oh God, one of mother's guidance people.' And then
... she used to give talks to schools. ... Right at the end we had
one wonderful holiday, Hetty and I, when the kids had grown
up more or less.[156] And we went on holiday on our own. It was
lovely. Walking the Bridleway, across the South of England. That
was lovely. And that was really sort of a second honeymoon. And
it was then, only after that, that the news came through that she
was not well. And she went into hospital and was diagnosed as
having cancer of the liver, which in those days was a sentence.

---

155 She worked for the National Marriage Guidance Council, which changed its name to
   Relate in 1988.
156 Jonathan, the youngest, would have been about 13.

And she knew, she was told by the doctor, and I was told – I was rung up at school actually – he said, 'I'm sorry, I've got bad news.' So I went up and saw her that evening in the hospital. And she said she'd arranged to come home, not wait in the hospital. They'd said she had about two months perhaps. And that evening I was doing a speech day in a girls' school. And I didn't cancel it. I thought, well, I'm not a bad actor. So I did my usual speech day nonsense. And Hetty came home and I actually dealt with her death, as far as the children were concerned, very badly. I'd decided it wasn't really a decision – it was just that I didn't want people to feel that I was any different, or I wasn't going to upset the school or anything like that.

The notice in the press was both brief and bleak:

RÉE. – On Sunday, 24th Dec., 1961, at 58, The Avenue, Watford, HETTY, wife of HARRY RÉE and daughter of Mr and Mrs E.W. Vine, of Beaconsfield, aged 49 years. Cremation private and no flowers.

There was no mention of the children, all three of whom were still living at home.

When I learned how Harry was handling the situation, I was in my mid-twenties and instantly judgemental. Hindsight suggests he knew that he had been profoundly wrong, but one should remember that this was 1961, not 2011. Harry again, in his own words:

… and I did the same with the children. I didn't tell them for some time. Didn't even tell Janet, who was 17. And Janet found out by reading a letter. A letter to me from somebody else. Dear Jan, I mean she was so upset, because she knew she shouldn't have read the letter and … she's a really lovely person. And when Hetty was ill she did a lot of the housework as well as her schoolwork. She was in her last year at Watford Girls' Grammar School. And then I asked her what she thought we ought to do about telling the boys. And I told Brian. But didn't tell Jonathan … I didn't tell him for ages. Which was dreadful.

Jonathan would have been 13 years old. Retrospectively, one has to wonder how Headmaster Rée would have advised a parent in a similar predicament. And Harry's mother had died only 15 years before, and very suddenly.

Hetty came back and stayed in bed. And we had a wonderful doctor who looked after her. In the end we had a nurse. And she died, terribly inconveniently poor dear, on Christmas Eve. ... And when she died – she'd said, 'Please, please, don't make any fuss.' ... And she died peacefully. The doctor saw to it, although she was in terrible discomfort and not in total control of her body. He was great. ... She wanted to be cremated. And so I told the undertakers, 'You can take away the body and see that it's cremated. I don't want anything else done.' And there was no funeral service. And I told the school ... I told members of the staff not to make any fuss. And I think looking back on it, it was OK for me, that was the way I wanted it. I didn't want a fuss and I knew Hetty didn't want a fuss. But from the children's point of view I think they needed some sort of recognition and celebration really, of her life.

The doctor may have been wonderful, but did he really talk with Harry, or the children? I doubt it. The 1988 interviewer asked, 'Had she talked much to the children while she was dying?' Harry:

Do you know, I don't know. Awful, isn't it. I think probably not. Her parents were still alive. They came to see her. I honestly don't know. Isn't that awful. No, it's one of the things I'm rather ashamed of, the way I dealt with Hetty's death.

What were her parents, both of whom were still alive, thinking and feeling, one has to wonder?

There were two very good things that happened, as far as she was concerned, before she died. One was the news that Janet had got into Oxford. ... And the other was I'd been offered the job at York, to run the Education Department, in the new University. And she knew both those things. It was something of a solace.

Lisa Vine writes:

Hetty was a very remarkable woman ... and when she died my poor grandmother [Kathleen] was so grief-stricken that she never recovered properly. Kathleen had had a very close relationship with her daughter who lived close by in Watford. My grandmother had lost her own mother at six and then her eldest son when he was 37, so you can imagine how awful it was for her. And 'Grandfa', as we called my grandfather, could be quite impatient with her. She later went into a home and was very sad. My father was her only living child left.

Hetty's death was made more unbearable for her family by Harry's decision not to have a funeral. ... As children, we were never allowed to go to those funerals in those days, so I did not realize how dreadful this was. But my father was so upset about it he could get very angry years after. And of course now I think, how could Harry be so insensitive? What about Hetty's parents? It was a lasting stain on him within the family, although more was felt than was said. It seems incredible to me now that a man can take a decision like that about his wife without consulting others. I think it was terrible for the children and devastating for my grandparents.

Lisa has subsequently emailed:

I hope I didn't sound too judgemental about Harry. I was very fond of him as an adult, though a bit scared of him as a child who was rather naughtier than his own children, and he was always telling me off! And of course that is how that generation grew up. ... He also told me that he hated saying goodbye. And that was how he rationalized it all: as part of being 'rational'.

Jill Pellew writes:

My parents were among those who were shocked and upset about his 'refusal' to bury Hetty or have any kind of remembrance ceremony for her.

Back to Lisa's email:

Harry ... certainly stayed in touch with all our family: he was never close to my parents as they were so different but he maintained contact. And he visited my grandparents with the children. My grandmother died in 1966, my grandfather in 1970. ... Harry was an encouragement to me when I wanted to go to university, against the wishes of my parents. And I did go, and it changed my life!

Harry's relationship with his niece Lisa Vine is a classic example of the contradictions embedded within him.

Wanting better to understand Harry's thoughts and actions from half a century ago, I discussed them with Stephen P. Hersh, a Washington-based psychiatrist, cancer and pain expert and close personal friend. He was able to put what I told him in context: 50 years ago, cancer was seen as leprosy; people used euphemisms; even people working at or visiting the National Cancer Institute would not use the word 'cancer', 'the C word'. Patients, quite often, would not be told they had cancer: this would be seen as cruelly adding to their burdens. And even into the 1990s, children might have been 'protected' by not being taken to funerals. Steve saw Harry's effective exclusion of Hetty's parents as 'eccentric', even by the standards of the time. And, for sure, he would have had difficulty giving sound advice as a headmaster.

Harry would have been psychologically traumatized, full of guilt, maybe somehow wishing Hetty to die but totally unable to admit it even to himself. (The final stages of liver cancer are messy.) He comes across to Steve as very controlled, very disciplined. And since he was not a believer, he could not blame God.

Hetty, in turn, knew his weaknesses and vulnerabilities and would have been focused on him rather than her children or parents, i.e. normal, while Harry was in extreme denial and torn up by his loss. During the last 30 years of his life, he couldn't quite allow himself to enter another wholly trusting relationship.

Meanwhile, the doctor, while treating Hetty, would almost certainly not have raised any issues with Harry. It would have been unusual for him to talk to family members: that was not his job as it would have been defined at that time.

Would the situation have been different if Hetty had been the survivor and Harry the cancer patient who died? In other words, did gender play a role? Quite possibly.

And did unresolved issues from the War play a role? Did Harry have what we would now call post-traumatic stress?[157] Steve thinks almost certainly, at least to some degree.

During his last years at Watford, Harry came to realize that grammar schools were no longer for him. 'I became the man who changed his mind.' Later, he would say to Dinah Brook of *The Guardian* and *The Observer*:

> I don't really think I have changed my attitude. Essentially I am
> and always have been an egalitarian.

More and more, he became uncomfortable representing the kind of institution he was no longer sure he believed in. But – and some of those

---

157 The disorder was not recognized by American psychiatrists until 1980.

who were there at the time would disagree with me – he was careful not to be seen denouncing the mission of the grammar school while still earning his bread and butter as a headmaster. Needless to say, some people, sensing his waning enthusiasm, were angry at his reluctance to continue on the bandwagon; others felt betrayed, especially retrospectively. True conversions do not always happen overnight, of course, yet most of us do not want our leaders to display ambivalence. Late in 1960, he wrote in a letter to me: 'I want to get away from Watford, of course, and, I agree, a comprehensive school is probably the place.' (I remember being overwhelmed by his frankness and by 'of course'.) By 1988, he was looking back:

> I realized that I couldn't go on teaching in grammar schools and giving myself to grammar schools. I was interviewed for Bristol Grammar School headship. And I suppose I wanted it, I would've liked to have gone there and converted it really, to being much less a direct grant school. ... But I don't think I would've been very good, I would've lost heart. Luckily I was turned down.

Bristol Grammar School chose Dr John Mackay, a respected Christian gentleman who stayed for 15 years: clearly, the governors did not want anyone remotely like Harry. He would have followed John Garrett, who had declined his services at Raynes Park almost a quarter of a century before. Garrett had moved on to be Headmaster of Bristol Grammar School for 17 years.

> I suppose in a way it would've been more sense if I'd tried to get to a comprehensive school straight away, but there weren't very many then. And I wanted to know about them. And I wanted to train young teachers to deal with the problems of the comprehensive school.

He was impatient to move on.

Not everyone seems to have been enchanted with Harry's efforts. David Hargreaves, whom I recall as a comprehensive school guru, wrote in 2010:

> I have not heard anyone mention Harry's name for some years now. I suspect very few active practitioners ... will remember him or even know of him. ... I knew him fairly well in the 1970s but was never a close friend. ... I once visited him in that amazing house on the hill where one had to walk through the fields to reach it. He was a remarkable man, fun and stimulating to

be with, and I much admired him and his work. Inevitably he remained very much on the outside to the academic education establishment of the time, who were very snooty about an ex-headmaster becoming a professor!

Sic transit. In 2009, Peter Wilby wrote of Hargreaves in *The Guardian*, 'In the 1980s, he was probably the most talked about educationist in the land.' In 1976, according to the same Peter Wilby, this time in *The Observer*, Harry

> still says grammar schools performed the vital function of opening up the universities to working-class entrants at a certain moment of history.

One is left with an interesting, unanswerable question: what kind of headmaster might he be today? How would he fare if he was a headmaster for a decade … 60-plus years later than Watford? Would his charm, energy and charisma somehow energize both staff and students, so that they took tests and rankings in their stride? Or would he alienate the powers that be with his stroppiness and, through his oppositional behaviour, beg to be dismissed? I think it would be the first: his sheer ability plus his charm, which his nephew Charles Swallow described as 'a dangerous commodity', plus his deep-seated desire to be middle-of-the-road after all the shouting would ensure his success. My concern: where are the independent-minded head teachers today with Harry Rée-like qualities?

In Eric Midwinter's words:

> His approach, of course, was one of insouciant and persuasive charm, an easy, almost benign mode that we could only envy.

At the 2014 centenary celebration, Eric quoted the Jerome Kern lyric from 1936 that Frank Sinatra sang:

> Now nothing's impossible, I've found for when my chin is in the ground,
> I pick myself up, dust myself off, and start all over again.
> Don't lose your confidence if you slip, be grateful for a pleasant trip,
> And pick yourself up, dust off, start over again.
> Work like a soul inspired until the battle of the day is won.

I did ask several people who had known him what kind of headmaster – or head teacher – Harry might be if he were to re-emerge in the second decade of the twenty-first century and elicited the following responses: Nigel Gann said he would delegate all the unpleasant stuff to a competent deputy; Eric Midwinter thought that 'he didn't lack spirit; he'd fight back'; Chris Bailey and Steve Plaice both said he'd either be working in the private sector or have gone into politics. (He seems never to have considered this option.) Nigel Wright, however, replied that:

> I don't think Harry would, in today's climate, have won over many people, nor do I think he would lose his cool and be destroyed. I think he would have continued to keep the flag of decency and enlightenment flying in his large network of personal relationships. And settled for that, waiting, as we all are, for something to turn up.

Chapter 10
York

Enter Dr Eric James, Lord James of Rusholme. Eric James, who had known Harry from his days at Bradford Grammar School, was, in his day, larger than life in the educational world. With a DPhil in chemistry (from Queen's College, Oxford), he was High Master of Manchester Grammar School (MGS) from 1945 until he became the founding Vice-Chancellor of the University of York. Harry would later say that 'MGS had operated much more like a university than a school'.[158] After Sussex, York was the second of the so-called plateglass universities that were established in the 1960s. Knighted in 1956 by the Eden government and named a life peer only three years later by the Macmillan government (both Conservative), James nevertheless saw himself as a Fabian socialist who believed passionately in equality of opportunity, if not equality of outcome.[159] In the House of Lords, he was a crossbencher, sitting with no political party.[160] He was very well known throughout England, partly because of his association with MGS, partly because of his titles – he was the only headmaster with a peerage – and partly because of his membership of the Brains' Trust on radio and television. He spoke passionately and frequently about grammar schools and academic standards. A Gladstonian liberal, he taught Plato to sixth formers and read Proust on the Manchester–London train. In a letter to Margaret Maden, Harry would write, 'Eric James wants to read Proust and Conrad.' He was a superb debater: I remember a 1960 confrontation in the MGS lecture theatre between him and the seemingly hapless A.D.C. Peterson (1908–1988), head of the Education Department at Oxford, sponsored by the Institute of Physics and the Physical Society, who got their money's worth. He came across as an invincible slayer of dragons.

---

158 From personal experience, I would agree that if he was referring to conversations in the common room then that was correct, but not if he was thinking of the boys and their teachers.

159 One wonders whether he knew that R.H. Tawney advocated as early as 1914 for 'not simply equality of opportunity but universality of provision' (Tawney, R.H. (1966) *The Radical Tradition: Twelve essays on politics, education and literature*. Edited by Rita Hinden. Harmondsworth: Penguin). One wonders also what he would have made of Eric Midwinter's powerful assertion that 'equality of opportunity without equality of environment is often a sham.'

160 The first life peers were appointed in 1958.

James believed that teachers should be 'educated' rather than 'trained'; I remember him as wholly dismissive of education as a discipline. In a telephone call, David Waddington, a chemist who joined the University of York in 1965 and retired in 2000, described James to me as sneering at educational research and supporting traditional subjects like chemistry and English; but he did want teacher training.

Like many others, I was surprised when he decided to have a department and therefore a professor of educational studies at York; I was even more surprised when he picked Harry. (These were two separate decisions, even though they may have been made within the same hour.) He must have come to the realization that the modern university had a responsibility to the secondary school world; and he must have known that, in a way he probably could not foresee, Harry would deliver for him. And he was confident enough to follow his gut. Alasdair Brown told me that he had heard more than once that Eric had offered Harry the job in a toilet.

I have asked several people who knew both men the obvious questions. Oliver James, Emeritus Professor of Hepatology at the University of Newcastle and Eric's son, writes in an email:

> Although he despised what was then going on in 'academic education' in the UK my dad was obviously profoundly interested in education and wrote/lectured about it very extensively. So I guess the answer may be that he wanted a 'different' education dept. Hence perhaps why he was keen to appoint Harry, who he knew was (a) inspirational, and (b) iconoclastic. I think it was to both of their credit that my dad sought Harry and Harry accepted.

Harry Judge, headmaster of a large and well-respected comprehensive school before he became head of the department of educational studies and a professor at Oxford (1973–88) writes:

1. Eric did *not* believe in education as a 'field of study' – neither do I, which is why we got on well. ... He saw Harry as a practitioner and an intellectual (in the best sense) who believed in real schools.
2. What they had in common originally was the championship of grammar schools versus public schools. ... They were headmaster allies in the 1950s. Eric more than once said to me that if all heads of comprehensive schools were like Harry R. or Harry J. [i.e. Judge], then he would believe in them too. BOTH Eric and Harry despised 'professors of education' and Harry had an uncomfortable time in York.

In the archives of the University of York, I found some notes from Eric James to Lord Robbins that reveal his thinking:

- Education departments … have … very low reputations.
- York cannot as a matter of principle send people into teaching without training.
- It must command the confidence of the schools.
- The education department must try to build up the confidence of other departments in the University.
- mention the possibility of H.A. Rée. … He is not a scholar, but he is one of the best-known headmasters in England, and is a good writer, speaker and broadcaster. Some think him *too* full of ideas, and certainly I do not always agree with him. But he has vision and vitality, and if he were appointed no one would have any doubt that York intended to take education seriously and was not going to be simply conventional.

When I asked Eric Midwinter (PhD, York), who knew both men, why he thought Eric had chosen Harry, he said, '50 per cent, he knew and trusted him; 50 per cent, he'd make a splash by getting a maverick.' He compared Eric James with the impresario who gets a top guy even if he personally doesn't think he's funny.

James's choice of Harry Rée may have been based on a personal relationship – impossible in today's world of affirmative action or positive discrimination, and rightly so – but it was not casual. His letter to Lord Robbins dates from August 1961. Harry's 'My answer to your question, will I come? is of course *yes*' came two-and-a-half months later.

In April of 1962, he was writing:

I am appalled at my ignorance of university organization and the amount I shall have to absorb quickly. … I do cling to practical experience.

In November, 1962, a full year after his enthusiastic *yes*, he wrote to Eric James from his house in Watford, practising typing and apologizing.

Eric was the third of Harry's hero-mentors: Henry Morris; John Newsom; and Eric James. Harry did not have many heroes, didn't see the world in terms of heroes, and certainly did not view himself as one. At Watford, several parents, staff members and boys did see him as a hero: was he even aware of that, and if he was aware, was he embarrassed, dismissive or uncomfortable?

Despite my contention that Harry was not keen on heroism, he did say, in his 1988 British Library interview:

> I'm a real sucker for heroes. Couldn't do without them. All through my life, I think, I've looked up to people. And they've been sort of models. I think at school, the boys at school whom I admired. Masters at school. There was a wonderful master at Shrewsbury. I've been rather rude about masters at Shrewsbury. ... And then, of course, at Cambridge, Henry Morris was a hero, and remained a hero all my life. I mean during the War, heroes no. ... And then I suppose John Newsom ... a wicked man in many ways. ... He gave us immense liberty. ... And then Eric James.

Somehow, the claim that he was a 'real sucker for heroes' doesn't ring true. Harry wanted to see himself as a 'stand-alone' character. In the 1988 interview, Harry went on to discuss his friendships with Edward Blishen and Francis Cammaerts. No wonder Edward, in his perceptive and loving obituary, referred to him as a 'gregarious loner'. And Jon Nixon was, I think, extraordinarily perceptive when he referred to him as 'needy'.

When the York appointment was announced, Dr Kenneth Urwin, General Secretary of the Association of University Teachers (AUT), wrote a letter to the *Times Educational Supplement* (*TES*) that many teachers in the land and certainly people who knew Harry must have read, querying how someone without traditional scholarly credentials could land such a job. Harry laughed it off, of course, but he was never totally comfortable with the professorial title. Oliver James emailed:

> Incidentally I believe that my dad got into trouble with the UGC for making his first two or three professorial appointments without going through too much in the way of due process. Couldn't happen now.

In 2008, David N. Smith wrote:

> Concerned that York should become prominent in teacher education, James had resolved to establish a chair of education. His choice of first professor was Harry Rée, headmaster of Watford Grammar School.
>
> News of Rée's appointment caused the *Times Educational Supplement* among others to question whether appointments of such prestige should be publicly advertised. Concerns were also voiced in Parliament, while the Association of University

Teachers (AUT) had previously written to James urging that 'all chairs should be advertised by a board including two outsiders'. James was unmoved. ... in Rée ... he believed he had 'got one of the liveliest minds in practical education'.[161]

Denis King, a wonderful French teacher at Watford, later headmaster of Clacton Grammar School, cheerfully asked Harry when he'd be delivering his inaugural lecture: he never did.[162] He was never quite confident enough to argue that, while maybe not a published scholar when he went to York, he was an intellectual and a voracious reader. Besides, he did prove, with his book on Henry Morris, that he could play the role of professor if he chose to. Chelly Halsey would write:

> Rée later came to believe that his academic elevation was a mistake mitigated somewhat by his appointment as provost of Derwent College.

And Nicole Ward Jouve writes:

> The university was in some way too theoretical, too removed from ordinary life, too narrow for him.

Harry was, of course, the first professor of education at York. But he was also the first professor of anything. Eric James made sure the appointment was confirmed and announced early, so that Hetty would know about it before she died. I was teaching at Manchester Grammar School at the time – Eric had not moved to York yet – and I will never forget him striding into the common room to tell me about it, pleased as Punch.

Those were the days before equal opportunities. Eric James, Harry Rée and their peers saw nothing wrong with selecting people for key positions whom they had known and observed and trusted for years: that was how one built institutions. And even though, inevitably, white males would tend to appoint white males with similar backgrounds, it wasn't all bad. One can argue the matter for ever, and people have.[163]

---

161 'Eric James and the "utopianist" campus: Biography, policy and the building of a new university during the 1960s', *History of Education*, 37 (1), 23–42.
162 The University's website now has the statement: 'Every member of the professoriate is eligible to give an inaugural lecture, but it is not obligatory.'
163 When Harry recruited me, then a student teacher, and all but offered me a job in 1958, he did write, 'Don't feel completely confident ... we must advertise ... It's possible that someone may apply who can teach Latin, French, science and P.T. ... and take rugger and hockey and cricket and who has already written two novels.' I never had either the courage or the chutzpah to ask about my competitors.

Jonathan M. Daube

Christopher Price writes:

He got the job through pure patronage. Knowing there was a gaggle of pedantic, well-qualified senior lecturers anxious for the job, Eric James ... decided to select his professor of education before anyone else, since there were no existing academics to help with the appointment.

Harry brought at least three characteristics with him to York: a reputation (war hero, public speaker); experience (headmaster, teacher, parent); and, perhaps most importantly, an attitude that he transmitted to students:

'You cannot be a teacher and a pessimist,' said Mr H.A. Rée, headmaster of Watford Grammar School and Professor-elect of Education at the new University of York.[164] He was speaking ... at the University of Exeter Institute of Education ... on 'The Hopes of a Reasonable Man'. ... the reasonable man was Mr Rée himself, although he expressed some apprehension at the nomenclature. Mr Rée described himself as an interminable optimist despite the Bomb and despite sick humour – 'What are you going to be if you grow up?' ... Mr Rée hoped to see 'excessive leaning on the crutch of examinations' disappear. ... 'Specialization would be forced out.' Mr Rée seemed to find much of his inspiration in the younger generation, in what he called the rebels 'twisting their way to Aldermaston'. They were responsible and honest, although they might lack stamina and imaginative generosity. Mr Rée's prognostications came thick and fast. ... Punishment would tend to wither away in the upper parts of schools. Children would begin to learn languages much earlier. Mr Rée hoped to see most history text books 'thrown out of the window'; to see compulsory games abolished, and to see some definite change in the compulsory form of morning worship. Mr Rée thought that the barriers between schools, between public school, grammar school and secondary modern school, would disappear 'in spirit if not in fact'. ... 'Wouldn't the *Educational Supplement* accuse you of talking comprehensive cant?' suggested a questioner. 'Or egalitarian cant', Mr Rée added, beaming.[165]

---

164 February 1962.
165 *Punch*, 14 February 1962.

In October 1960, in a letter to me, Harry referred to a Scottish piece in which Sir James Robertson, my headmaster – rector, actually – at the Aberdeen Grammar School, had written:

> It is said that many teachers like working towards examinations. There could be no more urgent reason for getting rid of them.[166]

Dame Margaret Miles, the famous comprehensive school headmistress, agreed:

> I have no objection to examinations as long as they are kept in their place and are used simply as a means of checking and testing and revising the work that has been done in a certain span of time. Once teaching becomes preparation for examinations, then education is lost sight of.[167]

Almost 55 years later, Harry might have been surprised at the company he was keeping. Tony Little, Headmaster at Eton (2002–15), recently said that:

> England's 'unimaginative' exam system is little changed from Victorian times and fails to prepare young people for modern working life.

He said:

> there was a risk that 'misleading' test scores may become more important than education itself, and warned against a narrow focus on topping rankings.

Headmaster Little, as Harry would have done, praised Rachel Tomlinson, head of the Barrowford School in Nelson, near Burnley, whose letter to pupils went viral when she wrote:

> … We are concerned that these tests do not always assess all of what it is that makes each of you special and unique.

> The people who create these tests and score them do not know each of you – the way your teachers do, the way I hope to, and certainly not the way your families do. They do not know that you can play a musical instrument or that you can dance or paint a picture. They do not know that your friends count on

---

166 Robertson, J. (1959) 'What are schools for?' *The Advancement of Science*, 62, 1–9.
167 Miles, M. (1966) *... And Gladly Teach: The adventure of teaching*. Reading: Educational Explorers.

you to be there for them or that your laughter can brighten the dreariest day.

George Walker, who knew Harry well both at Watford and at York, quoted him:

'When you meet a new class for the first time', Harry advised his student teachers, 'make the assumption that they are better than you are, will go further than you've gone, will do things you've only dreamed about. Then you'll start off with the right relationship.'

Harry would have enjoyed Anna Leonowens's lines in *The King and I*, quoted by Eric Midwinter at the celebration of his centenary:

It's a very ancient saying but a true and honest thought
That if you become a teacher by your pupils you'll be taught.

Eric went on to point out how sad it is that Michael Gove[168] needs to learn from a Broadway musical.

Back to George Walker:

Harry was a risk-taker and he would have little sympathy with the risk-averse, timid, multiply-insured environment that now cocoons and smothers much of education, replacing trust with tick boxes, eccentricity with conformity and professional pride with performance indicators. ... He had enormous confidence in the competence of young people. ... So I remember Harry as a sceptic, an optimist and a risk-taker but the most precious gift was his friendship.

At the 2014 celebration of the centenary of Harry's birth, George spoke of Harry's enormous faith in young people and his optimism: 'He was a phenomenal communicator.' He took risks, but he shielded others when they took risks. As recently as January 2015, *The Observer* opined that 'ours is an increasingly risk-averse society': Harry wouldn't have liked that.

He began in York, without secretarial assistance, at Micklegate House, 86 Micklegate, a building now occupied by Barron and Barron, chartered accountants.

At the age of 86, Harry Creaser, one of our Harry's very first colleagues, sent me his trenchant memories: 'I may add a more negative

---

168 Secretary of State for Education, 2010–14.

view', he readily admitted. 'We never fully clicked. By nature he was a solitary man …':

> Eric James and Eric Lucas taught … at Winchester and became great friends. James ended up as High Master of Manchester Grammar and Lucas was Professor of Education at Makerere College in Uganda 1951–71. … In 1956 I was appointed Lecturer in Education at Makerere. … Astonishingly by 1962 by accident, deaths, illness and colleagues leaving … I had become Dean of Education.
>
> I now jump over to UK. Eric James, controversially, appointed Harry as Professor of Education at York without even advertising the post and I am told that he said to Harry, 'I know nothing about teacher training, nor do you and you couldn't organize a ##### up in a brewery but I know a chap who does. He's Harry Creaser and he is in the middle of Africa; get a ticket and go see him – I'll fix it with Bernard de Bunsen the Vice Chancellor.'
>
> My wife and I had dinner with Bernard and others with Harry and we got at loggerheads as he shot off about what we should be doing in East Africa. … next night … we argued through the evening.

Creaser went on to recount how he did still get an offer to come to York:

> In 1963, I was interviewed by Harry, Eric and John West-Taylor[169] … Harry and I were the only tenants of a wing in King's Manor. It was a lovely setting and I thought we would spend time planning together. But Harry left it to me. He had so many interests going on …

I found a note from Harry to Eric James in the University of York archives:

> I didn't like him as much in York as in Makerere, and he is more conventional than I expected. … He is less lively than I had hoped.

We do get a picture of the developing curriculum, but:

> Harry was horrified lest it look like Teacher Training or worst of all Lesson preparation. (The favourite words of Harry: 'I've never prepared a lesson in my life.')

---

169 The first Registrar.

Needless to say, I didn't believe him then, and I don't believe him now. He prepared carefully, and I have seen notebooks that prove it. Creaser continues:

> I was the planner, Harry played it on his feet. We just couldn't fit. It was left to me and we both kept changing our minds. ... Harry was engrossed with the new Colleges. I am sure Eric and he had conceived them and Harry was to be the first provost. ...

Thelma Emmans wrote:

> Harry was brilliant at defusing difficult situations, e.g. when a group of Indian boys refused to accept as a tutor a young student from the Caribbean whose skin was darker than theirs (added to which she was female!).

Perhaps Harry was right to be concentrating more on building the colleges than the Education Department. Creaser felt:

> In retrospect the undergraduate education suffered most while the Colleges grew strongly.
>
> ... fortnightly essays and an end-of-term paper. Half-way through the first term under student pressure Harry, without consulting the Board of Studies, reduced it to two essays and a paper. ... Finally complete destruction of the whole plan in 1969. ... Another distraction was the Language Teaching Centre (LTC). Eric Hawkins was a language teacher who had become a Headmaster. ...

And Creaser went on to explain in considerable detail how the LTC, despite a wonderful new building, 'was a failure'. He ceased to be secretary to the Board of Studies, and unsurprisingly the two Harrys drifted apart. In a letter Harry wrote, 'Can you find a job for Harry Creaser – porter at the Hilton?' I don't think he meant Creaser harm, but they don't seem to have talked through their differences. However, Creaser was the first to admit:

> He was always ready to catch on to anything – a fount of ideas. Some were a success, sadly many failures. He never let any failures deter him and was always ready to try something else out. One weekend I found myself with Harry who had invited Yehudi Menuhin and his sister Hephzibah ... to hear Hephzibah's husband talk us into his ideas to stimulate pupils actually to do

something about which they felt strongly rather than talk.[170] It involved provoking pupils.

Harry didn't follow up; later he 'had forgotten about it and moved on to something else.' When I asked Peter Renshaw, who had headed the Menuhin School for almost a decade, about this, he wrote:

> I can certainly understand how Harry was not entirely sympathetic to Menuhin – they held very different views of the world! ... Richard Hauser was a social activist with pretty radical views on education. ... Hauser was a very strong-minded person who could be seen as a kind of 'social worker'. ... I suspect Harry found Hauser rather bigoted and uncompromising. I can't imagine Harry wanting to become involved with him.

Back to the other Harry, Harry Creaser:

> Harry felt strongly that Education Lecturers should actually teach a class in schools as part of the job and I agreed strongly. He started ... in a girls' grammar school ... eventually gave up.

> There were some embarrassing moments – but not many. ... one day we had an open lecture and Harry was in the chair. He introduced the lady speaker, stretched his legs out, lay back and fell asleep. The lady carried on but 20 minutes into her talk we heard gentle snores from Harry. ... I indicated to her to carry on which she did and the snores stopped. After 40 minutes she ended and Harry wakened to the applause, thanked her profusely and immediately asked the most relevant question.[171]

> Harry took an early retirement. ... I think he had had enough of Universities particularly York as it got bigger. ... I urged him not to go to the London comprehensive which he planned. I said, 'Harry they will eat you for breakfast.' He scoffed and pressed on. He lasted a term-and-a-half[172] ... They were exciting but irritating years. He was an enthusiast and leapt in with a wealth of ideas but often he had not worked it through. And that I think was his weakness. ... His great strength is that he never dwelt on

---

170 This would have been her second husband Richard J. Hauser, author of several books of a seemingly spiritual nature.
171 See below for a discussion of the possibility that Harry suffered from narcolepsy. See pages 203–4 for a discussion.
172 Actually, he lasted longer than that.

failure. When it didn't work he went on to some other new idea, and that is a strength we can all learn from him.

With no hard evidence, I am fairly sure that Eric James, who had an uncanny feel for how complex institutions can be made to work, decided that Harry needed someone like Harry Creaser, and then made it happen. It would be hard to argue that he was wrong. In May 1963, Creaser was appointed with an annual salary of £2,330.[173]

Not long after he arrived at York, Harry Rée summarized his approach to the training of teachers. He began by outlining three 'main ways by which students become qualified to teach', and I am amused to note that his piece is accompanied by a picture of Harry with jacket and tie! He also notes that 'Lord James, long before coming to York, was known to be dissatisfied with many aspects of these three methods', which were 'first through a college of education, secondly through a year's post-graduate training, and thirdly through the possession of a degree'. He then went on to describe a course that:

> enables students to study for their three years[174] one main academic subject alongside those who are working for a normal single-subject degree, but devoting a third of their time to subjects connected with education, such as psychology, philosophy and sociology. They emerge with an honours degree in say, Chemistry with Education, or English with Education. This link with other subject departments ensures that the Education Department remains closely woven into the fabric of the university, and that neither we nor our students can ever feel isolated or cut off in a kind of educational hot-house. All students are encouraged to approach education, not only through educational subjects, and not only through frequent visits to schools and contact with teachers, but through a study of literature lasting a whole year.

In a 1963 piece in the American *Saturday Review*, Harry wrote:

> York's programme offers the opportunity for students to major in one subject and to take a related subject at the same time, e.g. English with history; history with politics; mathematics with philosophy. ... Breaking away completely from previous

---

173 Equivalent to £45,000 in 2016.
174 The standard length of a bachelor's degree course in England and Wales.

university practice, York is offering a subsidiary course in education that can be taken alongside any other major subject.

One cannot stress enough how innovative and powerful these ideas continue to be. If you want to learn about London, read Charles Dickens; if you want to learn about South Africa, read Nadine Gordimer; if you want to learn about young people, read Camara Laye and – yes – Edward Blishen. Harry continued:

> ... particularly novels and short stories, such as *Lord of the Flies* and Moravia's *Two Adolescents*. These open up areas of imaginative experience often inaccessible to the student, except through books. This course was originally developed by Mr Edward Blishen, author of *Roaring Boys*.

> The three-year undergraduate course does not give an opportunity for prolonged teaching practice, essential for a teacher who is to be awarded a certificate. This, therefore, is done by students after graduation, when they remain attached to us for a fourth year, the first two terms of which are spent on practice in a school, or possibly in two different schools.

From 1963 to 1965, Harry persuaded his good friend Edward Blishen to come to York from time to time (he lived in the North London borough of Barnet), and, inevitably, Edward put him into more than one of his books. In *Donkey Work*, which came out in 1983, he describes himself as 'lecturer (who never lectured), part-time (very), at the new university of Ribchester'.[175]

Education at York was somewhat similar to Master of Arts in Teaching (MAT) programmes in the United States. And here comes another powerful Harry-innovation:

> Indeed, for those who may want to broaden their experience, one term may be spent attached to a welfare service (for example, in the children's department of a city, or with the Probation Service) ... We do not insist that students eventually teach, and we welcome the small minority who wish to go into social work of one kind or another.

---

175 Ribchester does exist: it is a village about 70 miles west of York.

Another great idea:

> If … the student on practice does decide to stay for two terms in the same school, often the school will be able to release a member of staff for the second term – to attend courses at the university, preparing materials for future teaching, completing a textbook, or catching up on essential reading.

> The final term of the fourth year is spent by students at the university, writing a thesis on a subject which will prove of value to them in their future career.

A copy of the syllabus from the 1960s, cyclostyled on a Gestetner, lists one weekly sociology lecture, one fortnightly novel lecture, a fortnightly seminar, a weekly open lecture, and a fortnightly tutorial with about four students in each group. Harry, the professor and department head, ran eight of the 18 tutorial groups. Each tutee had to write three essays per term. School visits were mandatory. In the second and third terms of their third year, students took what was called an 'assimilation course'. Harry indicated forthrightly that he was 'not satisfied with the present arrangement' of student assessment; nor were the students. The reading list is fascinating if a bit dated, including *Education and the Working Class* by Jackson and Marsden, *The Rise of the Meritocracy* by Michael Young, *The Uses of Literacy* by Richard Hoggart, *The Schools* by Martin Mayer, *The Crowther Report*, *The Comprehensive School* by Robin Pedley, *The Idea of a University* by John Henry Newman, *On Education* by Bertrand Russell, *Summerhill* by A.S. Neill, *Culture and Society* by Raymond Williams, etc. There is little from the United States and nothing from France or Germany. About 45 years after this syllabus was put together, and well over 3,000 miles from York, I heard a professor of education describing his as a 'multidisciplinary applied field': Harry was ahead of his time.

He asked his students to read the preface to George Bernard Shaw's 1909–10 play *Misalliance*, where they would encounter such statements as:

- Nobody knows the way a child should go.
- Hold yourself up as a warning, not as an example.
- There is no difference in principle between the rights of a child and those of an adult.
- There is … nothing on earth intended for innocent people as horrible as a school … It is a prison … more cruel than a prison.
- It is a ghastly business, quite beyond words, this schooling.

- I did not learn anything at school.
- None of my schoolmasters really cared a rap.
- My schooling did me a great deal of harm and no good whatever.
- I offered a handsome prize for the worst-behaved boy and girl on condition that a record should be kept of their subsequent careers and compared with the records of the best-behaved, in order to ascertain whether the school criterion of good conduct was valid out of school.
- What is the matter with our universities is that the students are school children, whereas it is of the very essence of university education that they should be adults.
- If our universities would exclude everybody who had not earned a living by his or her exertions for at least a couple of years, their effect would be vastly improved.
- Most of us live in a condition of quite unnecessary inhibition.

In October 1965, less than four years after Hetty's death, Harry was confronted with a terrible and challenging tragedy. His younger son Brian had finished his first year at Oxford; reading Philosophy, Politics and Economics (PPE) at St Catherine's College. It was the day before the beginning of his second year, and he was cycling from his digs into town. He turned right across a stream of traffic, and his head went through the windscreen of an oncoming car.

Brian lost consciousness for a whole month, much of which Harry spent at his bedside, not knowing whether his son would ever recover consciousness ... or how. He was at the Radcliffe Infirmary and, by immensely good fortune, his surgeon was the renowned Joe Pennybacker.[176]

Pennybacker told Harry that if Brian came out of it, and there were no guarantees, he would have the same basic characteristics as before: cheerfulness, a positive attitude, generosity of spirit, etc. And that is indeed what happened. Happily married to Anna, an American, with a thriving family, Brian now lives in Chatham, New York State. He has few memories from the accident, but he does recall being transported from Oxford to York on a stretcher and being deposited in Harry's living room. And Oxford did give him a degree.

---

176 Joseph Pennybacker (1907–1983) was an American from Somerset, Kentucky; a graduate of the University of Tennessee and the University of Edinburgh Medical School. A distinguished neurosurgeon, he had just returned from a trip to the US and was at home picking apples when he received a call to rush to the hospital. Brian continues to think of him with immense gratitude.

The question of course is: what did this experience do to Harry?

In the University of York archives, one can find a fascinating report entitled *General Remarks of the External Examiner* by Professor B.A. Fletcher of the University of Leeds, 'at the conclusion of a term of three years' and dated July 1968:

> There are two aspects of the course for undergraduates which I disliked at the outset of my work but which I have finally come to value highly. I therefore hope these will be kept on as firm and accepted parts of the course. They are:
>
> a) The first year introduction to the study of Education by a literary approach making use of stimulating works of fiction. I think this has proved to be an unrivalled method of engaging the interest of young students.
>
> b) The use of two terms of teaching practice in the final year of the course. I found the work of these students more than twice as good as those who had only had one term of practice.

Was Fletcher's mind really changed, or was he charmed by Harry?

Harry was named Provost of Derwent College fairly soon after his arrival at York. As Michael Beloff (later to be president of Trinity College, Oxford, and a well-known barrister and judge) reported in his 1968 book entitled *The Plateglass Universities*:

> Provost Rée framed his disciplinary code in the form of a letter to the students, and renamed rules 'reminders'. Thus it was stated: 'Men should be out of women's rooms, and women out of men's rooms by midnight. This regulation will be enforced, very largely, by public opinion. Students who do not feel able to accept its implications should not be in college.'

Beloff calls this gentle; I see it as tough: velvet glove maybe, but determined fist. I am reminded of Watford Grammar School's *School Rules*, which began:

> It cannot be emphasized too strongly that the supreme rule is one of courtesy and consideration for others. Granted this, the rest can be reduced to a minimum.

Caroline Royds was a student at Derwent College:

> He gave us a pastoral address ... and we all giggled because it was so very liberal in tone – he talked about 'jumping into bed'

as if it was possible – even OK! – all the while advocating sense and courtesy and respect for others.

I remember him with great affection as an utterly charming and lovely man.

Nicole Ward Jouve:

Magically or naturally, there was something special about Derwent, a friendly, relaxed, welcoming atmosphere. Somehow it was particularly pleasant to have meals there. Artists' exhibitions were encouraged …

According to Harry's successor, Ian Lister, Derwent College is still a very friendly place, 'with no b.s.'. Although Harry would, from time to time, purport to believe that university teaching was not real teaching, there is plenty of evidence that he understood how to handle traditional-aged undergraduates. Example: Nick Tucker, who taught psychology at York at the same time as Edward Blishen was teaching there, seems to have had some difficulty with a particular class: Harry, in a letter to him, reported on what he called 'my attempt to do some hypodermic therapy with seminar group two':

They all recognized the unsatisfactoriness of the situation, but didn't think it was so unsatisfactory as you do (because they don't *suffer* for the silences, they create them???) They think you are too kind. … They think you are omniscient – 'how *can* we contradict him – he knows the facts – he's the expert.' … They suggested that sometimes you asked such obvious questions they were silent because they couldn't believe you wanted such a simple answer!! (This is a familiar one, isn't it?) … I tried to induce them to show more aggression – even to sit forward rather than back. … It may all have been in vain, but things c'd hardly have been worse, c'd they – and I suspect that with the situation open you may see a big change – let's hope so. Bless you …

I think this tells us far more about Harry's insight and his style than it does about Nick's long-forgotten difficulty with a particular class.

In 1967, the *New Statesman* pontificated:

Headship, like marriage, is usually embarked upon without previous experience or training … courses for engaged headmasters are still rare.

At a time, then, when headship courses were not yet in vogue, Harry convened one at the University of York. In a statement for the attendees, he wrote:

> It has been argued that a school must have an aim, in the same way as a journey must have a destination. ... For a teacher true success ... implies purpose. ... Not only the Head ... must therefore make explicit the AIM of the school. ... But we must not stop there.

> From the aim can be derived the OBJECTIVES. ... From the objectives can be derived the MEANS appropriate to the defined objectives, and from these a determination of the best use of disposable resources – staff, accommodation, etc.[177]

> The teacher or administrator without such a plan in his mind is in danger of making ill-informed or half thought-out decisions, based on hunch, prejudice or habit. ...

> Would you ... send ... *two short pieces of work*. The first will be what you consider to be the general aim of your school, as you yourself conceive it ... not more than 200 words. Secondly, would you write down the objectives which arise ... under headings such as

> (1) Skills to be acquired by pupils
> (2) Personality traits – and attitudes
> (3) Abilities

As I write, every school in the English-speaking world seems to have its pithy mission statement on its website and, framed, on its walls. Again, Harry was ahead of his time. And surprisingly conservative in his approach. Not loose at all. In *The Plateglass Universities*, Beloff wrote:

> As Harry Rée, Professor of Education, said to me, 'Let's be thought of as conservative. Then we can get on with really exciting things.'

In many significant ways, Harry truly was conservative!

His boss, Eric James, as Eric Midwinter (PhD, York) put it in 2012, pretended York was 800 years old and recently discovered! Oxford with a smiling face? The University soon established five colleges; there are now

---

177 I think the reader would have understood his drift, despite the 'disposable' staff.

eight. In 1965, Harry became the first provost of Derwent College, a position he held for almost ten years. He had a simple philosophy that is still quoted: 'Treat everyone as an adult and respect your neighbour'. In the words of the website, 'His approach set a tone for the college and future provosts who have, like Harry, sought to encourage responsibility and respect within the college community.'

Harry always understood that it was the people who counted, the people he recruited and appointed, not so much the curriculum and the syllabi:

> So the people we appointed – I say 'we', because it was Eric James and I really. Eric was enormously interested in the education department at York. And he agreed that we needed to train people to work in comprehensive schools. The people we appointed were all teachers. None had taught in a comprehensive school. They'd all been grammar school teachers. There weren't many about at that time – 1961.[178] They were all practising teachers and teaching practice played a very large part.

According to Toby Weaver, the mandarin who worked at the Ministry of Education from 1946 to 1973, having taught both at a primary school and at Eton, there were only 20 genuinely comprehensive schools in the whole of England and Wales in 1951, the year Harry began at Watford.

Looking ahead to the demise of comprehensive education as Harry envisaged it, the numbers are ironic. Stephen Ball recently wrote:

> Whereas in 1965 a total of 8.5 per cent of the secondary age population was educated in 262 comprehensive schools, between 1966 and 1970 this rose from 12 per cent to 40 per cent, 50 per cent by 1973, 80 per cent by 1977 and 83 per cent by 1981. While in 1960 there were 3,000 grammar schools in England and Wales and 130 comprehensives, by 1990 there were over 3,000 comprehensives and only 150 grammar schools.

I think I can understand why Harry did not recruit anyone from the world of comprehensive schools, but did he try hard enough? Did he, unintentionally, tend to appoint people with experiences similar to his own? Why no one from a secondary modern school, or a primary school? Ian Lister describes Eric James as being in shock when Harry publicly supported the principles of the comprehensive school. (He shouldn't have been. After all, Harry

---

178 I assume he meant comprehensive schools.

famously changed his mind some time before he came to York.) Was Harry perhaps unwittingly constrained by his boss's views?

He went on:

> I managed to persuade Eric James to appoint an old friend of mine to come and run the language teaching centre at York – Eric Hawkins. He and I had been heads together. He had been head (1953–64) at Calday Grange Grammar School, the Wirral.

Patronage again, but it worked. I think Harry would have approved of later efforts to open access for women, members of traditionally underserved groups and others. But one can see how it is easier to create something new if you have known your colleagues for years and feel comfortable with them.

Some of his colleagues saw Harry as a visionary; others found it hard to cope with the constant stream of occasionally contradictory ideas. I always found the contradictions a comfort, feeling confirmed in my growing conviction that it's more than OK to think something and then to change one's mind.

Around 1970, Harry wrote a piece for a book entitled *Dear Lord James* about the education of teachers, 'Prospect: School in the 1980s':

> The teachers have left their platforms; they are working at desks, moving around. ... Everyone comes here: pregnant mothers come to the clinic ... mothers leave their toddlers at the playgroup, while they go to work or attend a class ... Old-age pensioners come to their club. ... There are halls, lounges and libraries, there are seminar rooms, workshops and laboratories, a restaurant and a bar ... a medical room and a gym. ... At weekends there is usually a wedding reception. ... Secondary students are increasingly expected to organize their own time ... they are free to come and go. ... At the beginning of each term all students will have had a private session with their tutors, and agreed the courses they will follow. ... The school day, for teachers, no longer consists of seven or eight 40-minute slots, during which 30 or more children have to be taught. ... Change in teachers' experience has been matched by a change in what is expected of teachers by children, by parents and by society in general. In the days when teaching children was all done in classrooms ... the first necessity ... was the power to dominate and to control the squad. ... The school marm and the martinet have joined the dodo. ... The school has been seen as not a mere work place, visited between nine o'clock

and four by conscripted children and salary-conscious adults, but a living collective.

Peter Renshaw quoted the very last sentence of the book, written by Harry, at the 2014 celebration of the centenary of his birth:

> We need to remind ourselves that education is wedded to the faith that the ideal and the actual can be made one – otherwise we flounder and perish.

Harry, if he had only known it, could have been describing a forward-looking community college with a magnet high school in the United States!

Thirty years earlier, in a book review for *Horizon*, Harry had written:

> Mr Jenkinson's book is a plea for the teachers to come down from their rostrums, to move among the crowd, to recognize the necessity for school stories. ... 'Tadpoles,' he says, 'do not flourish on dry land.' The examination system, the syllabus for School Certificate arranged by the Universities, is largely to blame. 'The don assassinates the schoolboy – at third hand. Murder is a fine art.'

In many ways, Alasdair Brown is the former student that anyone in education would dream of:

> teaching and managing in comprehensive schools, grammar schools, further education colleges, prisons and, latterly, independent sixth form colleges. ... full of incident, variety and challenge and it was Harry who started me off.

Besides, he is a good friend and former colleague of Harry's daughter Janet.

Alasdair was at York from 1964 to 1967:

> I was attracted ... by the buzz that surrounded the education department and intrigued by the personality of the man who led it. I would almost certainly not have thought about teaching as a career if I hadn't ... met Harry Rée.

> When I first noticed that there was a subject called Education at York, I could see how this could be an academic subject. ... Education was just a process ... My mother had taught me how to read. Primary school had got me through the 11-plus. A succession of haggard, bad-tempered men at my repressive, single-sex county grammar school had dictated sufficient notes

to allow me to get through ... And my headmaster had bullied me into submission about my luminous socks and the length of my hair.[179] ...

It was precisely that kind of complacency that Harry ... challenged. It had never occurred to me that the 11-plus was fundamentally unfair, that corporal punishment need not be a fact of school life ... Above all, it was a revelation to me that classrooms should be joyful places. Harry's department at the university was unique because it was the only one that related directly to our own experience.

It was basically Harry the man who was the role model that made me decide that school teaching was something I wanted to do. There were three things ...: his charm, his scruffiness, and his War record. At the age of 19, I did find it quite extraordinary that someone who had been a headmaster could be so warm, friendly and amusing. I had never met such a relaxed authority figure before. ... pleasingly transgressive ... signals which endorsed my resentments at the multitude of pointless restrictions to which I had been subjected at school.

And then there was the really interesting bit. The ultra-casual bohemian intellectual, prone to moments of ludicrous absentmindedness, had been a serious war hero. ... On a semi-conscious level, I think Harry operated for me as a strongly masculine role model who dispelled preconceptions that teaching was a stuffy, safe career option that real men didn't choose.

Any present-day inspector who jumped into a time machine to take a look at Harry's department would be amazed at the absence of nuts and bolts used in the training of teachers. Classroom management? Assessing progress? Written lesson objectives? Differentiation? Bloom's taxonomy? Skills-based learning? Where were they all? How to teach examination techniques? You have to be joking.

The 1988 Education [Reform] Act and the national curriculum that it mandated marked the beginning of the end for those who wanted to teach the Harry Rée way – that is with a measure of

---

179 This was at Newport Grammar School, near Saffron Walden.

originality, creativity and personal autonomy. This Act … tried as hard as it could to bury, once and for all, and for ever and ever, under layers and layers of concrete and stone, the heretical idea that the business of teaching and learning … could actually be fun. … Harry would have been dismayed at how daunting a prospect a teaching career can appear to today's graduates. … If they turned up for work at certain London comprehensive schools dressed like him, they would immediately find themselves in the headmaster's study being issued with a verbal warning. … People like Harry made it seem very cool indeed to be a teacher and in 1967 it was considered far more glamorous and exciting to work in a comprehensive school than as a mercenary purveyor of false consciousness in advertising, film or television.

Alasdair Brown mentioned scruffiness; others might have seen Harry as saving money and simply caring about other things. Similarly his dislike of wearing ties, like F.R. Leavis.

Beverley Naidoo, the noted writer from South Africa, now living in Bournemouth, is one of many, many individuals for whom Harry made a huge difference. She must have made an instant impact: there is a letter in the University of York archives from November 1964, from Harry to Eric:

Got a long letter from Robert Birley about a young lady who is being persecuted in South Africa. She told me how she was 'detained'.

This was a horrifically South African term, now part of history: she was detained in 1964 for 60 days. Her parents, understandably and rightly, wanted her out of the country. They took her to meet Sir Robert Birley, former headmaster of Eton College, who was a visiting professor at the University of the Witwatersrand, Johannesburg, from 1964 to 1967. Birley helped her and, later, her brother Paul, who was sentenced to two years imprisonment, with his contacts back in England, and she ended up with two choices: Lady Margaret Hall, Oxford, or the then-new University of York. LMH sent her a set of entrance examination papers in a sealed envelope; Harry wrote what she called an 'absolutely seminal letter' in which, among other things, he recommended that she read Camara Laye from Dakar (1928–1980), author of *The African Child*, and, of course, Edward Blishen. Guess where she went? Later, he would arrange her teaching practice at Crown Woods School, where Michael Marland was the head of the English Department.[180]

---

180 Marland was later to be Harry's headmaster at Woodberry Down School.

Harry, Beverley Naidoo went on, changed her view of education. She realized that she had been schooled, not educated, and she internalized the difference. Teaching, she learned, is, at least in part, about culture and class. She remembers the sea of desks meeting Blishen in *Roaring Boys*.

Beverley, who obtained her PhD at the University of Southampton in 1991, was, she said, shy during her time at York. But Harry made a 'huge, huge, huge, huge impression on me.' He was interested, vibrant, passionate, interested in real arguments. People like Harry, she says, are hard to find now. He had no affectation, and the intellect mattered. She sees Robert Birley and Harry Rée as essentially similar, always seeking responses, enjoying debates with no barriers, intellectually engaged, with a passion for justice. Today, on the other hand, she sees a lack of courage along with 'creeping privatization'.

Having experienced apartheid in South Africa first-hand, Beverley understands how Harry's wartime experiences may have influenced him. As she put it to me, 'he learned to contain himself'. She felt he understood her and her own reserve. More than occasional reserve is a way of coping.

It was during the York years that Harry married Peta Garrett, a marriage that did not end until his death, but which faded out. Peta, who still lives in York, did not share Harry's enthusiasm for Colt Park. Beneath all the bonhomie, Harry may have been lonely. Nicole Ward Jouve used the phrase 'lone wolf'. He reported the marriage to friends with unusual hesitancy, for example:

> I guess you'll approve of Peta – she's a-political and unconnected with education, shy and quiet with views about colours and shapes.[181] Tall, divorced with two very nice daughters (10 and 12) uneducated and cultivated and kind – sounds all right?

As has been mentioned above, Harry came across as fearless, a quality that many saw in him. Former Watford head boy Stuart Field told me, 'Harry was not bothered by the consequences of his actions; he was fearless.' He would take the risk of arriving late for the train, and he drove too fast. He was passionate about Europe and camping in France; didn't talk much about places outside Western Europe. He was very much a European, and you would never have known that, like both Winston Churchill and Harold Macmillan, he was half-American.

---

181 Her first husband had been an architect.

Beverley Naidoo made reference to Birley and Harry in a 2010 letter to the editor of *The Guardian* headed 'Library cuts hasten UK's cultural decline':

> Both understood the vital importance of reading and critical thought to the process of democracy. I came to understand this through the books they suggested I read, not for study but for interest and enlightenment. Coming from a society that placed little value on libraries and critical thinking, this made an impact on me. Cameron, Clegg and Gove have had all the benefit of their independent school libraries and professionally trained librarians. Now they are pulling up the ladder ...

Another student from the early days in York was Jeremy Cunningham, who retired in 2005 after 18 years heading two Oxfordshire schools and then went on to the Open University. He writes:

> I had a baptism of fire in the east end of London, in such a difficult school that paradoxically I was determined to make a career in teaching. ... I regarded myself as fairly radical and progressive ... there was an incredible atmosphere of optimism and determination. Harry came across as warm-hearted, urbane and modest. ... Like many charismatic people he had the knack of making one feel valued, and my confidence was increased by his supportive approach. ... teaching practice at Countesthorpe College, unquestionably the most radical and progressive state school in England.[182] ... After a few years in Japan, I returned to the comprehensive system, and joined Stantonbury Campus in the new town of Milton Keynes. ... One of the exciting developments there was the linking of community memory and history, with school drama, in the creation of documentary theatre, acted by all generations. This was absolutely in line with the approach to education fostered by Harry.
>
> After I was appointed to a headship ... Harry ... reminded me that education is not a Gradgrind affair, but a process of humanization. The most important task of a headteacher was to maintain the balance of individual and community needs; to listen to others and to keep the broadest possible view. For this there was one requirement only: 'Read widely'. I took this

---

182 Six miles from the centre of Leicester.

advice seriously, and I believe it made me a better head than I would otherwise have been. I learnt from his humility and lack of bombast, and his example kept me focusing on the real values in education.

Blair's 'Education, education, education' notoriously evaded the question 'for what?' The answer seemed to be reduced to 'competing with China and India'. The relentless pursuit of ever narrower target ranges during the late 1990s, with increased marketization of the state system attacked the tradition of a broad liberal and community education. It would have been good to have had Harry defending it.

Charles Swallow is both nephew and godson; son of Harry's older sister Irene, who outlived him by a year or so. On at least one occasion Harry, who was very fond of him, would refer to 'all the shy self-confidence of the public school boy' after decrying the public school boys, as a class, as being 'bloody secure behind their accents'. Charles writes:

> Harry had a profound influence on my career, and that of our son Mark, who is currently teaching in an Academy in a poor part of Bristol. Like Harry, I was privately educated. I taught history at Harrow from 1961–73. During that time Harry was becoming more and more active in promoting the comprehensive cause, particularly following Tony Crosland's circular of 1965 in which he ordered all LEAs[183] to make the State schools comprehensive. … a year's exchange in the USA. Over lunch with Harry in 1972 … he said why not try the State sector. I asked him where was the most revolutionary comprehensive in England. He said it was at Bicester. 1973 was the year that the school leaving age was raised from 15 to 16. I spent three rather turbulent years at Bicester wrestling with co-education, mixed ability classes, child-centred learning and an antipathy towards competition. … I agreed with Harry that to divide children into sheep and goats at the tender age of 11, on the basis of a rather spurious exam, was not only unreasonable but even more socially divisive than the chasm that existed between state and private. … In 1976 I was appointed … HM of Mount Grace (Comprehensive) School in Potters Bar. … The school was in the doldrums and I had been appointed

---

183 Local Education Authorities.

to clear it up. ... [After nine years] I resigned ... and bought an indoor tennis club in London (The Vanderbilt) which, together with my wife, I ran for the next 19 years.

Harry's view of my slightly unconventional career pattern was mixed. Unlike him ... I had remained politically a conservative and we sent our two children to Independent schools. I always felt, therefore, that Harry believed that I was only a partial convert to the state system.

I was saddened by the fact that the comprehensive ideal had become progressively identified with the Labour Party. ... It was a Conservative Minister of Education, Edward Boyle, who presided over the introduction of the first comprehensive schools in 1952. It was only after Crosland's rushed and ill-thought-out edict of 1965 that so many disastrous comprehensives were created. ... I think Harry perhaps felt I was the rat leaving the sinking ship!

When he was Professor of Education at York, Harry rushed around the country arguing that because there were a few conspicuous and inspirational Heads of State Schools all that was needed was for more to follow their example. The question remains – can you base a system on that principle?

... There are still 168 grammar schools left and all of them heavily oversubscribed and currently sending a disproportionate number of their pupils to Oxford and Cambridge. Harry would not have liked that.

A former colleague at York, Peter Hollindale, writes:

He was not a very hands-on Head of Department, and largely left people to do their own thing. ... As a professor he combined fresh ideas, impulsiveness, zest, and boredom, but he never ... regarded university teaching as real teaching. I did.

Chapter 11

Manifold causes

After he left Watford, that is, during the last 30 years or so of his life, Harry took on innumerable causes; maybe too many. In a 1965 talk, where he spoke, ambivalently and reluctantly, about his experiences in the War, he had said:

> I am a butterfly, I love dashing about from one place to another, from one idea to another for that matter, so the sort of thing I was doing in France suited me marvelously. I like people when I meet them, nearly everybody; I like the French.

This 1965 short paragraph is one of the very few instances where one can clearly see that the Harry Rée from, say, 1951 until 1991 were indeed the same person.

In a letter, he wrote, 'I'm obviously going through a pregnant phase – I've had another idea!'[184]

I have counted at least nine, most of them with ungainly acronyms: Agreement to Broaden the Curriculum (ABC), the Society of Teachers Opposed to Physical Punishment (STOPP), the Society for the Abolition of School Speech Days (SASSD), the Programme for Reform in Secondary Education (PRISE), the Society for the Promotion of Educational Reform Through Teacher Training (SPERTTT), Towards a New Education Act (TANEA) and the Voluntary Euthanasia Society (VES). STOPP, PRISE and SPERTTT, one could say, succeeded, at least to some degree, although one may ask whether corporal punishment would have vanished from the scene with or without STOPP's efforts. On the other hand, SASSD and TANEA were flops. There is no question that were Harry alive today, he would be a leading light in the New Visions for Education group, which includes Sir Tim Brighouse, Fred Jarvis, Margaret Maden, Peter Mortimore, Sir Peter Newsam, Tom Schuller, Margaret Tulloch and Geoff Whitty.

As Ian Lister described it, 'First there would be agonies about the acronym and then the duplicated broadsheets and meetings would follow.'

---

184 He was not alone. In her splendid biography of Barbara Wootton (1897–1988), *A Critical Woman*, Ann Oakley writes: 'It was a habit of the time to sign letters with one's friends; to invent and join campaigns; to name and re-name movements.'

He would go on what he described as 'missionary journeys', i.e. innumerable conferences, almost all of them in England.

Despite frequent visits to France and Germany, Scotland and Wales seemed to be outside his purview. Following Tim Brighouse's lead, I'd like to ask him why, in the riots of 6 to 11 August 2011, Edinburgh, Glasgow, Cardiff and Swansea were quiet. In an email, Brighouse confirms that Harry 'was very anglocentric'.

In the early 1960s, he was one of the 360 heads of secondary schools who signed the Agreement to Broaden the Curriculum (ABC). They agreed to insist on at least 25 per cent of the sixth form timetable being devoted to non-'A' level, i.e. non-specialist studies. Sadly, in the words of Denis Lawton,[185] 'The ABC faded away after a few years of good intentions.'[186]

As one might have expected, Harry was involved in the Schools Council, and more aware of the need for publicity and public relations than most. In his book, *The Life and Death of the Schools Council* (1985), Maurice Plaskow wrote:

> I remember Harry Rée suggesting in committee that, if the Council had confidence in its work it should promote it. It was as though he had uttered an obscene heresy. Foreign visitors could never understand the quaint English perversity in setting up a national agency, supported by the whole of the education service, which pretended that its curriculum offerings, painstakingly developed and carefully piloted by teachers, had no greater authority or credence than any textbook.

He was in on the ground floor when Gene Adams, a London teacher, founded the Society of Teachers Opposed to Physical Punishment (STOPP) in 1968, a year after the Plowden Report had come out against corporal punishment. In 1966, Dame Margaret Miles had written:

> There can be no modern educationist who accepts corporal punishment as a suitable means of correction in schools.[187]

About a quarter of a century before, Cyril Norwood, author of the Norwood Report, had been saying that:

---

185 Director of the Institute of Education, University of London, 1983–9.
186 ABC was outlined in the *Times Educational Supplement* of 27 January 1961, and is still worth looking at.
187 Miles, M. (1966) *... And Gladly Teach: The adventure of teaching*. Reading: Educational Explorers.

Masters must not on any account strike boys on the head, although he suggested that 'with little boys it is often judicious to give them a good shake'.

Barbara Wootton, by then Baroness Wootton of Abinger, introduced a bill into the House of Lords in 1973 that would have made corporal punishment illegal, but it did not achieve a second reading.

And yet, looking back, it is amazing how fast England moved from a culture where even pupils – prefects – in the most prestigious schools could administer corporal punishment, to the present, where the law of the land would put even a head teacher in jail for laying a hand on a child. By 1987, corporal punishment was abolished in state schools, by law; and 11 years later it was wholly abolished in the private sector.[188] STOPP, which never had more than 1,000 members, was wound up in 1986; its papers are deposited at the Institute of Education.

Colin Farrell has run a website since 1996 entitled *World Corporal Punishment Research*;[189] it now has over 3,200 pages. I asked him about the sheer speed with which the culture in the UK had changed. While warning me that 'there is still very far from being a consensus against CP across the public at large', he wrote:

> It was indeed a remarkably fast cultural change, but there have also been others – on racial sensitivities for instance, and perhaps most astonishingly the very rapid and profound shift in attitudes to smoking.

He went on to say that his 'own hunch is that at least three forces contributed to this':

(a) Left-wing activism infiltrating the National Union of Teachers (NUT) and the Labour Party in the 1970s
(b) The arrival of feminism, bringing about a world in which women have far more power and influence than they used to – CP was always, in my view, mainly a 'guy thing', which most women didn't understand
(c) Europe

Still puzzled by the sheer speed of the cultural change, I wrote to Tony Little, headmaster of Eton since 2002, who replied:

---

188 The actual House of Commons vote took place on 22 July 1986. 231 voted for the abolition; 230 did not. The Duke of York and Sarah Ferguson were married that day, and 12 MPs were supposedly stuck in traffic. How might they have voted?
189 www.corpun.com

I do not believe there are any formal dates when corporal punishment ceased at Eton. In a rather typically English way, the practice simply died out. I was a student myself at Eton in the late 1960s/early 1970s and beating was very rare then. Indeed, I cannot recall an actual case of a boy being beaten. Certainly the practice of older boys beating younger boys would have died out in the 1970s and, I suspect, caning ceased being used at all, even by the Head Master, by around 1980.

I am of a generation of teachers for whom the business of corporal punishment seems very strange indeed.

That last sentence is telling. It would have made Harry very happy.

Tim Card writes that beating was formally stopped in 1971. In his book *Eton Renewed: A history from 1860 to the present day* (1994), he discusses Anthony Chenevix-Trench[190] fairly forthrightly. Chenevix-Trench used the cane with great frequency, and Card records him as once remarking: 'A good thing the NSPCC do not know anything ...'. Amazingly, Chenevix-Trench was subsequently appointed to another headship, Fettes College in Edinburgh, in 1971. How times have changed!

Even though ... perhaps because ... he had been invited to innumerable speech days, all over England, Harry expressed boredom with them. So in 1965 he announced the creation of SASSD, the Society for the Abolition of School Speech Days. I don't think too many schools have given them up, even though Ian Lister would write:

He was in high demand as a speaker – his 'abolish school speech days' talk, which he gave at school speech days, was a favourite.

Six years earlier, the *Watford Observer* had editorialized:

Beaten at birth!

Parents who resign themselves annually to the platitudes and hard seats of schools' speech days will find much that is refreshing about the observations of Mr H.A. Rée ... Mr Rée warned of the dangers of self-satisfaction and complacency, and urged that young people be encouraged to seek wider experience and to meet people and situations beyond the confines of Watford High Street. ...

---

190 Headmaster from 1963 until he was asked to leave six years later.

The idea is good; it could be well received. But what steps will be taken to bring about such a scheme? Our guess is that it is beaten at birth – by COMPLACENCY!

The 1944 Education Act (often referred to as the Butler Act, after R.A. Butler) required compulsory daily prayer, 'a single act of worship', at all state-funded schools. There was a conscience clause, so that Jews and others could, at their parents' request, cool their heels outside, as I remember doing, but the intent of the law was that 'all pupils' should attend. In a 1964 letter to the *Times Educational Supplement*, Harry quoted at length from a piece a 'sincere and sensitive student' had written about the shallowness of 'Morning Assembly', with awkward hymns, no one saying 'Amen', the march of the prefects and meaningless announcements. He posed the dilemma of a candidate for a headship: 'What would his chances be today if he told the appointing committee that he would not take compulsory assembly?'[191]

In a set piece about seven months later, entitled 'Opium of the children; School assembly today', Harry raised several objections to the 20-year-old law, from the presumption that everyone is a Christian to the predicament of someone applying for a headship who might not be a believer. David Waddington tells a delightful story of Harry summing up after a week-long head teachers' seminar at the University of York and being quite dogmatic on the matter of daily assemblies. A young man rose to speak about how it was possible to make these affairs positive events that build community: he had seen it done – at Watford Grammar School (!) – which he had attended when Harry was its headmaster.

Norman Marrow, a Quaker, wrote:

From the very start he made his mark on school prayers (which hitherto had been very stereotyped, Bible and C of E prayer-book based). He spent a great deal of time and thought in planning a daily assembly at which the reading could be from a variety of sources ... At the same time he never claimed to be a devout Christian believer and, as time went on, he seemed to find it harder to continue in good conscience presiding at prayers. ... He invited five or six of his colleagues, including me, to share

---

191 Incidentally, in the Foreword of a 1969 book, i.e. a quarter of a century after the Butler Act, Lord Butler wrote: 'I have little doubt that the present Administration will try to find time to legislate on education, even though the 1944 Act has made everything possible that really needs doing at the present time.'

the work with him, making ourselves responsible for a week at a time.[192]

'What a bloody nuisance this Christianity is', I recall Harry saying, though I can't remember the context. John Law recalls Harry's matter-of-fact but 'utterly striking' reading of T.S. Eliot's *Journey of the Magi.*

Peter Wiles recalls Harry talking about CND, the Campaign for Nuclear Disarmament, in Assembly: how many school heads would have done that?

Many years later, George Walker, former head boy, told me:

Assembly was serious. Prefects would line up; the head boy would knock on Harry's door; noises of toilet flushing; and HAR would emerge. Once, he began Assembly in French and went on for several sentences.

This was confirmed by Bill Bailey.

The offending clause was amended (i.e. softened) in 1988 and finally repealed in 1996.

John Langton tells a tale from Harry's York days:

Harry was invited to be the chief after-dinner speaker at the annual banquet in York Art Gallery. He followed a visitor from the National Gallery of Wales whose little speech turned out to be an account of his meeting a one-time brother officer in the Cavalry in the desert during the Second World War. This was told in rather sentimental tones, revealing a certain gentlemanliness. When it came to Harry's turn, his speech was brief and given in cutting tones. He said he had never heard worse nonsense. He reminded his audience that he had set up an organization for the riddance of School Assemblies and he had now decided to set up a similar organization for the riddance of after-dinner speeches. He sat down to a stony silence.

In the early 1970s, rarely missing an opportunity to encourage something radical with like-minded people, Harry became a patron of what was to become the White Lion School, close to the Angel, Islington. He joined A.H. Halsey, Maurice Kogan, Royston Lambert, Ian Lister, A.S. Neill, Lady Plowden and Michael (later Lord) Young in 'giving the project a prestigious image and helping with early fund-raising efforts'.

---

192 Marrow, N. (2012) *Avi epistula: A grandfather's letter.* Online: *sine nomine.*

In 1975, Harry was one of the founders of PRISE (Programme for Reform in Secondary Education), which promulgated a Comprehensive School Charter. Among PRISE's beliefs were the following:

- Children want to learn
- Schools are there to help all children learn
- Children learn best when expectations are high; they play an active part in their own learning; they work co-operatively; parents are actively involved; their own culture and experience are valued
- We want schools which serve all children in the neighbourhood; are co-educational communities; are democratically run; actively promote the initiative of pupils and teachers; avoid fixing ability labels.

Eric Midwinter was to write:

> It is strange how the sexes mix freely in most primary schools and thereafter in colleges or places of employment but are, in between times, still segregated for the secondary years in many schools.[193]

Ian Lister, in a conversation in 2012, was to describe how unusually supportive the University of York, whose founding vice-chancellor's sole experience, after all, had been in boys' schools, was of the interests of women. 'Able middle-class women were the beneficiaries,' he said.

Philip Venning, who wrote for the *Times Educational Supplement* from 1970 to 1981, reported that 'PRISE slid rather awkwardly down the launching ramp ... with chains pulling in a variety of directions.' In addition to Harry, founding members included Caroline Benn, Gabriel Chanan, Maurice Kogan, Margaret Maden, Maurice Plaskow, and George and Zoe Varnava. Meetings were first held in Tony Benn's office at the House of Commons; later at the Camden Westminster Teachers' Centre where Zoe Varnava (then Zoe Image) was Deputy Warden. Margaret Maden wrote:

> PRISE was set up ... mainly as a vehicle for Harry's beliefs in the values enshrined in schools like Countesthorpe, Leicestershire ... It was also a kind of riposte to the Black Papers.[194]

Harry especially admired the 'lack of any fear or false respect' that he found at Countesthorpe.

PRISE would wind up in 1994, and its papers are at the Institute of Education. George Varnava, its chairman, writes that 'Years after PRISE

---

193 Eric Midwinter (1973) *Patterns of Community Education*. London: Ward Lock.
194 The primary goal of the so-called 'Black Papers' (beginning 1969) was to attack the Labour Party's promotion of comprehensive schools over grammar schools.

closed, there were attempts to revive the pressure under the name of REPRISE, but it didn't happen.' He continues:

> Harry was a most unassuming man, highly respected for his intellectual insight and a most significant contributor to the national education debate.

Then there was SPERTTT – a regrettable acronym, according to one Martyn Berry – the Society for the Promotion of Educational Reform Through Teacher Training. Maden writes:

> Harry liked to set up leftish, liberal campaigns and wanted them to have impact, be sociable, then wrap up. SPERTTT was established following a seminar at Bristol University in 1969.

Peter Renshaw retired in 2001 after almost two decades with the Guildhall School of Music and Drama in London.[195] He writes:

> SPERTTT grew out of a Colston Symposium on 'The Reform of Teacher Education' organized by Bill Taylor in Bristol. Several of us found it insufficiently radical and we got together in London to agree a plan of action. Initially the core group included Harry (who acted as Chair), Eric Robinson, Margaret Maden, Virginia Makins, Danny McDowell and later Tyrrell Burgess. There were no formal officers. ... Several of us organized local meetings of college/university lecturers, school teachers, local education authority administrators and students. ... The results of these sessions fed back into at least two national meetings. ... 1969/70 was the most active period and some of the thinking was fed into the book *Dear Lord James*, which was edited by Tyrrell Burgess. ... By the time the *James Report* came out, it was felt that SPERTTT had come to the end of its short life!

Harry must have seen the end coming when he wrote to Margaret Maden, 'SPERTTT could now metamorphose itself into a great pressure group for Paul Goodmanizing the schools'.

The Colston Symposium and what followed may not have been radical, but it provided something on which to build. In one of the speeches, Professor Roger Wilson of the University of Bristol, said:

---

195 He had been Principal of the Yehudi Menuhin School 1975–84.

Down through history the role of the teacher has been interpreted with reference to the lines to be learnt rather than by relationships to be established.

Renshaw's overview is helpful:

Harry Rée was an inspiring, romantic, visionary educationalist who ... was a maverick within the system. He firmly believed that education could transform the quality of young people's lives and that schools should be a vibrant hub within their own communities. ... practical idealism. In many ways Harry was unique. How many professors of education would return to the classroom to teach? ... He was a charismatic, idiosyncratic leader who always displayed courage if he felt something needed to be done. ... He was a person of action underpinned by values. ... He had little time for vacuous rhetoric. ... For him 'sacred cows' were anathema.

I found a delightful piece by Sydney Foxcroft, who was a Newcastle-based stringer for *The People*, a Sunday tabloid; it was entitled 'Is he just a mad professor?'

Hundreds of thousands of school-children will soon be hailing a new hero. ... What will bring him classroom acclaim in 1971 is a campaign he has just started – to give all 13-year-olds the option of dropping any school subject they dislike, *or dropping out of school entirely if they feel it is doing them no good.*

Harry proposed establishing community centres that teenagers could attend voluntarily. Foxcroft enjoyed reporting that most of Harry's colleagues thought his was a crazy dream. Sir Alec Clegg, Director of Education for the West Riding of Yorkshire 1945–74 and, in his day, one of England's most respected and forward-looking educators, argued for raising the school leaving age, while Henry Clother, head of public relations for the National Union of Teachers, argued that 'they are not going to have essential skilled jobs unless they stay on to the full school-leaving age.' 'The mad professor' was certainly throwing down a challenge to the educational community. And one could argue that Harry got at least half of what he wanted: today, many comprehensive schools and so-called community colleges look like the community centres he was advocating.

Then there was TANEA (Towards a New Education Act), which Harry did not live long enough to see fail. Tim Brighouse writes:

We argued passionately and persuasively that from 1940 until the 1980s all were clear about their respective roles ... and that this balance of power had been disturbed and lost in the earlier education acts of the 1980s and especially the 1988 Act. Harry gave his time unstintingly to chivvy people and organizations along. ... It is fair to say that TANEA took up a considerable amount of Harry's time and energies in what were to be his last three years of life.

As mentioned above, Harry had an interest since his acting days in Cambridge in how one approaches one's own death; doubtless influenced by what he had seen during the War and by the searing experience of Hetty's death. He seemed totally unafraid of death and had made preparations for his own ... if necessary. He said to Judith Hemming:

I've never known a moment's insecurity in my life.

This is hard to believe. He did not like the idea of growing old, mentioning this in conversation and in letters. In 1988, when Francis Cammaerts needed a hip operation and the doctors suggested postponement because of his 'dicky heart', Harry came across to me as scathing and somewhat cold:

Francis should have the operation, and if he doesn't come through, too bad! ... I'm sure I'd do my darndest to persuade a surgeon to have a go at the hip, and if I died under the operator, then, so what?

As early as 1978, when he was in his early sixties, he said, in a letter to John Collins, 'My life is drawing peacefully to a close. I have had a heart attack, but that's by the way.' 'I'm reaching the awkward age,' he wrote to Margaret Maden.

He served on the Board of the Voluntary Euthanasia Society (VES) and one year he delivered the keynote address to the annual general meeting at the House of Lords. As he put it in a letter to Margaret Maden:

We ought *all* to be able to go out like Auden – when and how we want – and 'on the Health'. ... We *must* change the attitude to euthanasia.

In a 1973 speech to the VES, he said:

There's a story about the Abbott of Downside School interviewing a couple of parents. The mother leant forward at one point and looking at him earnestly said, 'Father, what would you say exactly

that your school is educating the boys for?' 'Death', replied the
holy man.

Early in that same speech, Harry demonstrated his understanding of the
media and of how change happens:

> From experience I know that a school-based campaign is *not* the
> way to get changes in society. Teachers talking on sweets, sex or
> smoking do not make an impact when they are up against the
> press and television. ... Our message ... must end up by being
> carried by the media. And we must remember that it is the first
> step that matters.

He pointed out – and I think this is still true, about 40 years later – that
'people under 30 have rarely seen a dying person'. And he discussed three
forms of euthanasia: what he called passive euthanasia; 'positive action by
doctors to end a dying and suffering life'; and:

> I should like to put forward a third form of euthanasia which, I
> suspect, only a minority of members here would want to press
> for. This would make a reality of the right of adult individuals to
> decide when and how they die.

Rather than 'assisted suicide', he said, this should be called 'Socratic death'.
He described W.H. Auden's death in the Hotel Altenburgerhof in Vienna's
Walfischgasse only a month before his talk:

> After an evening when he had given much pleasure. He had a
> glass of whisky, went to sleep and never woke up. I know this
> was not suicide. What I am asking for is this sort of end to be
> available on demand ....

> Now I am well aware that to ask anybody to reproduce the
> public character of Socrates' death, where the principal actor is
> surrounded by his stoic friends, is perhaps asking too much. But
> the moral support and the sympathetic understanding of friends
> would surely be needed and Socrates himself seemed to need it.

In 1991, Gillian Tindall wrote Harry's obituary for the VES *Newsletter*:

> ... It was exactly the end for which he had hoped. He had been
> on medication for years for a heart condition about which he was
> almost smug, reckoning that this was going to be his escape route
> as and when he felt himself getting decrepit ... Death, which had

come within a finger's width of claiming him in 1943, and which took his wife with cancer while their three children were still in their teens, held no more fear for him; he was merely anxious not to be a nuisance …

Another story of recent years derives from … when he was staying at the house of French friends. After a convivial evening he retired to bed, then woke in the night with bad pains in his chest. Thinking 'This is IT' he took some of his pills, but also placed a notice outside the door politely warning his hosts that they might find him dead. Then, feeling that he'd done what he could to spare them undue shock, he relaxed – and fell asleep again. He woke in the morning, painless and much refreshed, to find the house in an uproar. The message had been interpreted as a suicide note. 'When I appeared', said Harry, 'they were at first relieved. Then quite cross with me.'

Harry was on the Board of the VES for some years.[196]

Interestingly, Harry and Gillian Tindall first met as a result of a novel she had published, not because of their mutual interest in euthanasia. In 1979, Tindall published *The Intruder*, which tells of a young British woman isolated in a small French village by the outbreak of the Second World War. Tindall writes in an email:

He had heard that I was in the same conference hall as he was and asked someone to introduce us. He came bouncing down from the platform, shook hands, congratulated me on *The Intruder*, and then said, 'But you're much younger than I thought you'd be!' He had assumed, I think, that the novel was autobiographical, whereas of course it is entirely imagined. But I was pleased with his reaction because it indicated to me that what I had imagined felt right and authentic to someone who had actually been in occupied France.[197]

Harry did like to write, and he wrote with ease. In 1962 and 1964, he composed two pieces for *Punch* entitled 'Which school, state or private?' and 'Class and distinction: Schoolsnobbery'.

In the first piece, Harry light-heartedly painted a picture of parents coming to take a look at his school:

---

196 Its name was changed to Dignity in Dying in 2005.
197 Gillian Tindall would have been barely seven years old at the end of the War.

'Of course we *had* hoped to send him to Gigglesbury, Headmaster; good school in my day, but with three children already ...' Mother chips in here and tries to right the boat: 'I don't like the idea of them going away quite so early, do you? And then with a good school like yours, just on our doorstep as it were, it seemed silly not to come and see you. I hope you don't mind.'

Harry listed the parents' questions and suggested his responses as they traipsed through the school; clearly he hoped that some of his readers would recognize themselves, their anxieties and their foibles. At one point, they

stop outside the CCF[198] hut and a couple of masters emerge, one impeccably RAF and the other shabbily Army.

Fifty years on, I can tell which masters he was thinking of (Lister or Topsfield, and Denis King); he must have had fun writing that. He talked about recruiting staff:

Often good ones leave industry to come teaching because it may not be so lucrative but is certainly more rewarding.

Harry ended the *Punch* article with a vignette worth pondering:

'Wouldn't you like to go to Watford Grammar School, darling?'
'Yes, *rather*, Mum ... at least, I think I would.'

'What don't you like about it, dear?'

Pause. Then words which surely condemn us all.

'It doesn't *sound* as good as Gigglesbury, does it, Dad?'

From 'Schoolsnobbery':

'When you prepare the envelopes for the 11-plus results, Beaglehole, you address the fathers of those who have passed as Esq.; plain Mr is used for the failures.'

Harry wrote wittily about boarding schools, especially for boys; Latin; uniforms; putting the kid down for a prestigious public school shortly after birth; replicating fathers' school experiences.

The trappings not only serve as life-lines, they serve as cloaks for educational nakedness and something to give warmth to inner

---

198 Combined Cadet Force; created in 1948.

insecurity. From these remote places come boys who insist sadly on saying: 'When I was at my public school.'

Another delightful vignette: Thelma Emmans writes:

> Not long before Harry went off to Woodberry Down he stopped me one afternoon in Heslington Village and asked me to give him an on-the-spot tutorial on how to teach French to less able pupils. At the time I was Head of Languages at Fulford School.[199] He used to come to Fulford to do some teaching but was not popular with the language staff because he frequently didn't turn up.

> By sheer chance a very old friend of mine was teaching at Woodberry Down when Harry was there. … I quote:

>> In spite of the fact that he had reached such dizzy heights he was a very unassuming colleague and never tried to pull rank. … it was an achievement on his part that he did not try to make his presence felt.

In 1977, when he was headquartered at Woodbury Down School, Harry wrote a piece for the *Times Educational Supplement* entitled 'A job for saints or superpersons …' in which he ruminated on the difficulty of being the head of a comprehensive school:

> Only a few schools have been able to develop a collective identity. … In the 'good old days' the head could embody the aims of the school. … each school was a cohesive, a convergent institution.

He made the point that staffs of comprehensive schools came from a variety of backgrounds and probably agreed on little. Thus 'the task of headship … can successfully be filled only by saints or superpersons'. He blamed the difficulties he saw on tensions within the staff room rather than on the incredible differences to be found between children and between parents … which he had been arguing elsewhere were exactly what made comprehensive schools so much more desirable than schools where one person thought or looked like another.

He quoted Ursula Brangwen's experience in D.H. Lawrence's *The Rainbow* (1915), teaching at Brinsley Street School in Ilkeston, where the headmaster was the thoroughly nasty Mr Harby. He must have assumed that his readers would be familiar with the book. As Harry made the point

---

199 A York comprehensive.

that the grammar and the secondary modern school cultures were meeting but not yet merging in the staff rooms, he deplored the trend towards management rather than colleagueship. One cannot help agreeing with him, but I query whether that trend, which has continued ridiculously in the years since his death, has much to do with whether schools are selective or not. He said, and he said it well:

> The head as manager has all too often replaced the head as colleague or partner. No question now of *primus inter pares*. A managerial hierarchy has been established, and a worker/boss, a we/they relationship has emerged between the 'teachers' and the 'hierarchy'. ... This situation need not last. Given time and retirement this difficult period should be short lived.

I hear the voice of the same author of *The Essential Grammar School* who argued that heads of schools should not have the authority to dismiss for incompetence.

A decade or so after he moved to York, Harry took some time out – he never really took time off – and returned to his old Cambridge college, St John's, to write about his hero, mentor and first employer, Henry Morris. Morris had died in 1961, in his early seventies, so Harry must have been thinking about writing while the memory was fresh. *Educator Extraordinary* was, to some extent, a labour of love; as Harry put it to me in a letter in April 1974, 'It's a meagre instalment on a debt I won't ever repay'.

Twenty-five years after Harry's book came out, in 1998, Tony Jeffs wrote a slim volume entitled *Henry Morris: Village colleges, community education and the ideal order*. While he describes Harry as Morris's 'principal biographer', he writes:

> Regretfully this is an exaggerated account of his contribution. Morris did not invent the community school, community education or lifelong education as many besides Rée have suggested. These, like many equally extravagant claims made on his behalf, are misleading.

Strangely, his book is an admiring tome that adds little.

Ian Martin would describe Harry as 'benign, patrician and very English (a bit like his hero Henry Morris).' Similarly, Nick Tucker wrote, 'He could ... be quite patrician in his attitudes.' Nicole Ward Jouve put it this way:

Harry was a patrician, of the chivalrous kind ... a kind of easy informal elegance with tweed jacket and open collar shirt, perfect manners which enabled him to remain aloof when he did not want to know or get involved.

Her husband Tony (Wilfrid Anthony) Ward, one of the founding members of the English Department at York, novelist and playwright, author of *Jenny's First Class Journey* and other tales, told Harry at the time that the book told him more about him (Harry) than about Henry Morris. The book's last paragraph does tell it all, when Harry enunciated:

two lessons which he ceaselessly taught, and which seemingly we still need to learn. First, he insisted in the need of [*sic*] all administrators, executives, decision takers, to base their action, not on efficiency (this, as he said, is attained by ants and bees), but on a philosophy which reminds them constantly what life here is for. Secondly he showed ... that the most maverick individual can work within the system, can bend it to constructive ends, and can yet retain humanity, integrity, and sensitivity.

Harry was to tell Margaret Maden that his whole philosophy was contained in that paragraph.

John Holloway, who had been a student of Harry's at Beckenham and Penge and who later became Professor of Modern English at Cambridge, wrote in a late 1971 letter to Harry:

He [Morris] would express his insights with a flashing clarity and a witty brio I have never begun to find elsewhere. I suppose he never persuaded anyone of anything; but his charisma, extraordinary in that it was boyish and magisterial all at once, filled me with a new sense of life, gave a new zest and generosity to one's seeing. ... He couldn't accept ageing.

He could have been describing Harry. Might Harry have been aware of this as he read? Holloway went on:

When I first knew him I was very naïve; didn't realize how little women meant to him (I knew men meant something but that's different), and used to feel great surprise that there wasn't some woman around to have her share of the good life! ... Probably I owe him more in terms of what I value in my own development than I owe anyone else (even you!). I hope I haven't lost – will never lose – some little spark anyhow of all that burned ... in him.

In a piece on Harry that she wrote in 2012, Margaret Maden began with the statement about the 'most maverick individual' and went on to say:

> Harry's abiding belief was that strong organizations, especially schools, are at their best when the staff collegium comprises decent – and preferably interesting – people.

How totally, totally different from Sir Michael Wilshaw, Chief Inspector of Schools in England and head of the Office for Standards in Education, Children's Services and Skills (Ofsted), who recently said, 'If anyone says to you that "staff morale is at an all-time low" you know you are doing something right.'[200]

I disagree with her description of Harry's view as 'rather quaint and romantic;' sadly, I agree with her characterization of today's schools as subject to 'the primacy of quantifiable objectives and performance measurement.' Surely we need to return to views that are quaint and romantic!

As suggested above, Harry saw himself as a gradualist, not a revolutionary, and the proof, if proof be needed, is in the paragraph below. Around this time, he wrote a piece entitled *Time to focus locally!* Harry the gradualist wrote:

> ... However, it needs to be said that some Tory LEAs are helpful and, within limits, generous. ... some [authorities] with strong Labour majorities are very much cooler in their support than are some Tory dominated ones. It shouldn't be forgotten that it was in a Tory authority that Community Education was born.

At the very beginning of the book, Harry wrote of his subject:

> He was an outsider. His public life was colourful, so was his private life. He was oddly enchanting and often maddening. ... Fiercely independent, but hating being alone. ... He remains a force today, and not a diminishing one.

He was, of course, describing himself. Tony Ward died in 1994; it would be a pleasure to tell him how profound his insight seems today.[201] I cannot help reading *Educator Extraordinary* without the assumption that, throughout the book, Harry is telling us about himself. He writes about Henry's 'convincing insouciance'. 'He abhorred the wasted life.' Was he at all aware of the extent to which he was like Henry Morris?

---

200 *The Guardian*, 23 January 2012.
201 I should note that it was Harry who told me of Tony Ward's comment.

Harry would have understood Alex Salmond, the First Minister of Scotland (2007–14), when he was quoted by *The Times* as saying:

> I've never thought of myself as revolutionary. But my grandad taught me if you are going to say radical things, say them in a suit.[202]

And several decades before, Dame Margaret Miles had written:

> I am not really a revolutionary; perhaps just a pragmatist who likes to look forward rather than back. 'Headmanship', like politics, involves the art of the possible.[203]

In October 1980, the *Times Educational Supplement* published a piece entitled 'The lost generation?' In it Harry began by describing a sixth former in late-1950s Watford Grammar School who came to see him, having been recommended to be made a prefect:

> He said he did not want to accept the privilege. I remember listening to his reasons with attention, curiosity, and, I admit, some surprise. He told me that he did not approve of authority in any form, and that the last thing he wanted to do was to give orders and to control younger boys ... They should be expected to discipline themselves ... In the years immediately following, the campaign to abolish school prefects took root and was often successful. I came round to favour it myself and I composed a paper called *The Death of Dad*: *Changing attitudes to authority*.

Harry used the title *The Death of Dad* for a broadcast in 1975. Later going on to reflect on 1968, once it was 12 years in the past, Harry wrote:

> The trouble comes from the word 'compromise'.

Harry wanted 'those who wish to keep their conscience pure' to engage in the real world.

John Holloway had written, 'Henry [Morris] was the most remarkable man I have ever known well ... Probably I owe him more ... than I owe anyone else.' But Sir Graham Savage, Chief Education Officer for the London County Council (LCC) 1940–51, opined that 'as a colleague ... he was occasionally amusing, for he could be provokingly witty, but for the most part he was maddening'. As he looked at Savage's comments, could

---

202 27 September 2011.
203 Miles, M. (1966) *... And Gladly Teach: The adventure of teaching*. Reading: Educational Explorers.

Harry have given a passing thought to the fact that one could have made a similar assessment of him, especially on a bad day?

Throughout *Educator Extraordinary*, we get a sense of where Harry got his first sense of the potential power of education; of the notion that education, properly understood, can be truly revolutionary:[204]

> We must reconstruct our conception of education 'so that it will be co-terminous with life.'

> 'We will lift the school leaving age to 90.'

And we get a sense of Morris's occasional bon mots:

> 'Who does your work when you are away from your office so often?' 'Precisely the same people who do it when I am not away,' replied Morris.

> 'It is not exactly pleasant work, this chasing rich people.'

Morris was gay (a word he would not have recognized in today's sense), an issue Harry faces head-on but with delicate understanding:

> A homosexual faces problems even today;[205] in the first half of the twentieth century, and especially for a man in public office, these problems were almost insuperable. He almost overcame them, to a large extent through a conscious effort at sublimation. He would, in fact, often and openly say, 'We must sublimate or perish.' He was therefore driven to concentrate almost to excess on his work, and on the pursuit of beauty in the arts. ... He strove to keep his emotions, as well as his mind, fully employed. In a programme for a teachers' course ... he arranged once for a significant quotation from Charles Darwin's autobiography to be prominently featured:
>
> > If I had to live my life again I would have made a rule to read some poetry and listen to some music at least once every week; for perhaps the parts of my brain now atrophied could thus have been kept alive through use. The loss of these tastes is a loss of happiness, and may possibly be injurious to intellect, and more probably to moral character, by enfeebling the emotional part of our nature.

---

204 A similar tradition can be traced in the United States from Thomas Jefferson's University of Virginia to the contemporary community college.
205 Written c. 1970.

But sublimation was not a total solution. Some time after the book came out, Harry wrote a sensitive and low-key letter to 'Walter and Betty', who seem to have been critical of the fact he had even mentioned the subject: 'By being open, and completely respectful about this side of Henry – the mention of which gives you such pain ...'. But he neither backed off nor apologized.

In mid-1971, George D. Edwards, Henry Morris's successor in Cambridgeshire, wrote to Harry:

> ... a gay man, a sad man – essentially, I think, a lonely man, forever missing (as more than once he confided in me) someone standing at his side in daily nearness to love. Lang held a special place in Henry's regard. Henry ascribed these words to the bachelor archbishop.[206]

Harry's book was published by Longman, where Sir John Newsom had become joint managing director after leaving Hertfordshire. Newsom died in 1971, of throat cancer, and there are tales of how Harry persuaded the publisher to take on the book in honour of Newsom. In 1984, Cambridge University Press published *The Henry Morris Collection*, edited by Harry with an introduction, 'His Life and Times'.

Reviews were positive. Brian Jackson described Harry's as a 'rare and personal book', but then told Henry Morris stories rather than actually reviewing the book. Stuart Maclure (editor of the *Times Educational Supplement* 1969–89) was more analytical, praising the 'warm and readable memoir'. He went on:

> If the book does somehow give the impression of slightness, it also conveys the author's enthusiasm for a worthy subject, one of whose characteristic qualities was gaiety in most senses of the world.

David Farnwell reported on a splendid party hosted by the Cambridge University Press at the Sawston Village College where Harry spoke

> ... referring at one point to Henry's yearning for a knighthood ... '*Silly man!*' (a welcome note of affectionate disrespect) and the roof of the hall did not fall in.[207] ... The book sold like hot

---

206 William Cosmo Gordon Lang (1864–1945) was Archbishop of York 1908–28 and Archbishop of Canterbury 1928–42. It is now generally assumed that he was a repressed homosexual. During the abdication crisis of 1936, he was strongly in favour of Edward VIII's departure.

207 Morris did receive a CBE in 1960, strongly supported by R.A. Butler.

cakes. Harry was on good form. (Why was no one else in open-neck shirt?)

The Henry Morris Collection could almost be read as a paean of praise for the community college (American, not British).[208] It asserts that:

- Education [is] coterminous with life.
- There would be no 'leaving school'! The child would enter at three and leave the college only in extreme old age.
- In all seriousness it might be said that the 'school leaving age' would be lifted to 90.

When Morris said, 'We must do away with the insulated school' (1926) and 'We must beware of thinking of education too much in terms of the school' (1941), we know exactly where Harry got some of his most visionary thinking. And remember: Morris's bosses were fairly conservative. Harry learned early in life how to cross aisles.

Eric Midwinter writes:

> What I do find slightly curious is that Harry did not appear, when at Watford, to do much to emulate Morris, his chief mentor. Or have I missed something? Did he try only to be scotched by antediluvian governors?

Soon after Morris's death in 1961, the Henry Morris Memorial Trust, of which Harry was a member, published a booklet entitled *Recalling Henry Morris 1889–1961*. In his Preface, Harry wrote of

> this important and very extraordinary man. His influence on people was enormous and on national education policy is lasting and benign.

Someone else wrote of his enthusiasm and the phrase 'infectious, vituperative vivacity' was used at his funeral. One can readily see where Harry got some of his qualities.

---

208 In England and Wales, a community college tends to be a sixth form college, a school for pupils aged 16–18, which may provide additional services. In the United States, on the other hand, a community college is an institution that provides the first two years of a four-year bachelor's degree, granting an associate's degree, plus continuing and adult education. Some further education colleges in the UK are somewhat similar to American community colleges. However, the biggest difference between British and American community colleges is that the latter are perceived and governed as part of the overall system of higher education, headed by presidents, but UK FE college principals are not vice-chancellors.

It was in the early 1960s, towards the end of his time at York, that Harry truly found his voice. In 1964, Peter Hall (now Sir Peter) of University College London, put together a book entitled *Labour's New Frontiers*, and invited Harry to contribute a chapter entitled 'Education policy'. Harry's 26 pages contain many of his basic beliefs, passionately and directly stated:

- Good teachers make good schools
- The major aim should be to abolish selection for secondary education
- Surgery is imperative.

On the other hand, he can, I think, be read by cautious bureaucrats:

> The educational–political axis is a fact, and the new Minister of Education must get things moving in universities, colleges and schools in the same way as, in 1945, Aneurin Bevan got things moving in hospitals, consulting rooms and surgeries.

I did not realize until recently how short ministers' terms were in those days ... and perhaps today. Michael Stewart was Minister of Education for a mere three months, from October 1964 to January 1965; and the sainted Tony Crosland got only 19 months, from January 1965 to August 1967. No wonder Harry felt urgency if the country was to 'remodel and reconstruct the whole national educational system'.

'Private schools', Harry argued, 'confer on their products ... so many free passes to power and privilege'. His passion showed through:

> The Grammar Schools as we now know them must begin to go, and the Prep Schools and Public Schools, having failed to wither away as many hoped they would when State Schools improved, must be removed from the educational scene.

> ... the two great evils which are found in our schools: segregation by intellect and segregation by wealth ... mad waste of human ability.

Harry's 'Education policy' is one of the few places where he discusses co-education:

> Of the 179 Direct Grant Schools, two only are co-educational ... single-sex schools reflect another form of our mania for segregation, which has little to commend it and much to be said against it. Local authorities should therefore be encouraged to apply a policy of desegregation to all their single sex schools.

Chapter 12

'Planned demotion'

Harry was getting restless at York, and he applied for the headship of Don Valley School, a comprehensive school in Doncaster. A letter to Margaret Maden suggests that he really wanted it. But I have seen the letter of application that he sent to Sir Alec Clegg, the chief education officer: it was short, almost slapdash, and made no attempt to explain why he wanted the job and how or why he might do it well. One of the many reasons he didn't make it was a local governor who simply could not comprehend how someone could be willing to contemplate a cut in pay. Sir Peter Newsam writes in an email:

> I do not think Harry would be able to function as a head these days. .. It was uncertain whether he could in 1970. ... Harry applied for a headship in Doncaster. It was a tough school in a tough area. He was easily the best qualified candidate academically and would be taking a drop in salary. He got nowhere with the governors. He wanted freedom to appoint staff (some governors in that area had nephews and nieces that needed special attention when applying for a job ...) And the drop in salary was fatal. 'Seems fishy to me,' one governor remarked. As I was advising the panel, I told Harry afterwards that he was well out of a school like that. He had been a distinguished head of a grammar school and what he called his 'planned demotion' would be better managed in London, where his influence outside the school would be important, as it was.

Interestingly, towards the end of his time as chief education officer of the Inner London Education Authority (ILEA), the second-largest school system in the world, 1980, when Newsam was sending a memorandum outlining his thoughts to a very few people, Harry, no longer a headmaster and no longer a professor, was on his list.

So towards the end of 1973, Harry announced that he was leaving his chair at York in order to become a half-time teacher at Woodberry Down Comprehensive School in Inner London. Woodberry Down, which opened in 1955 and closed, or transmogrified, in 1981, when it was amalgamated with another school, was regarded as a model, especially in its earlier days. The headmaster, from 1971 until it was fundamentally altered, was Michael Marland, who was described by Richard Aldrich in *The Guardian* as 'visionary, radical, colorful, charismatic.'[209] When he died in 2008, the obituarist in *The Independent* could have been writing about Harry:

> ... one of the educational pioneers of the second half of the twentieth century. He passionately believed that education was a leading force for social change.

Harry, heading for his sixtieth birthday, spoke at the time of 'planned self-demotion'.

As Nigel Gann pointed out to me almost 40 years later, he had to prepare to be rebuffed; he could have failed. His successor at York, Ian Lister, found the move hard to understand, while telling me that Harry had found it hard to find an acceptable role at York: he 'never taught a course' and 'didn't have a field'.

While not doubting Harry for a second, it needs to be said that he was becoming less comfortable as the University of York, inevitably, became somewhat bureaucratic. The vice-chancellor who had brought him there was heading towards retirement, leaving in 1973: it was becoming a different place.

At the end of 1973, the *Times Educational Supplement* printed a news item headed 'Professor Harry Rée's "self demotion"' in which Harry said he wanted to return to the classroom because 'things are coming to the boil, and I want to be in on them'.

> He particularly wants to observe the conflict between supporters of the tough 'right to learn' line, and those who 'want the schools to turn into youth clubs.' Woodberry Down's headmaster, Mr Michael Marland, says he is delighted at the prospect of Professor Rée coming to teach there, and will possibly use him in in-service training courses too.

As Colin Fletcher put it:

> His article on 'planned demotion' challenged everyone over 50. 'I'm going back to teaching, it's where I began and where I belong'.

---

209 *The Guardian*, 3 July 2008.

Given Harry's close and regular contacts with school classrooms even when he was a professor, I find Martin Berry off the mark in his 1971 review of *Dear Lord James* in the *New Scientist*. No one who knew Harry could have written:

> If I find ... Professor Harry Rée's contribution far too idealistic, it may be merely that my nose is kept too close to the grindstone of actual teaching for me to enjoy the bracing summit views experienced and discoursed upon by professors of education.

A little over two years after Harry moved from York to London, Peter Wilby[210] wrote in *The Observer*:

> When he was headmaster of Watford Grammar School ... he always favoured the C and D stream children. ... In the past he has been, by turns, conscientious objector and war hero, staunch defender of selection and campaigner for comprehensives, full-time classroom teacher and university professor ... His life is a series of intriguing changes of direction, admired by some as evidence of an open, unconforming mind, dismissed by others as nothing more than an eye for the latest bandwagon. Today he seems younger than his age [61], not so much in his kindly, weatherbeaten face as in his ease of manner and the freshness and vitality of his thinking:
>
>> I've never stayed longer than ten years in any job. I believe in planned demotion: if you're between 55 and 60 and in a position of responsibility, you should start to move down and make way for younger people. It's better than retirement.
>
> At Woodberry Down, he says, he has as much classroom trouble as the other teachers:
>
>> Teaching isn't a sedentary profession any more. The kids demand attention: you can't go into lessons any more and just mark books. I'm drained at the end of the day. Thank God I'm only teaching half-time.

---

210 Educational correspondent for *The New Statesman* in the 1970s and *The Sunday Times* in the 1980s; editor of the *New Statesman* 1998–2005, and still writing prolifically in *The Guardian*.

When he got to London, then, he found classroom teaching much harder work than he had expected ... and was honest enough to admit it, both to himself and to others. In the words of Jon Nixon:

> Woodberry Down – London's first purpose-built comprehensive school – faced huge social and educational challenges. The teachers were among the most dedicated I have ever met, but we were all seriously challenged. It was therefore hugely significant for all of us working there that a professor of education (they were a rarity in those days – now ten a penny!) should choose to join us. The fact that Harry himself clearly found the school extremely challenging – he, like the rest of us, found it difficult to cope – made his decision to join us all the more admirable. It was abundantly clear from the outset that he had come not to offer professorial advice but to join us in trying to make the school work for the pupils and for the local community.

Marland and he were not especially close: perhaps the school was not quite ample enough for them both. After all, Marland was in only his second year as a headmaster when Harry descended upon him. Knowing how legends can grow, I found it hard to believe Alasdair Brown when he told me that the kids had locked Harry in a cupboard ... I can, for sure, imagine him playing along ... but it could have happened.

Jon Nixon was head of drama at Woodberry Down. He describes how he first met Harry:

> It was the mid-1970s ... on a side road adjacent to Woodberry Down School. I had recently taken up post, was in my mid-twenties, and feeling rather out of my depth. As I straightened my car up I heard and felt a resounding THUD. I had inadvertently backed into the car behind. To make matters worse, the driver of the vehicle I had bumped into was in the car. I anticipated a difficult encounter and scrambled out of my car uttering grovelling apologies. From the other car emerged a sartorial figure whom I immediately recognized as the new and illustrious arrival in the Modern Language Department – Harry Rée. As I spluttered with embarrassment, Harry beamed at me with a broad smile, shook me by the hand, told me how pleased he was to meet me, and asked me about my work. As we walked into the school he said: 'Don't worry about the car, by the way. No real

damage!' I realized then that I had encountered someone who personified the virtue of magnanimity.

He sent me a thoughtful and perceptive email:

> I'm not sure how happy Harry was in his move to the London comprehensives. ... WD was London's first purpose-built comprehensive (as opposed to its first comprehensive) – along with Hackney Downs School down the road it had catered for a largely Jewish community, but by the time Harry (and I) arrived the Jewish community had moved up the road and the school served a predominantly Afro-Caribbean community (second generation). It was exciting, but exacting. I'm not sure how Harry coped.
>
> 1. Harry was adamant ... that French should be the first modern language at WD. Marland (the Head) was equally adamant that Spanish ... should be first. ... I think MM was probably right – but it caused some friction and no doubt it touched a deep chord in Harry's Francophile heart.
> 2. Harry felt the environment ... was hugely important – he wanted art work on the corridors, etc. ... When we became increasingly concerned about graffiti on the corridor walls, Harry suggested that we all carried spray paint round with us to blot out the graffiti and restore the walls to their pristine condition (a rather awful uniform ILEA yellow ...). He really believed (very William Morris!) that the environment mattered and that to be educationally functional it had to be attractive (if not quite beautiful).
> 3. He was wonderfully anarchic in his rejection of the organizational/managerial modes of thinking that were beginning to dominate ... in the 1970s. ... The staff room at WD provided the most intellectually stimulating forum I've ever been associated with – and I've held chairs at four UK universities. WD was heady stuff: at the forefront of every educational and political debate in the land.
>
> H. was a stylist – what he came to say was part of, and inseparable from, the beautifully ungroomed man that he was. He was (I think) on the intellectually anarchic side of socialism (at a time when these doctrinal distinctions mattered for those of us on the Left). He was kind and complicated and I think probably very

needy – although I was probably too young to understand that at the time.

In a later telephone conversation, having stressed that he had known Harry for a relatively short time, Nixon suggested that Harry may have become a fish out of water. Harry, he said, was imbued with the politics of the welfare state, whereas the new politics were more concerned with gender and race. No one understood the new Right and Margaret Thatcher, and no one took her seriously: a profound mistake. British culture had changed – maybe Stuart Hall could see it, but very few others. Interestingly, Edward Blishen, in *Donkey Work*, referred to 'Maurice's unifying view of British society'.[211]

According to her husband Nigel Gann, Cathy Wood recalls:

> One thing he did at Woodberry Down (partly to survive), but something that Cathy had discovered herself with recalcitrant boys, was to cook with them in the classroom – French recipes, of course. He and Cathy delightedly shared ideas of what you can cook with 20 odd teenagers on a spirit stove or having taken over the Home Economics room, while having discussions about and in French.

Harry never understood the taxpayer-voters described by his friend, the economist John Vaizey: 'The middle class believes itself to be poor and downtrodden, paying for a welfare state that others enjoy.' Nicole Ward Jouve:

> I still hear him saying how proud he was to pay his taxes, because they meant so much: schools, hospitals, care for the less well-off … Social solidarity at its most basic.

According to Nixon, Harry was a bit lost and unable to relate to the kids. In addition, he had almost a falling out with Michael Marland, whom Nixon described as obsessive, while Harry was a 'democratic anarchist':

> During the two days a week that Harry was at Woodberry Down, he had an enormous influence on the staff, especially the younger ones and the females; the culture of the staff room changed considerably when he was there and the tone was lifted. And there were the parties! Harry had no managerial responsibilities, of course, and was seen by some as a sage, or a 'fool' or jester.

---

211 The fictional 'Maurice' being Harry.

But he did display a profound understanding of his new setting. For example, in 1981, he wrote:

> Unlike many teachers in the past, who conscientiously excluded the child's home from their view of the child, they see the child at school as only a fraction of its whole being.

The left, said Nixon, was fragmented. In his day, Harry had ignored inadequate teachers 'because he could'. Marland did not, and Harry was violently opposed to his intolerance of poor teaching.[212] At least he was consistent (see pages 107–8) in that he had always valued colleagueship above the ability to confront inadequacies.

I asked Jon Nixon (this conversation took place in May 2012) whether there was anyone today remotely comparable to Harry. Tim Brighouse perhaps? Well, Jon responded, Tim is charismatic, flamboyant, and has a genius for working from the bottom up. He is also politically astute, charming, able to network, and a workaholic. Ian Lister could see the similarities between Harry and Tim (now Sir Tim) who 'dresses like a scarecrow' and thanks the dinner ladies as well as the big shots. Margaret Maden described both as pied pipers. Peter Wilby, while expressing genuine admiration for Tim's integrity and his ability to inspire teachers, feels that he has not taken Harry's journey, nor can he quite access media outlets like *The Guardian* in the way Harry did.

In a 2007 piece marking Brighouse's retirement as London schools tsar, Wilby wrote:

> The adjectives commonly attached to Tim Brighouse include charismatic, visionary, inspirational, even saintly. ...

> I ask Margaret Maden, who has known Brighouse for 30 years. 'There are lots of people who wouldn't be in teaching at all now if it weren't for him', she replies firmly.

> ... Neither recrimination nor hand-wringing are in his nature.

Maybe Michael Rosen (children's laureate, 2007–9), who was a sixth former for two years at Watford Grammar School, caught some of Harry's spunkiness when he wrote an open letter to Michael Gove, Secretary of State for Education in Cameron's cabinet, in October 2012. The letter begins:

---

212 See Marland's *The Craft of the Classroom*. As Alasdair Brown put it to me, 'he did know the business.'

I see you and Mr Clegg have spent time in a fantasy world where you have convinced yourself that bringing back things that have been shown to be useless is a great leap forward. ... So what underpins your walk back to the discredited past? ... The most significant factor in predicting attainment is family income.

Taylor-Gooby wrote:

Educational attainment is closely linked to income. ... A large number of studies indicate that more middle-class and better-off parents are able to gain advantage for their children by using their cultural capital and resources to locate the best schools, train their children for access and negotiate entry procedures, transport children and buy houses near prestigious schools, so that class advantage persists despite a universal right to schooling.[213]

And the letter ends with a reference to one of Gove's predecessors, Kenneth Baker, the bane of Harry's existence in the latter years of his life.

In 2013, Tim Hands, Master of Magdalen College School, Oxford, and that year's chair of the Headmasters' and Headmistresses' Conference, referred in a keynote speech to the 'Supreme Goviet': Harry would have liked that. *The Guardian* reported him as saying:

Love has disappeared from state-run education and children are suffering from the government's 'long interfering arm and dead restraining hand'...

Excessive interference and obsession with league tables ... 'emasculated the education system of this country'.

As a result, education 'is increasingly in the grip of central government and, worse, increasingly at the mercy of much-favoured commercial providers who would like to expand their operations.'

The story of the last 50 years is, I suggest, the intrusion of government and the disappearance of the child. More radically put, it is the intrusion of the state, and the disappearance of love.

Consider the source: as *The Guardian* pointed out, Dr Hands is the head of a highly selective school, founded in 1480 and charging £17,115 a year.

---

213 Taylor-Gooby, P. (2013) *The Double Crisis of the Welfare State and What We Can Do About It*. Basingstoke: Palgrave Macmillan.

In November, 2013, Dr Tristram Hunt, the new shadow Labour education secretary, criticized

> the Michael Gove model, of a competitive, atomistic school landscape where every school is an island, of a creative destruction approach to the school system …

> I think he's a very ideological figure. … And most educators and most in the teaching profession know that doubt is important. …

> It is teaching quality that is vital to improve schools.

Harry, ever the optimist, might think that the worm is turning.

Brian Simon hit the nail on the head in 1987 when he wrote:

> Fundamentally, the objective is, through downgrading and by-passing local authorities, to establish a whole mini-'system' of quasi-independent schools between the prestigious 'public' schools on the one hand, and local systems of primary and secondary schools on the other. These would serve the 'yuppie' (and other) strata between the working class and the really wealthy.[214]

He went on to say:

> Denis Lawton … director of London University's Institute of Education, and Clyde Chitty, write that 'a national standardization curriculum and external tests to assess achievement may well recreate the situation in late Victorian England when the vast majority of children were educated only to pass exams' (a reference to the 'payment by results' system). The proposal 'confuses education with training'. … 'A national curriculum continues to be viewed by politicians and civil servants as a convenient bureaucratic device for exercising control over what goes on in schools.'

'Payment by results' was introduced in England in the late 1860s and abolished around 1905.

Mary Evans quoted Kenneth Baker as saying that he hoped that schools would soon return to more 'rigour in their teaching and a greater emphasis, in the best Victorian sense, on the values of discipline'.[215]

214 Simon, B. (1987) 'Lessons in elitism', *Marxism Today*, September, 12–17.
215 Evans, M. (2004) *Killing Thinking: Death of the universities*. London: Continuum.

I wish Harry had lived to see Tim Brighouse's 2002 comment:

> Our national curriculum is more nationally prescriptive than any other state and is more so than the Stalinist regimes of the USSR.

Harry, who never hid his disdain for the direction in which Baker was headed in the late 1980s, would have loved Sir Peter Newsam's *Towards a Totalitarian Education System in England*, which was written in 2011:

> Over the past 40 years, the publicly funded schools in England have moved from being part of a democratically managed system to what is now becoming a totalitarian one. … What it by definition requires is for all decision-making, other than the trivial, to derive from a single source.

David Marquand put it this way:

> A centrally determined 'national curriculum' took control over school curricula away from teachers, and gave it to the Secretary of State. Schools were allowed (indeed, encouraged) to 'opt out' of local authority control, which, in practice, meant opting in to central government control.[216]

Stephen Ball wrote of '… national system locally administered' and the 'end of professional autonomy for teachers and schools'.

Jonathan Palmer thinks the educational establishment fought Baker too hard. So he got worse. Newsam described how the curriculum had been nationalized and the Secretary of State had effectively become the sole decision-maker. Harry had lost the battles and the war:

> Inspectors (HMIs, as we used to call them), local authorities, teacher unions, universities: all have been sidelined. The trains run on time, and competitiveness is the mantra.

Baker thought from the outset that 'Virtually everyone in University Education Departments … believes there must be prizes for everyone', belittling those with whom he disagreed. And he claimed that parents wanted to know where their schools stood in the league tables. 'I wanted', he said later:

---

216 Marquand, D. (2008) *Britain Since 1918: The strange career of British democracy*. London: Weidenfeld and Nicolson.

parents to be able to choose between comprehensive and grammar schools, between single sex and coeducational, between Church and non-denominational schools ...

How can one possibly have grammar and genuinely comprehensive schools in the same area?

In a piece entitled 'Why we make art and why it is taught', Richard Hickman, now at the University of Cambridge, wrote:

Schools ... are not geared to work through the feelings – the very opposite. They are designed to impart information, to reward exactitude, to inculcate skills and sometimes to develop curiosity. They are then expected to test the outcomes of their teaching and give numerical evidence for the success or failure of themselves or their pupils.

Harry would have related to that. He might, I suppose, be a misfit in the early twenty-first century. 'Deep down and all the way through', he was an educationist; neither a philosopher nor a historian. He believed in the intrinsic good of education and saw all people as potential learners. 'It's a great thing to be an educator', he would say; he wanted others to flourish through education. All of this was part of his fragile humanity.

Bruce Page[217] tells a delightful tale from Harry's Woodberry Down days:

I joined a group to which Harry was gleefully recounting the various dodges he used to park his car near the school in locations convenient to him and not approved by the various local authorities and landmeisters. Quite clearly he was making this his morning stimulation routine, and equally clearly his official pursuers were being driven to distraction. One could not but pity them. I had just read ... *SOE in France*[218], which has a good deal about Harry in it, and calls him (something like) 'perhaps the most naturally gifted subversive in a group notable for just that quality'. The luckless Hackney parking wardens, I thought. How could they know they were up against the man who had made monkeys of the Gestapo and the Vichy police for months on end? Shouldn't someone have told them that they would be better off not trying?

---

217 Later head of the *Sunday Times* 'Insight' team and editor of the *New Statesman* 1978–82.
218 M.R.D. Foot (1968) *SOE in France: An account of the work of the British Special Operations Executive in France 1940–1944*, London: HMSO.

The charisma remained intact. Lucy Hodges, now at the University of Buckingham, was a journalist; she edited the *Independent*'s weekly education supplement for nine years. She says in an email:

> Harry Rée was divine. I remember him as a sproglet. I was a young journalist on the *TES* in my twenties and Harry had retired from being a head teacher, or whatever big job he had risen to, and gone back into teaching. He was so charming and such a good man. ... He made a great impression on me. ... I think it was his goodness that shone through – the fact that he had given up a job as a professor to go and work in a comprehensive. I never forgot that. ... He represented a commitment to public service that was very present in the 1970s and that seems to have completely vanished.

On 21 January 1977, BBC Radio 3 transmitted an 18-minute broadcast entitled 'Planned demotion' that had been pre-recorded on 24 September. I do not know any reason for the four-month delay; nor do I know why *The Listener* declined to print it. A weekly magazine that was published from 1929 to 1991, *The Listener* would have given Harry a much wider audience than he received. As it turned out, the concept of planned demotion did not catch fire.[219]

Harry described how, shortly before his sixtieth birthday, he decided, as he put it, to stop being a chief and become an Indian. He was procrastinating more, dodging tough decisions, repeating himself, forgetting names, 'getting a bit bored'. But he still had energy and didn't want to retire or sit on committees, 'generously offering inappropriate and out-dated advice'. He could afford to live on less, and the days of exotic travel were probably over.[220]

So he decided to go back to the beginning. 'I wasn't looking for promotion and approval. It wouldn't even be the end of the world if I got the sack.' He would work half-time, and soon realized that he would be freer. 'I could say what I liked!'

Harry acknowledged that 'there were friends and colleagues who thought I was mad. ... They were all wrong.'

---

219 David Hargreaves wrote in *The Challenge for the Comprehensive School* (1982): 'We could also implement Harry Rée's ideas on 'planned demotion'.' He suggested, quite simply, that pensions should be fixed on the basis of one's best rather than one's last year. This is standard practice in several American states.

220 Though he did fly across the Atlantic to speak at my inauguration as a college president in 1988.

> Anyhow I've done it. About a couple of years ago I started at the bottom of the ladder for the second time in my life. It's not been all roses I must admit – the early days were far more difficult than I'd optimistically imagined. … By the end of each day I was dog tired.

Harry went on to describe how the world of school teaching had changed; fundamentally changed. In the old days 'doctors, parsons and teachers' were both respected and isolated. No more. Many children, perhaps a majority, treated school as if it were of no importance:

> One teacher explained it by saying that in her school the girls treated the staff in much the same way as they treated lamp posts – they avoided bumping into them.

So teachers had to be better prepared than they had been when Harry was at school, not droning on endlessly. Harry welcomed the fact that 'automatic, artificial respect has withered away'.

Harry welcomed most of the changes he saw, except the mistrust of authority. 'You can't trust the hierarchy', people were saying, reminding one of the Richard Nixon years in the United States. In Harry's words:

> I can't help feeling that today's almost universal suspicion of anybody with power is a dangerous growth – a malignant growth.

Some years later, David Marquand wrote of 'a culture of distrust, which is corroding the values of professionalism, citizenship, equity and service like acid in the water supply'.

Harry ended his talk with a recognition of some practical problems, e.g. 'the traditional pension scheme', but recommended planned demotion without reservation.

A year-and-a-half or so after the Radio 3 talk, and almost five years after his decision had initially been announced, the *Times Educational Supplement* published Harry's 'Why I planned my demotion'. No, he wasn't 'indulging my masochistic tendencies'; there were some good reasons, which he outlined. And, importantly for his readers, he had no regrets, even though:

> The actual teaching, I'll admit, wasn't often as satisfying as grammar school teaching had been.

He was reminded, he wrote:

> taken back 40 years at least – of how frightened one can be before taking certain classes where you're not sure what awful

thing may happen during the lesson; reminded of how far that fear extends backwards so that you feel it on the bus as you go to school; feel it worst during the night when you wake at 3 a.m. ... But actually nothing really awful did happen ...

Note that this is the only time, to my knowledge, that Harry ever wrote or spoke about his fears.

He told the tale of the 12-year-old girl who said, 'You don't laugh at the same things as we do, do you, sir?' He recalled telling student teachers that the second year would be much more 'satisfying' than the first: too true! And he mentioned his only regret at leaving the University of York: no secretary to help organize him.

He thought 'planned demotion' might be a good idea for people in any field:

> Doctors and consultants of both sexes can become nurses (but preferably not in the hospital they worked in); bank managers can become security officers; station masters move into the inquiry office.

I do think there was more to it. In the early 1970s, the *Sunday Telegraph* reported:

> Rée, now nearing 60, is a great disbeliever in the large scale pomposities and snobberies to be found in what the French, in their deadpan way, call la pédagogie. 'Most of the books written about education,' he once said, 'aren't worth reading.'

As he grew older, Harry became more and more committed to and articulate about community schools, community education, involvements with the local community. Back to what he had imbibed from Henry Morris. And it was my good fortune that I entered the world of American community colleges in 1978, never to think, even for a fleeting moment, of doing anything else with the rest of my life. Eric Midwinter and the late John Rennie were both key in the growth and development of the Community Education Development Centre (ContinYou), which is headquartered in Coventry and has offices in London, Cardiff and elsewhere. They recently wrote a paper entitled *Harry Rée: Community Education and the Rural-Urban Causeway* from which I quote liberally and shamelessly:

> His contributions were threefold. First, there was his constant sympathy and encouragement. ... Second, he gave valuable practical support. He was unfailing in helpful visits to projects

and in wise counsel. ... he was for several years the editor of the Community Education Development Centre (CEDC) newsletter. Third ... he offered a telling theoretical gloss. ... Harry Rée provided an intellectual conduit from the 'village college' concept of Henry Morris's 1930s Cambridgeshire and the urban community school concept pioneered by ... Eric Midwinter and John Rennie in Liverpool and Coventry. ... The sense of standing, however precariously, on the shoulders of the giant Henry Morris, foremost among British community educators, was a substantial psychological support.

... 'We must', he argued, 'do away with the insulated school', for he was, socially and culturally, the enemy of the school that withdrew children and encastled them, keeping the larger community at bay. Education, he believed, had to be 'coterminous with life ... we should abolish the barriers which separate education from all those activities which make up adult living.' ... 'education would not be a consequence of good government, but good government a consequence of education.'

The perfect community school was defined as one in which it was difficult to tell where the school finished and the community started. ... The other strand was to question the whole apparatus of the curriculum and to ask a similar kind of question to that posed by Henry Morris about the need to 'abolish the barriers that separate education' from everyday life. ...

From the stance of a Henry Morris or a Harry Rée, a national curriculum is as contrary a term as a professional foul or an antique reproduction.

The last 30 years have scarcely been a propitious time in Britain for community development of any kind, with community education something of a collateral sufferer. Nonetheless, and unhappily, the social dislocation that threatens much of present-day Britain, as it did 1930s rural Cambridgeshire, may be the imperative that calls for such ideals and practices to be re-discovered, at which point it may be vital that Harry Rée had the ingenuity and the enthusiasm and, above all, the passionate belief, to build that bridge between the bosky meadows of Cambridgeshire and the tough environs of downtown Liverpool and Coventry.

As Tessa Blackstone put it in the late 1990s:

> Slowly but relentlessly the predominant view of education as the preparation of young people for adult life is being replaced. What is emerging instead is a new concept of education as an experience that never ends but continues throughout people's lives. This is a much more dramatic change than appears at first sight. Indeed it is every bit as significant as the introduction of universal education in industrial societies in the latter half of the nineteenth century. For around a hundred years education has been focused on children and adolescents and a small minority of young adults. It has had a clear beginning in early childhood and a clear end, although the cut-off date has varied according to social class, gender and ability. It has for the most part been institutionalized in schools, colleges and universities and clearly separated from other activities; the task of education has largely been in the hands of full-time trained professionals.[221]

Colin Fletcher relates a delightful vignette from Harry's days with the Community Education Association:

> At the Plymouth AGM M... D... opened her Treasurer's report with 'I've been a hopeless treasurer. I really have ...' 'Yes,' said Harry firmly, gently and quietly. 'But you've always been a treasure.'

In 1985, Adriana Caudrey wrote a delightful piece for *New Society*, featuring Harry striding across the landscape and entitled 'Stirring up the schools':

> Harry Rée is the father figure of the community education movement. Or, more precisely, a permanent 'enfant terrible'.

She went on:

> 'I love putting all sorts of people together and stirring them up, m'dear,' Harry Rée muses mischievously. ... The bread-making process punctuates conversation in Rée's farmhouse, set among high limestone pavements and ash forests on the Yorkshire Dales.

She went on to describe how he attacked Baroness Warnock and 'orchestrates the campaign for community education':

---

221 Tessa Blackstone (1997) 'The boy who threw an inkwell: Bevan and education'. In Goodman, G. (ed.) *The State of the Nation: The political legacy of Aneurin Bevan.*

Rée has been the *enfant terrible* of the education system for more than 50 years – challenging, in turn, the public school, grammar school, university and comprehensive. ... 'You could say I've always bitten the hand that fed me.'

In 1961, restless Harry had written to me:

I find I am wedded to the cause of the underprivileged, probably for sentimental reasons, but it is in my gut. It struck me the other day how strange it is that in the 30s I went into grammar school teaching because I wanted to boost the products whom I felt were getting a raw deal – and that now in the 1960s I am finding myself uneasy in the G.S. world because I am rather ashamed of the g.s. products! ... The logical place for me to go would be a sec. mod. but I'm not good enough to do this.

In a letter to Margaret Maden, probably in the early 1970s, Harry wrote:

Looking back and writing my obit., I see what a sod I am, biting every damned hand which feeds me.

Harry would have been pleasantly surprised by a front-page story in the *Daily Telegraph* of 10 November 2013:

The dominance of a private-school educated elite and well-heeled middle class in the 'upper echelons' of public life in Britain is 'truly shocking', Sir John Major has said. ... He was appalled that 'every single sphere of British influence' in society is dominated by men and women who went to private school or who are from the 'affluent middle class'.

Former Prime Minister Major had attended a comprehensive school, the Rutlish School in south-west London, and left school with three 'O' levels. He continued:

I remember enough of my past to be outraged on behalf of the people abandoned when social mobility is lost. Our education system should help children out of the circumstances in which they were born, not lock them into the circumstances in which they were born.

Taylor-Gooby wrote:

It is hard to avoid the impression that some, at least, in government are seizing an opportunity to implement policies which deepen social divisions and undermine the contribution of common social provision, symbolized by the NHS, to social cohesion.[222]

Edward Blishen in 1983, describing 'Maurice':

> Recently he'd said that all his life he'd worked in institutions against which he'd turned: public schools, grammar schools, and now teacher training.

Back to Adriana Caudrey:

> Rée's quest for an egalitarian education system springs partly from a sense of *noblesse oblige*, created by the privileges of his own childhood. ... 'I felt awkward and embarrassed by my social position ...'

> Another clue to Rée's desire to mix people lies in his own parentage – a German-Jewish father and American mother ... He is conscious of the big part that community education can play in helping to bring together different ethnic groups. 'We are only just beginning to recognize what shits we have been to the gypsies.'

> 'Education is power,' says Rée. 'Education should extent to include environmental issues, conservation, pollution control and rent strikes.'

Caudrey went on to discuss the huge influence of Henry Morris and Harry's delight that someone thought his book was more about him than about Morris. She concluded:

> There's Rée, the grandfather, whose farmhouse is full of art works by his two young grand-daughters; Rée, the host, who throws house parties, mixing all sorts of people together, 'sometimes with disastrous effect'. Last, but not least, he bakes very good bread.

In 1980, Harry revisited the Cambridgeshire village colleges that Henry Morris had founded in the 1930s. Still enthused by Morris's 'high courage, vision and creative common sense', he was disappointed by some of the ordinariness that he saw, referring to 'this tired society of ours'. But he was still a believer.

Leslie Baruch Brent was sent from his home in Germany to England as part of the first Kindertransports. A distinguished immunologist and

---

222 Taylor-Gooby, P. (2013) *The Double Crisis of the Welfare State and What We Can Do About It*. Basingstoke: Palgrave Macmillan.

emeritus professor at the University of London, he was one of the many
people who contributed appreciations and obituaries after Harry's death
in 1991. I quote from *The Guardian*; the same page where Edward Blishen
and Francis Cammaerts also wrote:

> I knew Harry Rée as a fellow governor of Creighton School in
> Haringey where he emerged with a quiet and almost amused
> dignity despite injustice and injury done to him. In the 'winter
> of discontent' (1978/9), Haringey school caretakers went on
> strike and the schools were closed for a prolonged period. The
> Creighton governors passed a motion, proposed by me, asking
> the Education Committee to explore ways of safeguarding
> at least those children taking important examinations in the
> summer. Harry, Eva Holmes (an educational psychologist) and
> I were naturally supported by the Tory governors. Soon after,
> the Education Committee removed the three of us from the
> Governing Body behind our backs and our first intimation of it
> was a letter from Mrs Hattersley[223] thanking us for our work ...
> and regretting our inability to continue.
>
> Eva and I were outraged and Harry, too, felt that the local
> Labour Party had behaved appallingly. But whether from party
> loyalty or because by then he was unwilling to spend his energy
> on battling with third-raters, his attitude was that of a benign
> headmaster shaking his head over wrongdoings of some of his
> favourite pupils. How I wish I could have emulated him, for
> after much adrenalin our battle proved to be futile, even though
> Shirley Williams (Education Minister at the time) raised our case
> with the National Executive.

Several years later, Professor Brent retold the story in his autobiography,
Sunday's Child? A Memoir, which came out in 2009:

> Creighton School was large, and well run by the redoubtable
> Molly Hattersley, the wife of Roy, who was to become a minister
> in the next Labour government. ... party affiliations did not seem
> to matter very much as all governors were primarily interested in
> the welfare of the school. With the election of a new chairperson,
> Jane Chapman, the atmosphere changed and party politics became

---

223 The head teacher Molly Hattersley, wife of Roy Hattersley MP, who was then Secretary of
State for Prices and Consumer Protection.

paramount. She was extremely left-wing and either a member of, or sympathetic to, the 'Militant tendency', a shadowy bunch of neo-Communists who were infiltrating the Labour party ...

School caretakers began their strike in January 1979. ... After lengthy discussions a motion endorsing the caretakers' strike was blocked with the help of three Labour-appointed governors – Eva Holmes ... Harry Rée ... and me. ... I proposed a motion calling on the education committee to enter into discussions with the caretakers' union. ... This motion was passed with the support of Conservative and parent governors, as well as Harry Rée and Eva Holmes. At the time Rée was chairman of the Muswell Hill Labour Party ward and I was vice-chairman.

... In May I was astonished to receive a letter from Molly Hattersley expressing deep regret that I was no longer on the governing board and thanking me fulsomely for my services. 'The school will be the poorer without the benefit ...' Similar letters were received by Harry Rée and Eva Holmes. This was the first intimation we had of our removal, and we had not had the opportunity of defending ourselves against the charge of breaching the Labour party's guidelines. The three of us were deeply upset and sent a letter of protest to the leader of Haringey Council, Colin Ware. ... We asked four questions. Why were we removed? What constitutional procedures had been followed? Why had we been denied the right to be informed of the charge against us, and the opportunity of defending ourselves? And why were we not promptly informed once the decision was taken, apparently more than a week before Molly Hattersley had written to us on a purely personal basis? Support came from the Muswell Hill Branch in the form of an emergency resolution ...

We were not reinstated, although we were given the opportunity of stating our case to the executive committee of Haringey Labour Parties. ...

The whole issue soon became a political football. Harry Rée and I wanted to conduct our appeal quietly, but both the local and the national press ... got hold of the story and ran a number of articles ... all sympathetic to the dismissed governors. ... Eva Holmes made a formal complaint to the local ombudsman, who many months later found that Haringey Council had acted

illegally because they had removed us without a formal vote. ...
Creighton School parents supported us staunchly from the start ...

Shirley Williams took up our cause at a meeting of the national
executive, but according to her letter to me in October it was Tony
Benn and his left-wing supporters who ensured that the item was
not discussed ... She wrote, 'I really feel we must find some way
to fight back on this one ... I think your treatment was disgraceful
... it was even more disgraceful than you thought it was.'

Professor Brent was replaced by the Guyanese Bernie Grant, who later
became an MP.

Towards the end of 2011, i.e. over 30 years after the Creighton School
governors' fiasco, I obtained a copy of the nine-page *Report by the Local
Commissioner on an Investigation into Complaint 314/S/79 against The
London Borough of Haringey*. Dated 30 July 1980, it is signed by Baroness
Serota.[224] She wrote, in part:

The complainant was a governor of a school [Eva Holmes]
attended by three of her children ... She complains that there was
maladministration causing injustice in the way that she and two
other governors were dismissed and three new governors were
appointed.

After over six pages of recitation of facts, clearly set forth, the Baroness
moved to her conclusions:

... It cannot be good administration let alone fair to the
individuals concerned to appoint new governors before those
they are to replace have been removed from office or even told
that they are about to be removed.

I can well understand the feelings of the complainant when she
learnt ... in a letter from the headmistress of the school that she
was no longer a governor ...

I find that there was maladministration which caused injustice to
the complainant. I hope that in future any governors who may be

---

224 Bea Serota became a life peer in 1967, after a distinguished career of public service,
including vice-chairwoman of the Inner London Education Authority. She became deputy
speaker of the House of Lords and was the first ombudsman for local government. She
died in 2002.

considered for removal in such circumstances will be informed in advance.

But she did not propose reinstatement. Nigel Gann summarizes the story, mentioning Harry in particular, in his 1997 book, *Improving School Governance: How better governors make better schools.*

The tale is not clear to me, nor is Harry's role. In the spring of 2010, when I was trying to reach Molly Hattersley, I got an email from Roy Hattersley that read as follows:

> Molly Hattersley (head of Creighton School, now Fortismere, 1974–82) has asked me to reply to your note.
>
> *Harry Rée – for whom I had a high regard – was not a governor during my time as head of Creighton School.*

This is slightly puzzling, since no one objected when Professor Brent told the tale in *The Guardian* shortly after Harry's death.

I did manage to reach Dr Jane Chapman, who is now Professor of Communications at Lincoln University and Visiting Fellow at Wolfson College, Cambridge. Given the lapse of over 30 years, her lack of specific memories is understandable. She wrote:

> … at that time, issues of accountability by Labour governors to party policy were very important. This was in the context of a national obsession at the time with internal democracy and constitutional implications. The party required governing body members to vote in line with the council's controlling Labour Group – but for the life of me I can't remember what the particular issue was that Harry disagreed with and voted against.

Perhaps Professor Brent might be surprised to learn that Jane Chapman has long since lapsed as a member of the Labour Party.

Caroline Forbes, who became Harry's co-author, played a huge part in Harry's life at Colt Park. She knew him well: from his carefulness with small amounts of money to his falling asleep while driving! In his late twenties, he nodded off during lectures.

I recall dinner at the Rées in the late 1950s: Harry, sitting at one end of the table, fell asleep for a while; Hetty paid no attention; ditto her guests. And, as the reader will note, there are several tales of him napping at seemingly inappropriate times. Very few people knew then that there is quite a common condition called narcolepsy, and I am fairly sure that Harry had a form of it. The concept was first being formed in the mid-1960s; the

CPAP (continuous positive airwaves pressure) machine was invented for sleep apnoea in the early 1980s; the average general practitioner might have known about narcolepsy in the 1990s; and most of us might have heard mention of it by 2004–5.

The Mayo Clinic, in Rochester, Minnesota, says narcolepsy is 'a chronic sleep disorder characterized by overwhelming daytime drowsiness and sudden attacks of sleep' and says there's no known cure as yet.

So Harry's penchant, which we tended to smirk about because we didn't know how to respond, did have a reason. Even today, I have been told, narcolepsy and sleep apnoea are the most untreated diseases in the West, simply because of people's ignorance. Jane Steedman wrote in an email:

> I don't remember him worrying about it – 'useful to be able to catnap' and 'refreshing' are the only words I recall. ... Once, when he would be about 65 and teaching at Woodberry Down, we were about to set off for Colt Park ... a four-and-a-half-hour drive probably ... and he did ask me to watch him like a hawk for signs of sleepiness as he drove. He didn't fall asleep though. Many much younger teachers feel exhausted at half-term.

Edward Blishen almost certainly knew nothing about narcolepsy when describing 'Maurice' in *Donkey Work*:

> In being a member of an audience for anything whatever there's a kind of passivity that wasn't really in Maurice's range. The need for it quarrelled always with his need to take a hand. ... He fell back on his alternative impulse on public occasions, which was to drop suddenly asleep. I was to be with him on occasions of enormous dignity and importance and to be aware after five minutes that the shutters were up. For such moments, he'd perfected a small smile that was left hanging on his sleeping face, the equivalent of a notice saying CLOSED; but also a frozen feature that could be thawed out at the smallest hint that such a development was desirable. Then the small smile would instantly become a large and disarming one, and Maurice would look round for some clue to the connection between the moment before he fell asleep, and this moment of his waking up.

Caroline always felt better after having seen him. Sometimes, she said, he didn't like her friends and could act bored. He baked his own bread, which he sliced thin, and always started soup with an onion. (He hated English soup.) He tried never to be alone at Colt Park. I asked Caroline what drove

Harry: egalitarianism, she said, and the need of education for the working classes. Her son Tyler remembers being encouraged by Harry to eat raw bacon, to Caroline's dismay.

Harry's and Caroline's book *The Three Peaks of Yorkshire* was well received. It is organized around six walks, two each to the summits of Pen-y-Ghent, Ingleborough and Whernside. As Geoffrey Taylor said in a brief review:

> On each walk there are pauses to see how a lime-kiln or an ice-house worked, how a dry-stone wall is built, what effect the monasteries and granges had on the fell economy, and a score of other passing topics (the theory of the ram-pump, for example, for watering isolated farms).

In another review, Bert Lodge made a different point:

> The aim of the book is modest, not a traipse round the remoter edges of the world where you know the writer has never been but a potter really, not much more, round his neighbourhood. ... But the book isn't just an unorganized ramble.

I mentioned above that, like Winston Churchill and Harold Macmillan, Harry was half-American; in addition, he acquired an American daughter-in-law in 1983, and his nephew Philip Rée Mallinson has lived in the United States for most of his adult life and is an American citizen. Throughout his life, Harry was not especially interested in his American heritage and connections: he was very much a European.

I asked M.R.D. Foot whether, to his knowledge, it ever crossed Harry's mind that he, and presumably some members of his family, had the right to US citizenship, especially when he thought about the Hamburg branch, with its Jewish heritage. His response:

> I don't think he ever contemplated taking up American citizenship. The USA in those days seemed to every socialist to be the stronghold of capitalism, and he would have wanted no share in it.

Plus ça change.

Chapter 13
Who was the real Harry Rée?

Harry's last visit to the United States was in 1988, when he flew over to speak at my formal inauguration as a college president in Connecticut. After saying some nice things about me, he did mention specifically that he was half-American. 'My mother was born and bred in Scranton, Pennsylvania.' This was maybe his first public statement about his American antecedents; but even then he said nothing about the Dupont connection. (When I asked Ian Lister to speculate on why Harry seemingly had so little interest in things American, he simply said, 'They were very English.') Speaking at a community college (American style – and he did understand the difference between an American and an English so-called community college), he said, 'I am very closely involved in developing community education.' Perhaps I should have jumped up and asked people where the hell they thought I got my passion for community colleges! And he talked about Henry Morris:

> He was both a visionary and a practical person. In the 1920s he came back from the First World War. ... When his plans were turned down ... he bought himself carriage on a liner in Liverpool, and came to the States with letters of introduction to various foundations and trusts. And he came back with a cheque for $20,000. And in the 1930s, that was quite a lot of money. He waves the check in front of his committee, and they quite happily gave him permission to start building his community colleges – first ever in England, the first in Europe, and they were funded by Americans. ...

> Education both in the USA and in Britain has always been regarded as important. But in England we are concentrated, to our great disadvantage ... on educating well, very well indeed, only a small elite, allowing the standards obtained by the majority to remain scandalously low. ... If we ... fail to offer a high standard of education for such people, and concentrate on teaching only the elite, I fear for our future. We need badly to persuade everyone that education is a process which starts in the carrycot and only ends in the cemetery.

As it turns out, Harry had only three more years to live. And he chose the occasion to express beliefs he had honed over a lifetime, speaking passionately about imagination rather than the transmission of inert ideas, and arguing for a 'sense of public service' which, he thought, 'is being diminished and devalued in the dominant market economy'. Liz Peretz, who had conducted the British Library interviews, wrote in an email, 'He … wanted to tell me about his early understanding that public service was a guiding principle of life'.

Harry would have agreed 100 per cent with Iain Macleod, the Conservative British politician, when he said, 'you can't ask people to stand on their own two feet if you don't give them ground to stand on'.

Eric Midwinter reminds us of Bradley Headstone in Dickens's *Our Mutual Friend*, who represented everything that Harry despised:

> … he had acquired mechanically a great store of teacher's knowledge. He could do mental arithmetic mechanically, sing at sight mechanically, blow various wind instruments mechanically. … From his early childhood up, his mind had been a place of mechanical stowage …

Throughout his life, Harry read widely and voraciously: English, French, and some German; poetry and prose; fiction and magazines. He read even more widely than the people whom he would, in turn, advise to read widely. His taste was eclectic. This is a constant in his life, from school days to lively discussions with Hetty to the Colt Park period.

His daughter Janet remembers Harry encouraging her to read John Buchan (*The Thirty-Nine Steps* and *Greenmantle*) 'which I hated' and André Gide's *La Porte Etroite* (*Strait is the Gate*) and other novels – all in French. She comments:

> I think I remember these because I found them so hard. In general he was happy that I read anything, though when I was at Primary School I wasn't allowed any Enid Blyton and had to go to friends' houses to get my fix![225]

Son Brian recalls *Lavender's Blue*, a collection of nursery rhymes by Kathleen Lines and Harold Jones that first came out in 1954, when Brian would have been about nine years old. Then there were *Robinson Crusoe* and *Swallows*

---

225 Non-Commonwealth readers may not have heard of Enid Blyton (1897–1968), author of between 700 and 800 books, which sold more than 600 million copies over 40 years. And yet, it pleased most English teachers over the years to sneer at her writing, which remains little known in the United States.

and Amazons by Arthur Ransome: traditional stuff. Later there would be Wordsworth and his contemporaries, and Brian remembers 'a stream of Van der Post books lying about which have had the greatest of influence on my burgeoning consciousness'.

In a 1960 letter to John Collins, who was back in Australia, Harry mentioned *A Town Like Alice* by Nevil Shute, published in 1950, 'which I read because I've been looking for things to tempt Brian to read'. (By this time Brian would have been 15.)

Son Jonathan doesn't recall him recommending books:

> except that when I got interested in architecture and design (aged 12–14) he seemed pleased to lend me his pre-war books by, e.g., Maxwell Fry, and maybe Gropius and Corbusier. When travelling together we would talk a lot about elegant and inelegant design that we happened to see – houses, lamp posts, cars, bridges, motorways.

Hugo, the son of Harry's brother Eric, who died in 1943, recalls that Harry would occasionally play the role of surrogate father:

> On a visit to us (we lived in Seaford, a small seaside town in Sussex, best known at the time for its multitude of prep schools) he was appalled at my lack of structured reading, so gave me a list of books to read, asking me to write a commentary on each as I finished them, which he would read and in turn comment on. The first book was William Golding's *Lord of the Flies*, which opened my eyes and started an interest which has continued to this day. For that I will be eternally grateful to him.

Golding's best-known book first came out in 1954, with much attendant controversy. Harry had been a headmaster for about three years.

I have already mentioned an undated piece by Harry entitled *Books Are Teachers*, in which he tells us a great deal about himself:

> As I become old, the men of understanding are becoming less and less available, but not the books.

> The book I want to begin with has a dated title: *Through Literature to Life*. It appeared first as a serial in *The Teacher's World* in the late 1920s. The author was a popular novelist, Ernest Raymond.[226] ... It was the first chapter that moved me ...

---

226 1888–1974.

describing one of his memorable schoolmasters who obviously made a huge impression on the author, as he did – and still does – on me.

Rev Horace Dixon Elam, son of a chemist, had gone to Merchant Taylors' School and St John's College, Oxford. Since Harry's memory was playing tricks, I quote directly from Raymond:

> He did everything that was wrong and scandalous in the eyes of theorists. He was slovenly in his dress and dirty in his person; he was violent in temper and would thrash us in hot blood. … His language, when indignation overcame him, though brilliant with wit, malice, vindictiveness and humour, would certainly not have passed muster with the police in Victoria Park;[227] he was grossly unpunctual, wandering on splayed feet up to his class-room door long after other masters had taken their thrones and the corridors were silent. He had no dignity and no system in his conduct of a class, but would quite often go to sleep, with a handkerchief over his face, his chair tilted back, and his feet on his writing-desk; he would vilify the school and not a few of its masters. …

> By all theories such a man was the last person to whom adolescent boys should be trusted. … From such a man I, for one, should have learned nothing but good; learnt, in truth, almost everything that has been of value to me since. … We caught alight at such sizzling, spluttering enthusiasm; as he held forth on Micawber, Peggotty, Don Quixote, Uncle Toby, Hamlet, Tartuffe, Hogarth, Titian, Plato, Aristophanes, our imaginations flared up. … There was silence in Elam's classroom. … We hardly smiled when, in his gathering excitement, he stuttered for words, and even spat a little over the boys in the front row.

Harry asked, 'But how would he have emerged from his biennial appraisal?' Ernest Raymond was describing Elam, about whom he would later write a whole novel (*Mr Olim*, 1961). Elam joined the staff at St Paul's School[228] in 1884 and died in 1916. In many ways, Harry would have liked to be his clone.

Clearly, Elam played an enormous part in shaping Ernest Raymond. In a later chapter, he is described as 'the true begetter of this book'. Even

---

227 In the East End of London.
228 Where, ironically, Harry was later to be a student teacher.

though Raymond was well aware of 'the appalling worship of sport and the appalling contempt of scholarship', 'flogging by prefects', jingoism and the rest in the public schools of his day, he nevertheless was shaped by 'Elam … an unimportant master, a soured little clergyman'. 'In a word, he was undoubtedly mad.'

Raymond was 13 years old when he heard Elam saying:

> I don't care two-pence about giving you *facts* – anybody can give you *facts* – the official in the next class-room can do *that* and anybody can remember facts. *I'm* going to give you ideas. I don't think it matters much if the ideas are right, so long as they are ideas – so long as you *think* and *feel*. I don't want to teach you to *know*, but to *interpret*. See? Any fool can *know*. Wisdom comes when you begin to interpret. … Now run along to whoever's going to waste your next hour.

The memory of Elam, through Ernest Raymond, was crucial to Harry's thinking. Was Elam hovering in the background as Harry taught first-year boys once a week at Watford? Was Elam in his mind as he advised his students and protégées to 'read widely'?

> 'It's not examinations we ought to be aiming at, but the examined life. *Bios anexetastos ou biotos.*' 'An unexamined life is no life worth living.'

At Harry's centenary celebration, someone reminded us of Gerard Holmes's 1952 book, *The Idiot Teacher, A Book About Prestolee School and its Headmaster E.F. O'Neill.* If Henry Morris and Harry hadn't read the book, they surely should have!

Holmes quotes four proverbs of his subject:

'The passing of exams is not education.'

'Ask him something which he does not know, and see if he can find out.'

'Many teachers die in school but are not buried till later.'

'What we "can't do" is only what we have not done yet.'

'A school should be' … and there follows a list of 30 items, many of which Harry would have espoused. Examples:

- A workshop for young and old – of both sexes.
- A den of hobbies and indoor games.

- A studio for drawing, painting and plastics.
- A music studio.
- A hall for song and dance.
- A place for parties.
- A refreshment bar.

David Hockney had been one of Harry's pupils. Son Jonathan writes:

> In or around 1937, he was involved in a project called Lithographs for Schools, under the auspices of Contemporary Lithographs … He bought paintings in Bond Street galleries a bit, till he left Watford (Paul Nash, Philip Sutton, etc.) and he really minded how things look. He had bits of furniture that he'd designed in the 1930s, he bought with the greatest care, put flowers in rooms, etc: he was supported by Hetty in making the Watford house an oasis of good taste (in the style of austere modernism adapted to family life) and took enormous care furnishing his first house in York, abetted by me and Johnnie West Taylor, and also about the house he then moved into at Derwent Lodge. His second wife, Peta, was an interior designer by training and I think he liked that. I think they then started to fall out over questions of design (he would sacrifice comfort for beauty, she not) …
>
> He approved of classical music in a general sort of way, but was never particularly interested. … I was never aware of him going to a concert … and he certainly regarded opera as absurd, but he had a general liking for Bach and Mozart, especially the more dance-like parts. He once thought of taking up the double bass but … he was probably asked if he could fill a gap in the school orchestra.

Janet has a slightly different memory:

> Mozart above all, and especially the chamber music. He was an avid Radio 3 listener, and himself made countless tapes during his years at Colt Park, which I now have – recording concerts from the radio, the majority of which are Mozart, plus some Beethoven. He also liked Britten, and I well remember listening with him, in 1963 (I think) to the first performance from Coventry Cathedral, of Britten's *War Requiem*, of which he later bought the record.[229]

---

229 The first performance of *War Requiem* actually took place in 1962.

Harry read poetry throughout his life. Ernest Raymond had taught him well: 'Great literature is simply this', he had written, 'great emotion couched in great words'.

Harry would have been delighted that his friend Graham Mort, Professor of Creative Writing and Director of the Centre for Transcultural Writing and Research at the University of Lancaster, wrote as follows:

Metalwork

For Harry

Water's gleam is pewter
   the wood's alchemical copper
bronze and gold stripped
   from the trees' base metal
that iron-old assertion
   showing through as frost scrapes
back what is rich, trivial
   and new to some lost, deeper
trope. Everything becoming
   something else: lamentation
hope, the river falling into
   its own bass throat. Sea trout
and salmon – lashing silver
   tongues that tease the weir all
night – wait unpronounced
   in the lacquered pool where
drab trees reach and meld
   across the straits below and
days of tainted foam go by
   their dappled flux always unstill.
Now it's seen me, the heron
   will unweld: all elbows and knee
joints it ratchets the uncouth
   contraption of itself into a
nickel-plated sky. Flight
   seems a doubtful art, each
wing-beat provisionally
   inventing height; everything
tentative, untested, proto
   typical, unreal – except its bright
steel dart, acetylene eye.

In his essay *Books Are Teachers*, Harry movingly discussed writers who had influenced him when he was young. For example, there was a piece from the play *Cyrano de Bergerac* by Edmond Rostand. Cyrano is courting Roxane, and Harry had memorized the lines:

> Baiser. Le Mot est doux.
> Je ne vois pas pourquoi votre lèvre ne l'ose (…)
> Un baiser, mais à tout prendre, qu'est-ce?
> Un serment fait d'un peu plus près, une promesse
> Plus précise, un aveu qui veu se confirmer,
> Un point rose qu'on met sur l'i du verbe aimer (…)

Herewith Gladys Thomas's and Mary F. Guillamard's translation:

> A kiss. The word is sweet.
> I see not why your lip should shrink from it. (…)
> A kiss, when all is said, what is it?
> An oath that's ratified, a sealed promise,
> A heart's avowal claiming confirmation,
> A rose dot on the 'i' of 'adoration'.

Harry, in romantic mode and mood, went on to discuss Robert Louis Stevenson's *El Dorado*, written in 1881 as part of *Virginibus Puerisque*. The last paragraph, he opined, may be a bit cliché-ridden, but he 'hardly had to check a word when he recalled it' as he was writing.

One can, I think, see where Stevenson hit a chord with Harry:

> There is always a new horizon. … An aspiration is a joy forever, a possession as solid as a landed estate. … Desire and curiosity are the two eyes through which he sees the world in the most enchanted colours: it is they that make women beautiful or fossils interesting: and the man may squander his estate and come to beggary, but if he keeps these two amulets he is still rich in the possibilities of pleasures. … Happily we all shoot at the moon with ineffectual arrows … It is true that we shall never reach the goal. … To travel hopefully is a better thing than to arrive, and the true success is to labour.

Harry wasn't in the habit of telling jokes, nor was he a prankster; but he was full of *joie de vivre*. He had no time for joyless places where teachers have to wear suits. As Alasdair Brown put it to me in a recent conversation, 'Teachers should be joyful; now they're frightened.'

He went on to discuss his lifetime favourite poet, A.E. Housman, introduced to him by the same teacher. 'Housman', he said:

> introduced us to stoic reality and even a healthy cynicism about the world; about life and death; about love and the friendship that 'dared not speak its name'.

Was this caused, at least in part, by the fact that his mother died of cancer on his twelfth birthday? Harry quoted, presumably from memory:

> They hang us now in Shrewsbury jail:
>   The whistles blow forlorn,
> The trains all night groan on the rail
>   For men that die at morn.
>
> There sleeps in Shrewsbury jail tonight,
>   Or wakes, as may betide,
> A better lad, if things went right,
>   Than most that sleep outside.
>
> (A Shropshire Lad, 1896, IX)

> Oh, when I was in love with you
>   Then I was clean and brave,
> And miles around the wonder grew
>   How well did I behave.
> And now the fancy passes by,
>   And nothing will remain,
> And miles around they'll say that I
>   Am quite myself again.
>
> (A Shropshire Lad, XVIII)

> The troubles of our proud and angry dust
>   Are from eternity, and shall not fail.
> Bear them we can, and if we can we must.
>   Shoulder the sky, my lad, and drink your ale.
>
> (Last Poems, IX)

> Shot? So quick, so clean an ending?
>   Oh that was right, lad, that was brave:
> Yours was not an ill for mending,
>   'Twas best to take it to the grave.
>
> (A Shropshire Lad, XLIV)

'Housman's harsh pessimism', Harry wrote:

> although it touched a chord, wasn't wholly acceptable. (I've often thought I'm essentially an optimistic pessimist!) But for a long time I've felt that a person's attitude to life is closely related to their attitude to death, and it's probably the latter which rules the former. So, once again I return to Stevenson … deals openly, cheerfully and sensibly with the fact of Death. 'It is better to live and be done with it than to die daily in the sickroom.'

But Harry kept returning to Housman. At the end of her obituary of Harry, Gillian Tindall quoted a poem that he had jotted down for her several years before, from memory. I find the differences between Housman's poem as written and as remembered by Harry interesting; here follow both:

Housman:

> Good creatures, do you love your lives
>   And have you ears for sense?
> Here is a knife like other knives,
>   That cost me eighteen pence.
> I need but stick it in my heart
>   And down will come the sky,
> And earth's foundations will depart
>   And all you folk will die.
>
> (*More Poems*, XXVI)

Housman, as recalled by Harry:

> Good people, do you love your life
> And have you ears for sense?
> Here is a knife like other knives,
> It cost me eighteen pence.
> I needs but stick it in my heart
> And down would fall the sky,
> And earth's foundations would depart
> And all you folk would die!

Pippa Warin recalled Harry's love of T.S. Eliot's poem 'A cooking egg', which begins with two lines from a fifteenth-century poem by François Villon called 'The Testament'. He admired the work of Herbert Read (1893–1968), who visited the University of York at least once. Jonathan remembers accompanying Harry to tea with Read 'in his lovely place in the

Yorkshire Dales' when he was about 14 years old. Read described himself as an anarchist, though he nevertheless accepted a knighthood in 1953. Harry especially enjoyed a slim volume, minimally punctuated, that appeared in 1956, entitled *Moon's Farm and Poems Mostly Elegiac*.

Janet wrote:

> He himself read avidly and widely. He loved the poetry of A.E. Housman, Wordsworth, T.S. Eliot, Auden. I have letters he wrote … in the late 1950s/early 1960s, where he and my mother are both reading, and disagreeing about, C.P. Snow and Lawrence Durrell. These letters are bursting with excitement at articles he read – in *The New Statesman*, *The Listener*, *Encounter*, etc. Huxley features widely.

> I think he would describe himself as an eclectic and speedy reader – not poring over or studying a book, but getting a strong and immediate impression and talking passionately about it. He kept notebooks where, as a young man, he would transcribe passages from writing that had strongly affected him.

Excitement is a constant theme in Harry's life. As Beverley Naidoo puts it – and she learned this from Harry – 'Teachers need to be excited about learning'.

He may not have been in the habit of poring over or studying a book, but there is, according to Margaret Maden, at least one book that he read regularly, over several years: *A Fortunate Man* by John Berger,[230] with photographs by the Swiss-German Jean Mohr. First published in 1967, the book has been described as calm, intelligent, low-key, peaceful and perceptive. It is a study of the everyday life of John Sassell, who was a general practitioner in the Forest of Dean.

Berger wrote movingly about Sassell's transformation from someone who thrives on emergencies to an empathetic listener; an older brother rather than a paternalistic expert. The book is, in part, about the redemptive qualities of community.

In 1974, Dr Sassell committed suicide, 'frightened in case a patient comes into the surgery with a problem I can't solve'. One can only speculate about his inner tensions, and I wonder what effect this dramatic end may have had on Harry the reader. The doctor portrayed in Berger's book is … at

---

230 Painter, art critic, novelist and poet (1926–2017).

least superficially ... so different from Harry that I wonder what drew him to it. Some quotations may help:

> Sassall is ... a man doing what he wants. Or, to be more accurate, a man pursuing what he wishes to pursue.

> Sassall, except when involved in the actual treatment of patients, is the most impatient man I know. He is incapable of waiting and doing nothing. (p. 131)

> Sassall has to a large extent liberated himself ... in the eyes of his patients from the conventions of social etiquette. He has done this by becoming unconventional. Yet the unconventional doctor is a traditional figure. (p. 97)

> He cures others to cure himself. (p. 77)

> He suffers the doubts and enjoys the reputation of a professional idealist. (p. 133)

> His appetite for knowledge is insatiable. (p. 143)

> From time to time Sassall becomes deeply depressed. The depression may last one, two or three months. (p. 144)

Keith Emmans, who served under Harry's chairmanship on the Board of Studies of the Education Department at York, said, 'He was always quoting *Huckleberry Finn*'. One wonders, of course, to what extent the use of the 'N' word would have bothered Harry, as it should have even in the 1950s and 1960s. Similarly: what was he thinking when he recommended that his students read Alberto Moravia's *Two Adolescents, The Stories of Agostino and Luca*, which first came out in 1950? The book is replete with the words 'negro' and 'nigger'; Homs, the black boy, is usually referred to as 'the Negro', where all the white boys are called by their names. The racism is not subtle, e.g. 'Agostino drew back from the Negro, as from the touch of a reptile.' And sometimes Homs is referred to as 'The Moor'. (The translator, Beryl de Zoete, died in 1962, so it is far too late to ask any questions.)

He read *Fathers and Children* (1862) by Ivan Turgenev and *Childhood, Boyhood, and Youth* (1852–6) by Leo Tolstoy.

Harry could be quite direct. Years ago, he urged me to read *Contrary Imaginations: A psychological study of the young student*, by Liam Hudson, who was professor of education at the University of Edinburgh. 'This is a fascinating and provoking book. Whether it is important is open to doubt'.

Harry especially enjoyed *Kiss Kiss*, Roald Dahl's fourth collection of short stories (1960). The 11 stories, most of which you can't put down, ranged from the outrageously unbelievable 'Pig' to 'The Champion of the World', which is plain funny. Dahl has been accused of both racism and sexism; rather, there are stereotypes throughout the stories: Irish cops; wives serving their husbands; McPottle, the Scottish nurse; etc. But the macabre stories are totally gripping.

He recommended *Footsteps, Adventures of a Romantic Biographer*, by Richard Holmes, which came out in 1985. France is central to the book, as are both Shelley and Robert Louis Stevenson. And it is Holmes who said:

> If you are only a scholar your story will be dead but if you are only a storyteller then it will be ludicrous.

Among contemporary novels he enjoyed was *The Book of Ebenezer Le Page*, a fictionalized autobiography of an archetypal Guernseyan by G.B. Edwards. It was published posthumously in 1981, five years after the author's death, with an introduction by John Fowles. William Golding praised it unreservedly. I wonder whether part of the appeal for Harry was the French influence on the writing.

He enjoyed the Irish writer Jennifer Johnston's *The Railway Station Man*, which came out in 1984. (It is a pity that Harry did not live to see the 1992 film, with Julie Christie as Helen Cuffe and Donald Sutherland as Roger Hawthorne, the Second World War hero who lost an eye and an arm at the Battle of Arnhem.) Among the themes that Harry may have related to are happiness is precarious, and love is fleeting.

He would have recommended *Frost in May* by Antonia White[231] for its penetrating, searing story of how a convent school could destroy one of its pupils. The book first came out in 1933 and was revived by Virago in the late 1970s. A thinly disguised autobiography, it should be read by educators as well as anyone who thinks that religious beliefs are simple. For example, Léonie, one of the girls in the convent school, explains: 'It's only a dogma that hell exists; it isn't a dogma that there's anybody in it'. In 1985, *The Observer* reviewed a memoir by White's daughter: it produced, Hilary Spurling wrote, 'a sensation of appalled and fascinated revulsion'.

I do not understand the appeal of F.M. Mayor's *The Rector's Daughter*, a gruelling, delicate and sensitively written novel that was first published by the Hogarth Press in 1924, then by Virago in 1987. Caroline Forbes reports that Harry loved it. It tells the tale of Mary Jocelyn, her very traditional

---

231 1899–1980.

and emotionally very restrained clergyman father, and how she makes it through relationships that come to naught. It discusses 'Father's want of feeling', how 'Canon Jocelyn's circle really enjoyed dullness', and quotes Mary: 'Father is so far above me in mind, I can't be much of a companion for him.' Mr Herbert, the clergyman who ends up marrying someone else, says, 'I don't believe discussion ever has done any good to anybody'. 'It could not be expected from one of his generation that he would apologize.' Elegantly written, yes, but what would Harry have taken away from his reading? For sure, it cannot have fed his general optimism, that optimism that so many people saw in him.

Harry hugely admired *Kindergarten*, Peter Rushforth's first novel, which first came out in 1979 and won the Hawthornden Prize; it demonstrates a subtle and unsentimental understanding of the Holocaust. Rushforth taught for many years at the Friends' School in Great Ayton and lived in Castleton, North Yorkshire. Caroline Forbes writes, 'Harry sought him out and called in, but he wasn't especially friendly, which disappointed Harry'.

His tastes were, as I have said, eclectic. For example, he read *The Heart is a Lonely Hunter* (1940), by Carson McCullers. He enjoyed *Acts of Worship* (1965), seven short stories by Yukio Mishima.

He read *The Lives of Lee Miller* (1985) by Antony Penrose, who was her son. American-born Lee Miller, a depressed alcoholic, died of cancer after a life that one can only describe as hectic, courageous and totally unpredictable from day to day. Penrose, who was alienated from her during most of their lives together, described her as 'a paradox of irascibility and effusive warmth, of powerful talent and hopeless incapability'. Towards the end of the book – and this may have intrigued Harry – he wrote that 'She faced her death fearlessly and with both interest and candour, as at the beginning of a great new adventure.'

Harry recommended the novelist Janet Frame[232] to Australian John Collins, maybe, in part, because she was a New Zealander. But I am sure he was intrigued by her life story: following years in a psychiatric hospital, she was scheduled for a lobotomy that was cancelled when, just days before the procedure, her debut publication of short stories won an unexpected national literary prize.

We should not be surprised that Harry read Hugh Tinker's *A Message from the Falklands*, letters and poems compiled after his son David was killed during the conflict in June 1982.

---

232 1924–2004.

Chapter 14
Death and legacy

Harry died on Friday 17 May 1991. Only 11 days before, he had spoken at the unveiling, by the Queen Mother (who brought her piper with her), of the 'F' Section Memorial at Valençay in the Loire Valley (see J.D. Sainsbury's brief *The F Section Memorial*, 1992). The memorial commemorates 104 members of the SOE who gave their lives for the liberation of France. Nephew Philip Rée Mallinson reports that Harry was 'furious' that he had been chosen, feeling that many others deserved this top spot and casting conversational aspersions on the Queen Mother. But – middle-of-the-road to the end? – he went.

Since this was Harry's last speech, given in the presence of François Mitterand, President of the French Republic, it is worth quoting in full. I am indebted to my lifelong friend Michel Lemosse for help with the translation:

> Ministers, Your Majesty, Your Excellency, Ladies and Gentlemen.
>
> Speaking on the occasion of this ceremony is a great honour for me, and a very moving assignment. Having myself been a member of this 'F' Section, like those whose names are carved on these steles, and, to tell the truth, having served with some amongst them in the Franche Comté in 1943, I will try to speak on their behalf – both men and women – as well as for their families, and also for us ourselves – the Buckmaster agents – who, God knows why, have had the good fortune to return here after the War.
>
> First of all, I should like to thank all those responsible for setting up this Memorial, and to convey to the Mayor of the Town of Valençay, and actually to the French, our gratitude for having recorded the sacrifice of those who are commemorated here, most of whom died in concentration camps, as did so many members of the French Resistance. Furthermore, I should like to express simple thanks to France for having, in this manner, expressed her appreciation for the contribution which we were trying to make to the common cause – that is to say – to liberation.
>
> We of Section 'F' belonged to several nationalities; our temperaments, our qualities were exceptionally diverse. However,

I would dare to say that we shared a common feeling, a feeling of affection, empathy, and – how should I put it? – love for France and, in addition to this, a respect for her qualities and her traditions.

Finally, on this occasion, I should like to express more than a hope, rather an article of faith. Serving in the ranks of the French Resistance, and at the same time dependent on British authorities, we never harboured a feeling of divided loyalty – on the contrary, we experienced a bilateral loyalty. It is this common spirit which is confirmed by this Memorial at Valençay. And I am certain that out of this common spirit will emerge a similar understanding, an auspicious outcome, for both France and Great Britain. For, as in the past, to ensure the progressive welfare of our two countries, we will always have a need for one another.

Long live France.

Long live Great Britain.

Harry was unafraid of dying: of that I am convinced. You would occasionally get the sense that he was preparing you for his death; perhaps he was preparing himself. For sure, he did not want to grow old and feeble. Nigel Gann recalls a visit to Colt Park:

He took us up the hill behind his farmhouse in the mid-1980s and said that, when the doctor told him his heart wouldn't last any longer, he would take a bottle of whisky up to the top and wait. … His beliefs are a constant inspiration to us, and to my work, in very different times.

Ian Lister remembered Harry's harshly dismissive comments after a funeral: '… dead; they're shit.'

When people die in the United States, the media report the event as soon as they can; frequently the family will print its version of the life of the dearly departed on the obituary page. If the person is at all well known, then, in the United Kingdom, the print press will wait a few days and then publish a thoughtful, and occasionally critical, account of the life, with a discussion of that life's significance. So we should not be surprised that the major London-based papers all printed lengthy, specially commissioned obituaries of Harry – what did surprise me at the time was the sheer number of obituaries and the speed with which they appeared. It is very rare for so many personal tributes to appear in the pages of Britain's quality newspapers so soon after the publication of an obituary.

In order of publication, there were obituaries and/or letters in *The Guardian*, *The Daily Telegraph*, *The Independent*, *The Times*, the *Times Educational Supplement*, *L'Est Républicain*, *The Craven Herald and Pioneer*, *Education* and the *VES Newsletter*.

Anne Corbett, a former journalist and now a visiting fellow at the European Institute at the London School of Economics, captured Harry's essence in *The Guardian*, only three days after he died. 'He led several lives,' she wrote, 'and all of them with panache.' Having listed some of his major accomplishments, she went on, 'these were all aspects of a coherent whole'. Her last paragraph reads, in part:

> He was never a conventional part of the educational establishment which did not like his untidy suits and no doubt feared his subversive style. It was his capacity for friendship which gave him influence. ... We were friends because he was he and I was I.

At the 2014 celebration of the centenary of Harry's birth, Anne referred to the last words in George Eliot's *Middlemarch*:

> The effect of her being on those around her was incalculably diffusive: for the growing good of the world is partly dependent on unhistoric acts; and that things are not so ill with you and me as they might have been, is half owing to the number who lived faithfully a hidden life, and rest in unvisited tombs.

This had been one of Harry's favourite quotations, and was included in a hand-out at the October 1991 celebration of his life.

There was an interesting error in the obituary in *The Daily Telegraph* – author unknown to me – his mother was not French. (Well, the Duponts did originate from France, but that was in the early nineteenth century.) Otherwise, the obituary is an unexceptional summary of the life.

The Independent wisely asked two people to write about Harry rather than the usual one: Professor Brian Simon, a well-known advocate of comprehensive schools, son of Lord and Lady Simon of Wythenshawe and, according to Nigel Gann, a pupil at the same nursery school Harry went to; and M.R.D. Foot, author of *S.O.E. in France* and much else. Professor Foot made the same, understandable, error as *The Daily Telegraph*: French was not 'his mother's native tongue'. He found the speech quoted above 'magically good', after summarizing Harry's war years in admirable and intelligible detail. Professor Simon began with Harry's 'most formative influence', Henry Morris, giving Harry full credit for his effective commitment to community education. In one of his many books, referring specifically to 1965, he had written:

> Harry Rée was to play an important part in the move to comprehensive education from this time on – and especially in the development of comprehensive schools as community schools.

The Times, also, thought his mother was French. The obituary (author unknown) provides a good summary of the life and adds:

> Although not a man for conventional religion and not an admirer of the church as an institution, he cared deeply for the life of the spirit. He was to be found at the Le Bec Monastery in Normandy, making friends with the monks and attending the services.

Halsey would write:

> Somewhere on his travels he left behind the conventional religion of his childhood. But he retained and developed a deep spirituality, disguised by frequent laughter and punctuated by an irreverence towards the pomposities of this world – a hugely refreshing inspiration for children of all ages. He was a true son of the ethical socialist tradition.

Three days after Anne Corbett's obituary, which she said she wrote in four hours, *The Guardian* printed 'Appreciations' by Edward Blishen, Francis Cammaerts and Leslie Brent, under the title 'Gregarious loner, great teacher'. Edward, who might have been the prime author of this biography had he not become ill and died, understood his friend:

> Visit him and within an hour your lap would be heavy with pieces it was imperative you should read. From then on you'd be part of his amazing network of friends and acquaintances. ... More wonderfully than anyone else I've known or can imagine, Harry was a spreader of ideas. ... He was the gustiest of men: always gustily coming, gustily going.

> Under the bustle ... there was quietness and delicacy. I thought of him as a gregarious loner: passionate for company, passionate for solitude.

Francis Cammaerts wrote of Harry's idealism. But 'he rejected the idea of the heroic man or woman', and he did have one hero: Henry Morris. And Professor Leslie Brent, briefly describing the Creighton School contretemps

Jonathan M. Daube

outlined above, said Harry 'emerged with a quiet and almost amused dignity'.

The *Times Educational Supplement* published five tributes to Harry, by Tim Brighouse, Anne Corbett, Margaret Maden, Sir Richard O'Brien and George Walker. Tim Brighouse first met Harry in 1976, when he was teaching at Woodberry Down and was 'the inspiration, conscience and moving force of TANEA. … He was the most extraordinary person and teacher I have ever met, and the finest friend'. Anne Corbett referred to 'Harry's unusually un-insular attitudes'; she explained how, in France, 'almost everyone of his generation had been faced with the choice of whether to collaborate or to resist'. Margaret Maden, whom Anne would later describe as 'always political', met Harry in 1967 in Bristol when SPERTTT was created, then PRISE. She described him as 'ruthlessly honest'. Richard O'Brien wrote of 'those marvellous letters':

> The last letter I received included these subjects: walking on Mull, the unveiling by the Queen Mother of the monument to English members of the French Resistance at Valençay, thanks for books, Iona (too many people), a talk to primary school heads, the new Education Commission, and (as always) an account of the latest doings at Colt Park, his farmhouse in the Yorkshire dales.

George Walker met Harry when he was ten and 'a precocious applicant to Watford Grammar School'. At Watford, Harry 'was mercurial, inspirational, probably infuriating to those who had to work with him'.

Perhaps not surprisingly, the obituary in *L'Est Républicain* (Région Franche-Comté) says nothing about his career in England while referring glowingly to his heroism in France. Surprisingly, I could find almost no obituaries in the French press. Jonathan Rée suggests that this could be because, for many years after the War, it was uncommon for patriotic French to allow that anyone other than fellow-patriots was involved in the Resistance. Even M.R.D. Foot's book was embargoed for many years. Michel Lemosse tells me that not even Francis Cammaerts, who lived for his last two decades in the south of France, was noted in the French press when he died.

The headline in *The Craven Herald and Pioneer*, a weekly published in Skipton and covering North Yorkshire, read 'Harry Rée, an unassuming man':

> Harry Rée will never be remembered for smart dress. … He taught voluntarily at Settle High School on occasion, was a

governor there and at Settle Middle School, and taught German
once a week at Ingleborough Community Centre. ... He was a
committed and active Socialist.

After a balanced summary of his career, the *Herald and Pioneer* went on:

It was said he was a great seed sower, who recognized potential in
people and did all he could to make sure it was realized.

Roger Halsam, then the headmaster at Settle High School:

said he had been a tremendous influence on the governors and
helped make staff appointments.

Alan King, the warden at Ingleborough Community Centre, reported that

recently he had done a lot of work for the University of the
Third Age. He was also trying to twin Ingleton with a small
French town.

The University of the Third Age began in France in 1973; by the early
1980s it was well established in the UK. Ingleton became twinned with
La Chapelle-des-Marais, a town of 3,500 people in the Loire-Atlantique
Department, in 1993, a couple of years after Harry died. King added, 'He
was a superb friend'.

Within a week of Harry's death, the letters were beginning to appear.
Laurie Taylor, well known for his long-running 'Poppletonian' column in the
Times Higher Education Supplement[233] and one-time head of the sociology
department at the University of York, wrote in *The Independent*:

What keeps breaking through is the sound of his laughter. What
made him laugh was any form of pomposity, but in particular the
imbecilities perpetrated by professors and university committees.
It was laughter which escalated, going up in pitch as absurdity
was piled on absurdity, until his dozens of laugh lines were
squeezed tight together and he began springing up and down
with delight on one of the notoriously unsprung armchairs in
the big cold room at Colt Park. ... He was loved by everyone
who believed that universities were primarily about intellectual
freedom and sociability rather than professional advancement or
narrow vocational training.

---

233 Since 2008, simply *Times Higher Education* or *THE*.

Brian Hicks, in a brief letter to *The Guardian,* deplored Harry's departure from this world

> at the very time that this odious government, culturally and morally barren, announces its intention to cease funding adult education ...

Tudor David, editor of the weekly *Education*, described Harry as

> one of the most influential and distinguished figures on the English educational landscape this century. ... Above all else a committed teacher.

Harry's career was described as 'remarkably fecund':

> He began to wonder, at York, if he was really equipped to teach teachers since he had never taught in a comprehensive. ... His adherence to the comprehensive principle never faltered.

After giving due recognition to both Henry Morris and John Newsom, David concluded:

> But he was always very much his own man, never fitting, as many thought he should, into the mould of the educational establishment.

Frank Pedley, another passionate supporter of comprehensive schools who retired to the Yorkshire Dales, described Harry in the same issue of *Education* as a 'real character' and noted:

> the way in which his lively, quicksilver mind captivated people of all walks of life. ... He saw life as a whole, not compartmentalized, and as a consequence he was able to make an immense and global impact on the educational world.

The Guardian printed three short but significant letters:
   Henry Cleere wrote:

> Harry Rée was a brilliant teacher who inspired one small boy whom he taught between 1937–40 with a deep-seated and abiding love for French language and culture, as well as an appreciation of the true meaning of freedom.

Hilary Taylor:

> Harry was all that you describe but also a splendid cook.

And Laurence Kitchin:

> The magnificent Harry Rée also served on the committee of the
> Voluntary Euthanasia Society – another example of his wide-
> reaching humanity.

John Holloway, poet and English professor at Cambridge, wrote in *The Independent*:

> Something should perhaps be said of Harry Rée's earliest years
> as a teacher. In 1937 he came as the first of a new generation
> to my south-east London suburban secondary school.[234] He was
> full of high spirits, sharp iconoclastic informality, and kindliness;
> and he transformed our pleasant but somewhat colourless
> atmosphere into energetic liveliness and exuberant good humour.
> He entertained the older boys in groups at his flat, and I vividly
> recall his delicious cooking, and how he taught me to make an
> excellent French dressing for salad. All my life I have looked back
> to his inspiring example.

Nicole Ward Jouve recalled:

> Harry was a brilliant cook; it was unusual in men in those days.
> I can still remember the sweet and sour red cabbage pot, whose
> recipe I got and used!

Bob Finch, a colleague at York, was writing a 'Last Word' for the *Times Educational Supplement*. He described:

> … sitting at my kitchen table trying to decipher his spidery scrawl.
> It was essential to stick at this task because Harry's letters were
> liable to contain instructions, commands and requests alongside
> the gossip, scandal and wonderfully funny (and libellous)
> comments about well-known people. …

> He had so much life in him that he took over small parts of other
> people's lives, and an extraordinary number of people of all ages
> fell under his spell. He could be tough with you if he thought
> you were going down the wrong track but his approval, when it
> came, was total and no one ever laughed louder or longer than
> Harry at other people's stories.

---

234 Beckenham and Penge County School for Boys.

On the one occasion when we discussed death, he told me: 'Through the exit with panache, Bob, that's the secret. No clinging on to the door frame, straight through, with panache.'

I'm so glad that he brought it off.

In a 2012 exchange of emails, Bob wrote:

> Harry changed my life. He offered instant friendship followed by a challenge to make more of myself so I could do more for society/others. ... My kids adored him. He was THE most remarkable man and a jewel of a friend. Magnetism. Generosity. Laughter. Loyalty.

> More specifically. The Home and School Council (invented by Michael Young) needed a university base. One Feb. morning in 1967 I sat in my car outside Derwent College ... when Harry emerged. It was 8 a.m. My brief was to visit York, Leeds and Sheffield and settle on one. I got no further than York. Harry gave me a room, found me a secretary and subsumed the project into the university before lunch!

At the 2014 celebration of the centenary of Harry's birth, it was Bob Finch who said, 'friendship with Harry wasn't for wimps'.

Ian Lister, the successor to Harry's chair at York, wrote:

> He was a humanist and a reformer who developed and changed his views throughout his life. ... I last saw Harry at a conference ... when the assembled worthies showed in speech after speech just how dull the world of education has become. ... I said to Harry that having them all collected together might have some potential. Harry's eyes lit up at the thought of an act of God striking a blow for educational reform. At creative sabotage Harry had no peer.

Neil Hart, whom Harry had appointed as a history teacher at Watford Grammar School in the late 1950s and who later became deputy head and, for a brief time, headmaster, wrote in the centenary edition (1992) of the school magazine, *The Fullerian*. He commented on Harry's portrait:

> Alongside the formal portraits of his predecessors, his unconventional appearance, including open-necked shirt, demonstrates his impatience with what he saw as unnecessary pomp and circumstance. Yet, whilst here, he respected the

traditions of the school which he held in trust; assemblies, for example, were very formal and he would appear, flanked by staff and prefects, not only with gown but also with mortar-board which he would doff in solemn salute to the school before beginning prayers.

Neil went on to mention Harry's 'sheer magnetism, deep human sympathies and radical imagination'. He went on:

> Harry did not please everyone. ... Not all the staff were comfortable with his easy manner and informality and by a tendency to treat teachers and boys alike. Yet his real message was that all members of the school were of equal worth. ... He was capable of very great kindness without being soft, he made great demands but was remarkably non-judgemental, he had a strong sense of fairness and an instinctive sympathy for the underdog.

> ... The death of Harry's wife, Hetty, whose own contribution to his and the School's success was so very great, changed him. He showed great courage and dignity ... Yet it was clear that an important part of him was missing.

Chelly Halsey described Harry as 'one of the best-loved men of his generation'.

I asked Charles Swallow, Harry's nephew and godson and himself a headmaster for eight years – almost as long as his uncle Harry – what a young teacher today should make of his uncle, and these points were part of his response:

- Harry had a sort of missionary zeal which is always attractive to the young.
- Teaching for him was essentially a vocation.
- He was part of that band of returning War heroes who wanted to transform the society for which they had been fighting.
- Harry believed that teachers should be passionate about their subject and have a genuine interest in helping young minds to develop.
- He was unimpressed by institutional rules (e.g. the Church of England in which he had been brought up).
- He was impatient about convention but more Christian than most Christians, by which I mean his disregard of self and his understanding of the concept of love. I never met anyone who disliked Harry.

- Harry had no interest in money and loathed the moneyed Establishment, as he and many others could confirm. ... I don't think Harry begrudged his parents' comparative wealth. Nor would he, I believe, have distinguished between his father's earned wealth and his mother's inherited wealth. As his socialist convictions grew and as his wartime experiences caused him to long for a 'better' society so his thoughts turned to the future without any feeling of embarrassment or shame about the advantages of his past.
- He continued to love and feel affection for his parents and siblings even though he would not have chosen ...
- Harry wanted a society based on the Utopian ideals of Morris and his village colleges. Learning should be a lifelong aim.
- It was strange in a way that Harry's natural diffidence, personal modesty and total lack of conceit concealed ... fearlessness. ... There was no aggression in the promulgation of his ideals. He would just feel rather sad about people who could not see his point!
- Who is to say whether Harry was right or wrong? He had a devoted band of supporters and he was certainly inspirational in both his speeches, articles and his way of life. As Nigel Gann and his wife Cathy Wood put it, teaching was, for him, a way of life, not a job; a calling, as previous generations might have said. Perhaps in the post-war years if governments had injected new ideas and more resources into the secondary modern schools and the technical schools envisaged by Butler the story might have been different. The sullen anger directed towards the 11-plus would not have been so bitter. But all that gives rise to the British obsession with Class ...

Toby Weaver, who served at the highest levels of the Ministry of Education and the Department of Education and Science 1946–73, wrote:

> There was a general belief, I believe totally false, that children were divided into three kinds. It was sort of Platonic. There were golden children, and silver children, and iron children. The golden children were capable of going to a grammar school, they had minds, they could have abstract thinking. The technical children, so to speak, were technically oriented, and all the rest, they couldn't handle ideas, they had to have concrete notions.

When Harry died, some people who knew him well thought he had committed suicide. So did I. But we were probably wrong. It was a heart attack, in his house where he was alone at the time, and he had tickets for another trip to France. Son Jonathan writes:

I think the suicide story is incredible, because if he'd wanted to take his own life he would have explained what he was doing and thought about how he wanted to be found.

Suffice it to say that one shouldn't jump to the conclusion that he committed suicide simply because he could have and because he did not look forward to old age. George Walker adds:

Quite simply, he was lucky to be alive and much of his life was a celebration of his good fortune.

Son Jonathan made the point in 2014 that Harry had been extremely close to being killed more than once. Hence what Jonathan called his 'survivor recklessness'.[235]

Tim Edwards, a lifelong friend from when we taught together at Manchester Grammar School, became a fellow-Hertfordshire headmaster just before Harry left for York. Harry nominated him for membership of the All Souls Group, a peculiarly English invention: it was first put together in 1941, under the aegis of W.G.S. Adams, who was then Warden of All Souls College, Oxford, and meets about three times a year under the Chatham House Rule, discussing educational issues of the day. And they would meet at Fred and Ann Jarvis's Christmas parties.[236] Tim writes:

I always found him interesting and stimulating, provocative whenever possible and especially if on an inappropriate occasion. ... He was very good at identifying forward-looking younger people in the educational scene. ... He possessed a wonderful understanding of young people and their needs, while his capacity to talk at their level without the remotest hint of patronage was always an example to aim at, though very hard indeed to match. ... I can never forget ... the voice, the modesty, the gentleness of his treatment of friends and his vigorous contempt for those whose views he opposed or disputed. ... Harry was the epitome of an educational activist and networker with huge physical and intellectual energy who served young people in a wonderful and selfless way.

Patrick Nuttgens, Professor of Architecture at York and later the first director of Leeds Polytechnic, wrote of:

---

235 NB: not guilt.
236 Fred Jarvis was General Secretary of the National Union of Teachers 1975–89.

elements of the bizarre, the absurd, the provocative, the endlessly generous and always the unexpected that one has come to expect of Harry.

The theme of hesitant modesty comes up continually. As Harry's son Jonathan pointed out in his concluding remarks at the 2014 celebration, his mantra was 'Please do not make a fuss.'

Harry seems to have had all his mid-life crises about the same time: Hetty's death; Janet's health scare; Brian's accident; the move from headmastering to professing; the physical move from Watford to York; Henry Morris's death; and the shift in support of the grammar to the comprehensive school.

He emerged from the War heavily and appropriately decorated, but received nothing thereafter from a grateful nation. I always thought that he and Francis Cammaerts should have been knighted: not only for their significant contributions *after* the War, but also for being who they were. I am reminded of Bertrand Russell's quirky idea, first articulated in *Education and the Social Order*, that certain persons 'will be allowed to place after their names the letters LT, meaning "licensed to think"'.

If I could pose some questions to Harry now, with the benefit of hindsight, I would ask few factual questions. But I would probe with him the extent to which he was aware of the perceptions of others, from his mother-in-law to the many who, like me, were hugely influenced by him. And to the extent that he was aware, what were his thoughts? (And if he wasn't aware, why the hell not?) Did these thoughts change with time?

He was a complex person. I am reminded of Section 51 of Walt Whitman's *Song of Myself*, written when the poet was in his late thirties and published in 1855:

> Do I contradict myself?
> Very well then I contradict myself,
> I am large, I contain multitudes.

During the two-plus years when I saw Harry almost every working day, he was an authority figure, a headmaster, and many of my colleagues, wanting the Head to be the same from one day to the next, expressed frustration with what they saw as contradictions, changes in viewpoint, unpredictability. After all, as Auden and Worsley had written just before the Second World War, 'The word "headmaster" has a frightening association for most'.[237]

---

237 W.H. Auden and T.C. Worsley (1939) *Education Today and Tomorrow*. London: Hogarth Press, 13.

Some saw Harry as a weak manager, others as a courageous leader; for sure, he was a frequent subject of discussion in the staff room: was he aware of that, and if so, to what extent did he care?

His roots were Mancunian, Bradfordian, Danish, Jewish, Christian, Salopian, Cantabridgian, Alsatian (maybe), French (possibly), Hamburgian, Pennsylvanian but he was 100 per cent European. The family he was born into was important to him, as were his three children. At least two of his siblings worked in schools, and all three of his children taught and/or worked with people; none of them went into 'business'.

Harry's attitudes to wealth were ambivalent. Listening to him, you would think he was hostile to the effortless wealth represented by the Dupont connection or Shrewsbury School, and yet he seems to have accepted money from his parents and never to have had financial worries.

As described above, Harry's description of the role of sex in his life, from the Craig School to Colt Park, was straightforward, with no attempts to hide anything. His single-sex boarding schools both led to homosexual encounters; in Cambridge, his sexuality seems to have been quiescent; then Hetty came along. In later life, he had more female friends and relationships than male. Hetty was the love of his life, which would have moved in somewhat different directions had she lived. And yet, in 1988, he confessed that he still did not quite know what love meant. I am convinced that Hetty's death continued to be the most devastating single event in his life; nothing in the War was comparable.

Given his profound love for Janet, his eldest child and only daughter, I am still puzzled that the single-sex aspect of many of Britain's most prestigious schools did not seem to have bothered him.

Throughout his life, Harry was building community. He was an inveterate letter-writer, as was his mother, connecting people with each other and sharing details of what he had been reading. Sometimes these letters would be indiscreet; he trusted people not to blab in the wrong places – or he didn't care. He would, I think, have enjoyed using email; we would have missed his unique handwriting. A minor annoyance: he would date his letters with the day and the month but not the year.

Both his father and his grandfather were community-minded and dedicated to public service. Harry, in turn, both learned from Henry Morris and understood the American community college as it developed after the Second World War and especially in the 1960s. He believed in a society where rich and poor, young and old, engage in learning activities from the cradle to the grave and where they gravitate to and coexist in the same building. He would have been very disturbed by today's increasing gap between rich and poor. He was always interested in design, whether it be a village college in Cambridgeshire or his own Colt Park.

He was an intellectual, a public intellectual, the kind of person Coleridge had in mind when he coined the word 'clerisy' around 1830. And yet, he was never comfortable with the title of professor. He read voraciously and widely, urging others to do likewise. He loved argument, and his conversation was always lively. One might have thought that he would enjoy university common rooms and even Oxbridge high tables, but he didn't. When Eric James created Oxford-like colleges at the new University of York, he wasn't wholly comfortable. I am not clear why Harry was such a reluctant academic, even when, with his Henry Morris book, he had proved that he could do it: perhaps he felt that being a professor would distance him from ordinary people, perhaps he simply preferred to be a journalist. And yet, his enthusiasm for the written word was hugely important for both the public and the private persona that were Harry Rée. And, as Peter Wilby reminded me, Harry was a surprisingly private person.

One of the themes we would discuss endlessly at Watford Grammar School was: was Harry radical or middle-of-the-road? At the time, I thought he was pretty radical; now I am not so sure. Eric Midwinter writes:

> My own view is that he had the wit and gifts to try and work within the system, chiefly on pragmatic grounds. I remember being at conferences, some of them with Harry, when speaker after speaker would rise and call for revolution. ... It was all eyewash.

Jon Nixon, speaking in 2014, described Harry as a 'practical idealist ... very grounded.' 'We can't be powerful on our own; only together.'

When he was asked to speak at Valençay, he complained that he was in no way the best choice, that the Queen Mother represented outdated values, etc. And yet, he went, was charming, and delivered an unexceptionable speech. Could this be a metaphor for how he should be perceived?

Similarly, he did glory in being unconventional, not wearing a tie for the portrait that was to be hung in the Hall at Watford. And yet, one of the many reasons he bought Colt Park was so he could house some of his parents' Victorian furniture from Manchester.

The family sold Colt Park, understandably, and his granddaughter Harriet recently found that it was on sale for over half a million pounds. The outside looks as I remember it; the inside precious and twee.

Harry would have understood the need to sell. He was an optimist, like his friend Francis Cammaerts, and a visionary; an enthusiast, both for people and for causes. He wanted the world to be a better place, and he despised people who talked a good game but did little.

Describing his father's optimism, Jonathan described the only time he ever observed Harry in 'utter pain and despair'. It was January 1960, when he learned on the radio – the wireless – of the death of Albert Camus, who was a mere 11 months older than Harry.

As Margaret Maden pointed out, he was unthreatened by staff who were better than him. He put enormous energy into projects, travelling throughout England to conferences and writing, writing, writing. At the celebration of the centenary of his birth, Tim Brighouse used the words, 'hope, enthusiasm and energy'. Harry never really retired.

He liked to shock people out of what we would call their comfort zones, but he never knowingly hurt anyone. I am reminded of Ludwig Wittgenstein when he said that his main task was:

> to teach you to pass from a piece of disguised nonsense to something that is patent nonsense.[238]

Harry was, I think, a model in that he was not afraid to change his mind if he felt the facts warranted. As I explained above, this would often confuse people, occasionally annoying them. He went from conscientious objector to War hero, from defender of the essential grammar school to spokesperson for the comprehensive school. These changes took place over relatively short time periods, adding to the confusion. Yes, he shifted from grammar to comprehensive schools, but his basic principles did not shift. Equity. Equality. As Tim Brighouse beautifully put it at the centenary of his birth, he was finding a gap in the metaphorical hedge.

Some people chose to think that he played with ideas; I always saw him as an intensely serious person. He was not the kind who would tell or listen much to jokes.

Not all of Harry's writing was both brilliant and memorable: I have already opined that *The Essential Grammar School* is as poor as *Educator Extraordinary* is superb. On 19 October 1980, he wrote 'A comprehensively revealing view' for the *Times Educational Supplement*. Demonstrating balance, wisdom and a passionate backward look at his life's work as well as an optimistic view of the future, he began:

> I have spent the past five years as an ordinary teacher in a Hackney comprehensive school. I retire now after a life which

---

238 *Philosophical Investigations* (1953).

covers public and grammar schools, Cambridge and a new university, but was not confined to education.

'Not confined to education': nicely understated. He had just turned 66. 'I have always been proud to work in the state education system': needed to be said then; needs to be said now. He went on to paint the big picture, acknowledging problems, without exaggerations:

> Many causes of the faults and difficulties are not only ephemeral, they lie outside the school, or beyond the power of the school to control. But first it should be said that the mixing in one school of children from widely different backgrounds and with a huge range of intellectual gifts and interests, has been one of the least of the difficulties.

He discussed teachers:

> learning to meet tensions and to control potential conflict with patience and tolerance, rather than with aggression of incitement to fear.

Teachers, he continued, were exhausted! And we know that, even though he was a part-timer, he too was exhausted. Parents, on the whole, were grateful for what was being done for their children. Community was being built. Staff rooms, consisting of people with public or grammar school backgrounds on the one hand, people from secondary modern schools on the other, were coming together. There were pressures from outside (though little did Harry know how these would increase in the next quarter-century).

Harry articulated his core belief, namely that:

> learning goes on outside as well as inside the classroom, that the duty of the teacher is to get the children to want to learn, and that learning is a lifetime activity.

In one of the best pieces he ever wrote, Harry warned of 'the spectre of Disraeli's two nations', first articulated in 1845, when the rich get richer and the poor get poorer, seeing the comprehensive school as the one place where societal gaps could be bridged.

And yet, Nigel Gann felt that he did not understand poverty. In fact, Gann places Harry in a tradition that goes back to Matthew Arnold, a romantic tradition of upper-class, privately educated English males. There's the sonnet, *To A Republican Friend*, from 1848, that begins, 'God knows it, I am with you', and ends, 'Then am I yours, and what you feel, I share.'

Everybody who knew him, especially in his post-Watford years, would emphasize his 'capacity for friendship', to use Anne Corbett's phrase. He was a networker – 'the supreme networker', according to Margaret Maden – a constant encourager, a friend. He used food and cooking as a way of bringing people together. Pippa Warin confirmed, as did many others, the centrality of friendship in Harry's life.

He hated to be alone, and Colt Park was almost always full of people coming and going. Edward Blishen called him a 'gregarious loner'. Jon Nixon went as far as to label him needy. David Green thought that Harry's vision was close to that of Hector, the teacher in Alan Bennett's *The History Boys*. For sure, it is ironic that the film of the play was made on location at Watford Grammar School.

Harry makes an appearance, thinly disguised as Maurice Lee, in Edward Blishen's *The Penny World*, which came out the year before he died:

> I remember my friend Maurice Lee, in a television debate, offering ideas as he always did, ideas that smiled and were warm, and how in that setting, which implied the superiority of cold if not frozen opinion, he was bested again and again, in terms of chill logic, by another debater who drew his ideas, stiff with frost, out of the refrigerator of his mind. I thought it should have been taking place in Maurice's huge farmhouse kitchen; and Maurice should, while talking and listening, have been hurling bits of this and that into pan or saucepan, tasting, exclaiming, as I'd seen him do time and again. I thought of the warmth that was implied when you said people had bedroom eyes: in that way, Maurice had classroom eyes. His educational ideas were like his dishes, you tossed in this and that and tasted and swore and sometimes it didn't work out and you threw it away and started again.
>
> Imagine discussing education in terms, not simply of happiness, but of bedrooms and bean soup, in that grey radio discussion!
>
> Oh education, poor education! I thought …

In an earlier book, Edward referred to

> great quantities of jugged hare, pickled walnuts in syrup, and whisky, wine and brandy.

Needless to say, the total adds up to far more than the discrete parts. He was a lifelong learner, so of course he changed with time; mostly for the better. His life had a focus, the betterment of society and the encouragement of individuals; and people were enriched by his influence. The famous quotation from Horace Mann fits Harry Rée more than anyone I have ever known.

So what have I learned from Harry, whom I first encountered as an impressionable 19-year-old?

1. Don't be afraid to take sensible risks.
2. Trust your hunches and instincts.
3. Think boldly.
4. Practise what you preach.
5. Take your work seriously, take other people seriously, but not yourself.
6. Trust your colleagues, co-workers and employees almost more than you should.
7. Treat people who disagree with you with respect.
8. Read voraciously and widely. Write.
9. Steep yourself in other cultures.
10. Laugh.

If Harry had had but one or two of the characteristics outlined above, he would still have been quite extraordinary; what made him unique was the combination of qualities he exhibited throughout his life.

1. He could change his mind when the facts warranted. Some people chose to think that he was not totally serious, that he would follow whims. *Au contraire*. As I have tried to demonstrate, he was profoundly serious: his passionate support of comprehensive schools followed his wholehearted support of grammar schools only after he had studied the facts.
2. He was an intellectual, a voracious reader who wanted others to be readers. Despite the Henry Morris book, which proved that he could be as professorial as any of his colleagues, he never saw himself as a scholar, but was 100 per cent the intellectual who reflects and then acts on what he reads and hears.
3. He was what we would today call the supreme networker, constantly putting people in touch with each other, always refreshing his contacts. I don't think he ever had a physical rolodex on his desk, but he had one in his head. He would have been the ultimate emailer.
4. He seemed fearless. As his daughter Janet put it to Alasdair Brown, Harry 'never experienced a moment of self-doubt'. I still do not know how I feel about that! For sure, as someone who knew him pretty well put it, he was in charge of his life.

And, consciously or not, he could be mysterious. He avoided talking about his wartime adventures, yet did discuss them with some. He never spoke about his Jewish ancestry ... well, hardly ever! You would never have known that he had an American mother and could have claimed American citizenship at any time. And when he was a headmaster, I don't think anyone knew that he had undergone a year of teacher training before the War.

His last battle, tilting at windmills as he fully recognized, was the preparation of a letter to Kenneth Baker, who was the Tory Secretary of State for Education and Science (1986–9).[239] 1988 turned out to be the year when the State took over education; since then, as Michel Lemosse remarked to me, chief education officers are bypassed and unknown. That same year, Tim Brighouse, then Chief Education Officer for Oxfordshire, pointed out that power was being devolved to the heads of individual schools and scooped up by central government, leaving chief education officers out in the cold. 'The Age of Paradox', he called it, 'Centralization and De-centralization':

> The worlds of Sylvester [Bristol], Longland [Derbyshire], Newsom [Hertfordshire] and Chorlton [Oxfordshire] were lodged in a deferential age. ... The charismatic officer 'willed', and the squirearchy agreed.[240]

Today, for sure, there is no one on the scene to compare with Alexander, Newsom, Clegg [West Riding of Yorkshire], Baraclough, Mason [Leicestershire] 'and the rest'. In the late 1980s, any reader of the *Times Educational Supplement* would have recognized most of these names.

Baker devoted four chapters in *The Turbulent Years* to his years in education. Nary a mention of Harry; but he did excoriate 'left-wing dogma', as well as 'problem-solving' and 'child-centred', which he described as euphemisms. 'Too many LEAs', he said, 'are imposing their own political prejudices upon the system in their charge'. And he went on:

> Once established the curriculum will have to be inspected on a more regular basis than now. We will need a much enlarged national inspectorate. This will mean taking into Central Government employment the local inspectors and advisors.

239 Now Lord Baker of Dorking. In an email in 2012, Lord Baker wrote that he had no recollection of Harry's views in the late 1980s.
240 Brighouse, T. (1988) 'Politicising the manager or managing the politicians? Can the headteacher succeed where the education officer failed?' *Educational Management Administration and Leadership*, 16, 97–103.

It will be necessary to have some reserve powers for the LEAs and even the Secretary of State to make appointments to Governing Bodies which get into difficulties or which are being subverted by political groups.

In 1992, Brian Simon was to write:

I ... received a letter from Harry Rée, written just a few weeks before he died. He commented on the fact that I ended my book *Education and Social Order, 1940–1990* ... on an optimistic note, and says, 'as, in public, I still do – but I'm beginning to have my doubts'. He goes on:

The almost certain economic decline will, I fear, buttress the moral decline (can we doubt that?). Signs of hope, I agree, are there – especially in the fine teachers who have stayed on, determined to exert themselves heroically on behalf of their students – and there'll always be such. But I fear that the Tory changes of the 80s will have inflicted a permanent blow to our health as a nation. Kenneth Baker owes us an abject apology.

I am grateful to Sir Peter Newsam for introducing me to a wonderful book that, it turns out, Harry had also read. *What Is and What Might Be: A study of education in general and elementary education in particular,* came out in 1914, i.e. before the First World War and before Harry was born. The author, Edmond Holmes, could have been writing yesterday:

1. My aim in writing this book, is to show that ... the prevalent tendency to pay undue regard to outward and visible 'results' and to neglect what is inward and vital, is the source of most of the defects that vitiate Education in this country.
2. The function of education is to foster growth.
3. The process of growing must be done by the growing organism, by the child, let us say, and by no one else.
4. The examination system controls education, and in doing so arrests the self-development of the child.
5. When the education given in a school is dominated by a periodical examination on a prescribed syllabus, suppression of a child's natural activities becomes the central feature of the teacher's programme.

Was Edmond Holmes Harry's role model and not Henry Morris after all?

Finding a gap in the hedge
A tribute to Harry Rée

When Jonathan invited me to give this talk, I rather casually accepted. I say 'rather casually', because as the day has approached I have realized how important it is to other people and that the chances of my letting them down and Harry's memory were rather too great to be *too* casual.

What I want to avoid in this tribute is nostalgia. There is nothing worse, it seems to me (and as I am sure it was to Harry), than to give in to that tendency which so afflicts the old, of regretting some golden age, which probably glistered but certainly was not all gold. My particular older generation is prone to see the years between Butler's 1944 Act and Baker's 1988 through rose-tinted spectacles.

For all that we achieved in those years – discovering and campaigning for comprehensive rather than selective schools, realizing the importance of community education (in both of which causes Harry played a significant leading role) or transforming our understanding of what was possible in primary schools and in particular promoting the expressive arts through education (and Harry played a big role there too) – for all that and much else, there were downsides. Immigrant pupils placed at the back of the class and in the lower streams and given nicknames by teachers who found their real names too much bother is one example. Another was our treatment of girls. Take the extraordinary ILEA experience of having to argue with DFE as we expanded Kidbrooke as it went co-ed in the 1970s – that it needed more laboratories only to be told that we were overestimating need because we hadn't allowed for the fact that 'many girls can't do science'. It was a view which chimed with the plea of the Association of Headmistresses in the 1940s, that the old school certificate should be modified because intellectually girls 'cannot do maths and science'. Or marking girls down in the old 11+ because they scored too highly, as I saw happen in Buckinghamshire in the late '60s.

No; we treated girls almost as badly as pupils from ethnic minorities.

On a daily basis too many pupils of all ages had to put up with being treated with a scathing indignity, which is not tolerated in most classrooms today, from a sizeable minority of poor teachers whose sarcasm sometimes permeated the ethos of a whole school, as HMI reports of the time illustrate all too clearly.

The habits of such staff betrayed the efforts of people like Harry – and I am sure many others in this room – whose career provided a beacon of hope, enthusiasm and energy, which touched so many. Indeed, Harry spent much of his life trying to address the vital issue of improving the quality of teachers, and through the many people he influenced his legacy lies at least and in considerable part in the way today's children are treated with dignity in the overwhelming majority of schools and by teachers whose skill and expertise increases even as the respect for politicians who berate those teachers declines.

So this is not an occasion for looking back with nostalgia about a golden age. Harry, who for example in his accounts of Shrewsbury in his teenage years certainly did not regret a far-off golden age, provides us with a different example: 'There's a lot to be gained, however, from studying the lives of great people who provide us with models of how to live a fulfilling life and in doing so contribute so much to others' fulfilment.' So although Harry would not have approved of nostalgia, he would have approved of what we shall say both about himself – of course with that mischievous grin – and about the issues he felt strongly about, namely equity, equality and egalitarianism. At least that's what he urged me to campaign for as, post-1988, we formed TANEA (Towards a New Education Act), and as he gently chided me for giving up a 'real job' to join a university. I have always regretted that he didn't live long enough to see that I heeded his advice on this, as I did on so many other issues and occasions.

I called this talk 'Finding a gap in the hedge' because that's what people do who want to continue to pursue their goal but find that their previous direction towards a desired goal is suddenly blocked. Harry demonstrated that ability. For example, in the interests of equality and equity, the author of *The Essential Grammar School* later became the champion of community comprehensive schools. He recognized the importance of context both of time and of place in deciding what to do about a particular timeless value such as equity or equality. Such issues require different solutions according to the time, the place and the people. From Penge, through Bradford and Watford Grammar Schools, to Derwent College at York and Woodbury Down, and above all at Colt Park, Harry was so adept at effortlessly understanding those three variable elements of context and, whatever they were, of carrying out that elusive art of changing cultures in order to further a strategic issue based on unshakable principles.

In short, metaphorically speaking, they 'Find a gap in the hedge'. For unless you are an expert in that, you stand no chance of shifting the pattern of events in your preferred direction. Harry was a supreme expert in finding which gap to scramble through and when. Moreover, he would appear ever optimistic and always inspiring, albeit looking slightly dishevelled – but always in a mysteriously posh way – on the other side, where he would provide the energy and rations for us all to resume our travel in hope and expectation. Harry was no Bourbon in that he never forgot but always learnt; nevertheless, he was always a person for the present and the future.

And he was a blessed communicator.

I recall him sending me an account of a conversation with his great friend Edward Blishen as they contemplated a third Conservative term. Consider the communicator:

> I'm distressed in a manner only to be defined by using words such as 'honour', 'magnanimity', 'vision'. Who in his worst dreams would have guessed that we'd fall into the hands of patently dishonest and personally disgusting mediocrities, or that we'd enter a phase in our history in which blatant venality and nastiness were rewarded? What seems to have been destroyed, for the moment, is every trace of national generosity, for the moment imagination has been surgically removed from national life. One trouble is that generosity and imagination need to be embodied and given voice and there is no sign of that voice.
>
> I'm reminded of the speech of the dying Gaunt,
>
> ... this dear dear land,
>
> *Is now leased out, I die pronouncing it,*
>
> *Like to a tenement or pelting farm;*
>
> *England ... is now bound in with shame*
>
> *With inky blots and rotten parchment bonds*
>
> The country is turned into a thieves' kitchen. We were discussing the other night where we would go if they get in again. Not that we would go anywhere. Our place is here. But the thought of what they'd do if their vandal unpleasantness and insolence were assented to for a third time is not to be borne.

And so it was to our great advantage that Harry addressed the issues of the then present and the then future – as he did so tirelessly in the last years of his life, which is when I knew him well.

What did he reveal of his beliefs? Well, there's another session which will illuminate our understanding far more than I shall do here. But it seemed to me from his actions and his conversations that he cared passionately about equity and equality. Indeed, in the piece he gave me and which I have quoted involving Edward Blishen, you can guess other things he cared strongly about too, not least generosity of spirit.

We once discussed another passage of prose, this time from William Temple, which provides clues perhaps about why he chose education rather than broadcasting as a career. It certainly influenced me, and I can remember talking about it with him; indeed, it may have been Harry who gave it to me. Consider:

> Until Education has done more work than it has had an opportunity of doing, you cannot have a society organised on the basis of justice, for this reason.... that there will always be a strain between what is due to a man in view of his humanity with all his powers and capabilities and what is due to him at the moment of time as a member of society with all his faculties still undeveloped, with many of his tastes warped, with his powers largely crushed.

> Are you going to treat a man as what he is or what he might be? Morality, I think, requires that you should treat him as what he might be, as what he might become ... and business requires that you should treat him as he is.

> You cannot get rid of that strain except by raising what he is to the level of what he might be. That is the whole work of education. Give him the full development of his powers and there will no longer be that conflict between the man as he is and the man as he might become.

> And so you can have no justice as the basis of your social life until education has done its full work. And then again, you can have no real freedom, because until a man's whole personality has developed, he cannot be free in his own life ... And you cannot have political freedom any more than you can have moral freedom until people's powers are developed, for the simple reason that over and over again we find men with a cause which

is just... are unable to state it in a way which might enable it to prevail ... there exists a form of mental slavery which is as real as any economic form ... We are pledged to destroy it ... it you want human liberty, you must have educated people.

There are plenty of clues there as to his beliefs ... social justice, political freedom, individual freedom in the sense of being able to argue a case which is just, and much more contentiously the tension expressed by the phrases 'morality requires we should treat people as they might become but business requires you treat them as they are'. Is there a clue in that phrase about all our mistrust of the intrusion of market forces into education?

If my estimate of Harry's beliefs is correct – and they are backed by his own written work – and bearing in mind he was a person for the future not the past, what would he be urging us to do if he were here today?

I want to advance the proposition that today Harry would be addressing four issues. Well, remembering Harry, I wager it would have been more. But these four would have been near the top of his list.

First, his lifetime commitment to equality and equity would have him at the forefront of those arguing passionately for changes to the schooling system, so that those gaining least from it should get a better deal. Those of us who get hot under the collar about admission arrangements for secondary schools, which, in urban though not rural contexts, continue to disadvantage children coming from the most challenged areas, would have had some support and advice from Harry. As we would have had in attempts to reform the exam system which Gove has changed to the immense disadvantage of those who find learning based on memorized facts and theories most difficult and who, as we know, are apt to come from the most disadvantaged families.

Secondly, his fear of attacks on local government as the first step on a downward path towards totalitarianism and dictatorship – which of course he had witnessed in Hitler's Germany and Mussolini's Italy, and which he specifically remarked upon in his biography of Henry Morris – would have had him even more outraged than he was when he died about the centralization of powers in education to a largely unaccountable secretary of state. Of course, then the process had only just started, for through the 1988 Act the Secretary of State acquired only 200 powers. Now he has more than 2,000.

Thirdly, there is an urgent need to address the question of the supply and subsequent training of teachers and above all ensure that they are as trusted for their skill, integrity and generosity of spirit by politicians acting nationally in the same way as they undoubtedly are by the parents in the school where they teach. Much of Harry's career was devoted to promoting just that.

Fourth, finally and perhaps most importantly, Harry would be campaigning to restore respect for public service, which all those who became adults in the twenty-five years after the Second World War took for granted as part of the 'British Values' which schools are now being told to promote. Inevitably in doing so we must consider whether as we are so often told things really are done best by the private for profit sector rather than through publicly provided and run services.

So three priorities for each of the first three of those four issues and one for the last:

Our first was what do we do about egalitarianism, not of course on the wider front, though Piketty, Danny Dorling and others have suggested ways in which progressive taxation would make such a difference and help create a fairer society. And I cannot believe that Harry would support student fees and loans rather than a graduate tax. But that's not today's bag, and I shall focus on schools and therefore on that stage in life where we treat people not *as they are* but *as they might become*, and where life's chances are largely made or lost.

My three Rée priorities for that are:

1. Let the admission arrangements for all schools be determined locally and democratically, not by the schools themselves. After priority for children with SEND and those "Looked After", let the first priority be an entitlement for the children of parents that they should attend the school closest to their home unless capacity makes that impossible. There will be different ways of securing equity according to whether it is a rural or urban set of schools. One further point demands notice. Is it a British value that parents of a particular faith should have priority in admission to an aided school of that faith? We are uncertain in practice. It is not so in Northern Ireland and Scotland but it is so in England and Wales.

2. Change level two exams – GCSE or equivalent – to ones which are accumulated when youngsters are ready, rather than at a predetermined point, and are criterion rather than normatively referenced. (Harry would be as outraged, as I am, by the OFQUAL's breathtaking edict that pupil performance at 11 should govern the number receiving certain grades at 16. Teachers' skills, not to mention pupils' efforts,

are apparently irrelevant! I am amazed that nobody has commented on that.)

3. Change school accountability by reforming Ofsted and changing the habits of publication of school results. On the first, restore HMI's role in advising the Secretary of State on policy and establish their role as validators of a tough externally moderated school review process run regionally by a democratically accountable school improvement service and by re-establishing their role as collectors of evidence through national surveys of school practice. Publish school report cards giving a comprehensive picture including exam and test results of school performance. Always have the data showing a three-year rolling average.

Now let me turn to the three priorities for the second theme, namely the need to ensure healthy democratic and local influence. Of course, the Scottish debate has brought this to long overdue public attention. The powers of local government have been steadily eroded, especially in education, and with that process an increasing alienation from Westminster and their central micro-management, which induces a sense of powerlessness that is the enemy of democracy itself. It looks as though quite properly Scotland, Wales and Northern Ireland are going to have 'devo-max'. What happens in England will have to bear in mind that we are a very large population – over 45 million – to have all our services determined in minute detail by a national English government. I am assuming at the very least some local tax raising powers and a revenue support grant system to mirror a Barnet-type formula.

In the three 'Rée' priorities, here, I have assumed that the outcome of any constitutional debate will be the establishment of a strong local government, if not exactly in its present form.

1. Give existing local authorities the responsibility for providing all SEND services to schools, and the responsibility of running 'admission to school' arrangements and ensuring that there is a properly-funded youth service and sufficient facilities for beyond school education.

2. Ensure the existing LAs have the right to nominate at least one governor to every Academy, Free and other school governing body, with a duty to blow the whistle on any inappropriate governor behaviour. (The Trojan Horse fiasco demands nothing less.) Give the LAs the duty to run the 'contracts', at present administered by the Secretary of State, with existing Academies and Free Schools.

3. Run School Improvement services and school accountability arrangements on a regional basis, which would be democratically

controlled in the way that Police Authorities used to be held locally accountable.

The third set of 'Rée' issues concerns teachers.

1. Establish a National College of Teaching – one might call it the Harry Rée National College – and charge it with all the powers cherished by other professional bodies usually called Royal Colleges. Amongst those powers would be the responsibility to advise on a three-year basis the Secretary of State publicly about the standards of initial education and training and the numbers needed in training and how that training should be organized.

2. Reform exams so that all exams are nationally set, internally assessed and marked by teachers, but externally moderated, backed by each school having within their ranks a Chartered assessor and with each group of schools holding a licence to assess.

3. Establish a ring-fenced pool of expenditure for proper professional development for teachers.

On the last issue of the place of public service, I don't know where to start. In parts of the United Kingdom, principally Scotland, it is alive and well, but south of the border it seems to have been clinically excised from our life. We were talking the other day. Was it so strong in our youth,, when all those leaving university considered public service as the 'thing to do' – the preferred destination – because of the Empire, with its voracious need for public service boosted in India for so many years, long ago, by the curious hybrid of the East India Company? Was it just a post-war dream that saw the water, coal, gas and electricity part of the public service before they were sold off to guarantee private profits from the poor at an annual rate of 5%? And as a result, was it that so many of us – rich and poor, skilled and unskilled – were in the public service, that we could see we were trying to help others and were rewarded for our efforts, whereas now our successors work in 'for profit' private companies that march to a different and more selfish drum beat? Whatever it is, private profit undermines the moral purpose of all we try to do in schools. It is for that reason that I suggest here just one Rée priority.

1. In outsourcing and the provision of services to schools, make it a legal requirement that providers are not for-profit enterprises, with Charity Commission registration.

As I said at the beginning, Harry would be demanding change on many other fronts as well as these ten. For instance he wouldn't have been quiet on the place of religion in school, or the privatization of the universities ... he would have been a great blogger and tweeter. Amazing to think he died before the mobile phone and the pervasive internet-based technologies. He would have loved them and used them to such good effect.

Above all, Harry was a passionate teacher who had an enviable command of questioning and of storytelling.

Anyway, enough of me putting words into his mouth.

I said at the beginning that I had accepted Jonathan's invitation rather casually. I hope Harry would have approved nevertheless. He certainly had to rely on his intuition rather than his intellect more than once, and make instinctive decisions, which in retrospect always seemed the right ones. Well, as an expert finder of gaps through hedges, he needed to be blessed with that instinctive and intuitive talent among his many other ones, and I want to end this keynote with a recording of Harry at his best – moving, inspiring, speculating, motivating. So over to Harry to tell us a story about another part of his life.

And as you listen, reflect on what we would all have lost if Madame Fuiette in the Jura had chosen to make a different decision in 1943. And we shall hear all about those achievements as the day unfolds, and as all of us agree because we have been influenced by Harry and his example, we shall not give up on realizing our aims, albeit in our different context. So here is Harry telling a story as only a brilliant teacher can.[241]

Tim Brighouse, 11 October 2014

---

241 The audience then heard a recording of the radio talk mentioned on p. 43, fn. 73.

Index